The BREAKTHROUGH
Covenant Partner

Millennium
Journal

A Day-By-Day Devotional Countdown

RESULTS
PUBLISHING

ISBN: 1-880244-43-8
Copyright © 1998 by Rod Parsley.

Published by:
Results Publishing
P.O. Box 32903
Columbus, Ohio 43232-0903 USA

The *Breakthrough Covenant Partner Millennium Journal* is for you, your family, your church and your friends. Use it to journal what God is doing in and through you.

As the curtain on this millennium pulls shut, one day at a time in 1999, you are living in the most exciting time of history. Just beyond your view, the King of kings and Lord of lords is poised to usher in the mightiest army in all eternity.

You are called to be a radical believer, part of a revolutionary church that marches gloriously into battle lifting high the standard of Jesus Christ. This year declare:

- No Retreats and Defeats!
- No Bondage or Sickness!
- No Famine or Drought!
- No Debt or Lack!
- No Compromise or Holding Back!

God is doing a new thing in your life—step into His glory, newness and holiness.

Each day I will share with you fresh revelation and inspiring insights for living in Christ's abundance and the power of the Holy Ghost. Jesus is returning for a radical, revolutionary bride without spot or blemish. Get ready. Prepare for the Bridegroom.

You are a part of the remnant church—the church within a church, the revolutionary soldier amidst complacent, sleepy-eyed pew sitters. You are called to be the radical, sold-out, blood-bought Christian who rebukes every worldly compromise, crushes Satan's head at every opportunity and takes back what the enemy has stolen!

Daily write down what the Spirit speaks to your heart. Record His piercing Word. Pray in the Spirit for Jesus' anointing and fiery passion to transform you into a mighty warrior triumphantly marching into the dawn of the millennium.

Millennial Countdown

But I will sing of thy power; yea, I will sing aloud of thy mercy in the morning: for thou hast been my defense and refuge in the day of my trouble.
(Psalm 59:16)

Your morning has come. A cloud the size of a man's hand is rising on the horizon. Laden with wind, rain and fire, it is gathering above you. Glory and honor will crown your life while signs and wonders will follow you into the four corners of the earth. Today dawns a millennial countdown.

God is calling you to raise high the standard for living in this final generation. The time has come to plant your flag, possess your land, raise the standard and march under the banner of the King of kings.

Your time as a standard bearer for the King has arrived. The heavens are opening. The wind of the Holy Spirit is blowing. Holy fire is consuming all that is dross and refining all that is gold. The latter and the former rains are falling. You will reap before the sower's seed hits the ground.

"The time to raise the standard for Christ dawns today for you."

Faith is Knowing God

And they that know thy name will put their trust in thee: for thou, LORD, hast not forsaken them that seek thee. (Psalm 9:10)

Dr. Sumrall was my spiritual mentor, my pastor, my friend—a man of faith and destiny.

In the early years of my ministry, after a service in which he had preached for me, I apologized to Dr. Sumrall for not being better prepared for him. I said, "Dr. Sumrall, I am just going to have to increase my faith and get a bigger place. Then when you come we can have room to accommodate the people, and your products won't get blown over by the wind."

In Dr. Sumrall's unique fashion, he spoke directly to me and said, "Hmm. You don't need more faith."

I said, "No, Sir, you are right. Thank you." My inexperience was sitting across the table from this man of great wisdom and experience.

He said, "What you need is to know what faith is."

"Yes, Sir, I would like to know," I responded eagerly.

He answered, "Faith is simply knowing God."

"By faith, we know and trust God."

Spring Up O Well!

Spring up, O well; sing ye unto it. (Numbers 21:17)

Jesus also declares, "But whosoever drinketh of the water that I shall give him shall never thirst; but the water that I shall give him shall be in him a well of water springing up into everlasting life" (John 4:14). Stop drinking from the old wells of your past traditions and worldly preoccupations. Refuse to drink the stagnant, sin-infested, putrid waters of this world. Instead, dig new wells deep into the waters of God.

Sing a new song unto the Lord as Israel did: "Then Israel sang this song, Spring up, O well; sing ye unto it" (Numbers 21:17). Christ is the well of living water springing up within us.

We must allow His well to flow continually and eternally from within us through the Holy Spirit. "He that believeth on me [Jesus], as the Scripture hath said, out of his belly shall flow rivers of living water. (But this spake he of the Spirit, which they that believe on him should receive)" (John 7:38, 39).

_____

_____

_____

_____

_____

_____

_____

_____

_____

_____

"Let God's well of water spring up within you."

The Final Act Of Human Drama

Wherefore seeing we also are compassed about with so great a cloud of witnesses, let us lay aside every weight, and the sin which doth so easily beset us, and let us run with patience the race that is set before us.
(Hebrews 12:1)

The citizens of heaven sit on the edge of their seats. As if viewing a thrilling suspense story, they peer through the portals of eternity onto the stage of time to witness the final scene of the human drama. The curtain has risen on the final act. Will the lead character rise to the occasion? It's time for us to unveil the character of the lead player.

The end of this eternal drama for the hearts and souls of humanity rests with us. Throughout the ages saints have journeyed through wildernesses, crossed deserts, faced hostile animals and governments and sacrificed their lives so we might have this moment in spiritual history. The call to bring in the harvest, win the battle and possess the land rests with us—the final generation.

To us the sword has been passed. In this hour we are anointed to raise high the standard of Jesus Christ and proclaim the Gospel with Pentecostal power.

"A cloud of witnesses has gathered to see you finish the race."

Get Ready!

Watch therefore: for ye know not what hour your Lord doth come (Matthew 24:42)

How are you sleeping at night? Do you rest well knowing that your day was filled with the Lord, or does a restlessness pervade your nights gripped by the icy tentacles of fear, causing you to wake up in cold sweats?

Like it or not, history avalanches around you toward the precipice of eternity. As quickly as a blink of the eye, the end could overtake you.

Are you ready?

The Lord is coming again . . . soon! Jesus warned us to gird our loins, keep our lights burning and to be ready and watching for the Bridegroom. As His bride, we must be alert and prepared (Luke 12:35,36). "Remember therefore how thou has received and heard, and hold fast, and repent. If therefore thou shalt not watch, I will come on thee as a thief, and thou shalt not know what hour I will come upon thee" (Revelation 3:3).

It's approaching midnight. Are you prepared to receive your Bridegroom and His blessing? Or will you be caught sleeping and lacking? The final watch is approaching. Are you ready?

_____

_____

_____

_____

_____

_____

_____

_____

_____

_____

"Tomorrow may be too late. Be ready now to meet Jesus."

The Revolution Has Begun!

Who is she that looketh forth as the morning, fair as the moon, clear as the sun, and terrible as an army with banners? (Song of Solomon 6:10)

This war that rages in the final day, before eternity, has a specific battle plan. First, the enemy has been identified and his strategies unmasked. "Put on the whole armour of God, that ye may be able to stand against the wiles of the devil" (Ephesians 6:11). The enemy is Satan, whose tactics include accusing the saints (Revelation 12:10).

Second, the revolution's outcome has already been determined. While the outcome of the American Revolutionary War hung in the balance for months, the outcome of this final day revolutionary war has already been revealed. The army of saints in the true Church of Jesus Christ will overcome and defeat Satan. He will be cast into a lake of everlasting fire for eternity (Revelation 20).

Third and finally, we must be prepared to wage war. The lazy, nonchalant attitude of many toward evangelism, conversion, repentance, revival, renewal, and holiness must be radically changed and altered by our God who is a consuming fire (Hebrews 12:29).

Are you ready for the revolution? How do you enlist in this awesome army that marches "fair as the moon, clear as the sun, and terrible as an army with banners?" (Song of Solomon 6:10) Into some armies soldiers are drafted; for others, soldiers volunteer. The only way to enter the Lord's victorious army is to surrender. Radically surrender to the Lord of the battle, the King of kings, Jesus.

_____

_____

_____

_____

_____

"Radically surrender and prepare to march in the Lord's army."

The Only Way is Jesus

Jesus saith unto him, I am the way, the truth, and the life: no man cometh unto the Father, but by me. (John 14:6)

Neither Buddha, Mohammed or Krishna could have saved my friends, me or you. The millions who have surrendered to their philosophies and religion receive just that: philosophy and religion. I like the bumper stickers often seen around Christmas time, "Wise Men Still Seek Him." In this last day, before eternity, we need to possess enough wisdom to do one thing right—seek the only One who can save and change our lives.

Jesus Christ is the only One who has the power to give us new life. Whoever the Son sets free, is free indeed (John 8:36) because Jesus became flesh (John 1:14) and dwelt among us to give us eternal life. Everyone in the end time army must be set free by Jesus.

Jesus doesn't require hard works that produce fruitless religion. We don't have to pay thousands of dollars to travel to "holy" earthly places to throw rocks at stone pillars representing Satan, wash in the "holy" rivers, shave our heads or grow beards. When we surrender, Jesus sends the Holy Spirit to restore us to life.

_____

_____

_____

_____

_____

_____

_____

_____

_____

"Only one way exists to get to heaven—Jesus."

The Love of God

God is love. In this was manifested the love of God toward us, because that God sent his only begotten Son into the world, that we might live through him. Herein is love, not that we loved God, but that he loved us, and sent his Son to be the propitiation for our sins. (1 John 4:8b–10)

Religion is man seeking God. Christianity isn't about religion but about relationship. Desiring a covenant relationship with us, God seeks us out. He loves us unselfishly and unconditionally. Being in covenant relationship with Him doesn't do anything for God. He does not need us, nor can we do anything for Him. Rather, God pursues us out of agape—unconditional love. In fact, He is driven to give to us.

I love my wife, Joni, with unconditional love. That means I love her whether or not she acts loving toward me. It also means that I love her whether or not I feel like it. I am in covenant relationship with her through marriage. I have promised to love her "for better or worse." And I am a driven husband. I am driven to give her love, material necessities and every luxury I can lavish upon her. The covenant I have with Joni imparts my every blessing to her.

In a much greater way, God is driven to give to us. His very nature of love compels Him to be a giver. The Father gave His Son to save us. That gift is the greatest act of unconditional love in eternity.

_____

_____

_____

_____

_____

_____

_____

_____

_____

"God's love in Christ seeks you out to save, deliver and heal you."

Fear's Power Has Been Broken

For God hath not given us the spirit of fear; but of power, and of love, and of a sound mind. (2 Timothy 1:7)

Fear makes us hide in the shadows. Lurking in the shadows are all the lies and half-truths that chain our lives to the past and shatter all our dreams of new tomorrows. Mephibosheth (2 Samuel 9) believed the lie that a physical handicap and a sinful ancestor had ruined his potential and promise. So he hid behind the lie and avoided the struggle and pain of facing the truth and changing his life.

Is there a lie that you are hiding behind? An abusive relationship? A handicap? A sinful past? An unconfessed, dark sin? An emotional hurt? A mental lapse? Maybe you crawl into the secret world of the Internet and exchange your identity for another. Wrapped in this deceptive game, do you continue to tell yourself the lie that you are nobody and that nobody cares? By believing this lie, you are accepting the curse and denying your blessing.

The power and love of God, coupled with the mind of Christ, can break the bondage of fear in your life. You have nothing or no one to fear!

"Live in faith not in fear."

A New Creation

Therefore if any man be in Christ, he is a new creature: old things are passed away; behold, all things are become new. (2 Corinthians 5:17)

Social commentators have labeled this present generation of youth as Generation X. They are not Baby Boomers or Busters. They seem to have no purpose or direction. No name seems appropriate for this generation of mixed cultures and ideas, so they are simply designated as "X." Mephibosheth may have been the first member of Generation X. Children poked fun at him. Women laughed at him. Men ignored him. He was living in a Jewish ghetto on the outskirts of nowhere—a place called Lo-debar. For him, annihilation would have been welcomed. His life was a living hell, not inflicted by others but by the prison of his own torturous thoughts. He was "Ex," ex-royalty.

How horrible that sounds. "Ex" means nobody. As an "ex," ex-wife, ex-husband, ex-employee, you are defined by what you are not, instead of by what you are. You were somebody, but now you wear the scarlet letter of "X," sown on the fabric of your soul for all to see and scorn.

You are not an "X." In Christ, you are a new creation (2 Corinthians 5:17). The old has passed away and all things are becoming new. Stop listening to the labels the world gives you, and claim what Jesus has given you!

_____

_____

_____

_____

_____

_____

_____

_____

" Refuse to be an 'Ex.' You are a new creation in Christ. "

Don't Sell Out

And the LORD shall make thee the head, and not the tail; and thou shalt be above only, and thou shalt not be beneath; if that thou hearken unto the commandments of the LORD thy God, which I command thee this day, to observe and to do them. (Deuteronomy 28:13)

People may intimidate us. The opinions of others may be even more important to us than God's opinion of us. Some love the praise of men more than the praise of God (John 12:43). As a result, they retreat from any criticism or persecution. They go out of their way to please those whom they esteem and to placate those whom they fear. They accept the crutches of humiliation instead of standing firm on the solid support of God's truth.

If you find yourself running from intimidation, you will always be crippled by the opinions of others. Refuse to be intimated by or to sell out to your circumstances.

Mephibosheth of the Bible dwelt in the house of Machir, which means "sold out." He had sold out to his circumstances. Have you ever said, "Well, under the circumstances, I'm doing okay"?

The Bible declares that you are more than a conqueror (Romans 8:37). You are the head and not the tail. You are above and not beneath. But if your circumstances dictate your lifestyle instead of your position, then you will sell out your birthright for your current situation instead of waiting for your future promise. Don't settle for anything less than what God wants for your life.

_____

_____

_____

_____

_____

_____

_____

_____

"Forsake the praise of men. Only desire to please God."

Receive Jesus as Lord and Savior

For whosoever shall call upon the name of the Lord shall be saved. (Romans 10:13)

If you have already received Jesus as Savior, allow Him to show you what He wants you to do. Stay surrendered. Jesus has the answer for whatever you're going through.

If you haven't received Jesus yet, pause right now and let down all your defenses. Why not stop running? Why not say "Yes" to God? Before you turn another page, you can surrender your life to Jesus and be filled with the Holy Spirit's power to change your life. He will change you from the inside out and equip you to spend eternity with Him.

Are you ready? Pray out loud with complete and radical surrender:

"Father God, I repent of my sins right now before you and ask you to forgive me, a sinner, through the sacrificial offering and blood of Jesus Christ. I surrender all to you now, in Jesus' name, and promise to follow you all the days of my life. I pray this, Heavenly Father, in Jesus' name. Amen."

If you prayed this prayer for the first time, I want to welcome you to the family of God! Scripture tells us all of heaven is rejoicing over your decision for Christ . . . and so do I! Now I invite you to say, *"I'm going to serve God and not the devil. I'm going to live life and experience God's blessing, in Jesus' name."*

_____

_____

_____

_____

_____

_____

_____

_____

_____

_____

" Confess Jesus as the Lord and Savior of your life. "

The Last Day Before Eternity

But every man in his own order: Christ the firstfruits; afterward they that are Christ's at his coming. Then cometh the end, when he shall have delivered up the kingdom of God, even the Father; when he shall have put down all rule and all authority and power. For he must reign, till he hath put all enemies under his feet. The last enemy that shall be destroyed is death. (1 Corinthians 15:23-26)

There is a coming day—the last day before eternity—when all who have surrendered to God's love through Christ will receive another divine life change. And since the dark day of Adam's transgression in the garden, God has been preparing humanity for this, according to His time.

God wills that every human being be given the time and truth necessary to prepare for this powerful transition which will occur at the last ticking moment before time, as we know it, ceases to be. For those who are unprepared, eternal separation from God meted out by the Judge they rejected as King, awaits them. In this life, there is a heaven to be gained and a hell to be shunned.

By the time any of us face eternity, less than a 100 years have usually passed. This is less than one-tenth of what Scripture reveals as the length of one of God's days: "But, beloved, be not ignorant of this one thing, that one day is with the Lord as a thousand years, and a thousand years as one day" (2 Peter 3:8). So for each of us, life is but a vapor that appears and fades away. Live each day knowing it could be the last day before eternity!

_____

_____

_____

_____

_____

_____

"You are living in the last days; live boldly for Christ!"

Miracles Are For Today

This beginning of miracles did Jesus in Cana of Galilee, and manifested forth his glory; and his disciples believed on him. (John 2:11)

Jesus' first miracle was to turn water to wine. What Jesus began is not finished; the Miracle-worker has never changed: "Jesus Christ the same yesterday to day and forever" (Hebrews 13:8).

The last miracle did not end with the last apostle named in the Bible; for this to be true there would have to be a complete absence of miracles. Even one miracle would disprove this erroneous statement.

In Mark 16:15-20, Jesus confirmed that miracles are not special gifts for a few, but they are for all believers. Those claiming that the age of miracles has ended deny the power of prayer. For God to hear and answer your prayer is a miracle.

When you pray, expect God to hear and answer your prayer. Healing is for today. Deliverance is for today. Signs and wonders are for today! Write down some miracles God has manifested in your life recently.

_____

_____

_____

_____

_____

_____

_____

_____

_____

_____

_____

_____

"In the revolutionary church, miracles are commonplace."

Under Christ's Banner

Lift ye up a banner upon the high mountain, exalt the voice unto them, shake the hand, that they may go into the gates of the nobles. (Isaiah 13:2)

The Bible has much to say about banners and standards—flags, if you will. Who is lifting up banners and whose banners are they flying? The church raises high the banner of Christ!

However, not everyone who shows up for church on Sunday morning to go through the rigors of religiosity and march to the cadences and creeds of men is part of the true church of Jesus Christ. She is the church within a church. The kingdom within a kingdom. The people of God within a people. The living water within a desert. A remnant church called to be a mighty army marching into the world under Christ's banner.

There is a problem in America. Yes, we may raise a national flag or banner at our sporting events and political rallies. Nonetheless, within the hearts of many who stand under that banner exists confusion, a lack of vision and a wavering commitment to our nation's standard.

There is a problem in the church. We, too, are having difficulty seeing our standard. We need to fix our eyes on the banner of Christ over us because we are to be a terrible army (Song of Solomon 6:10). The army with banners is a terror to the forces of darkness and the alien armies of the Antichrist, which are arrayed against the body of Christ. The enemy is marching against the Lord Jesus Christ and against his anointed standard bearers, the church.

Take your place in the remnant Church!

"March under Christ's banner into battle."

Joy Comes in the Morning

For his anger endureth but a moment; in his favour is life: weeping may endure for a night, but joy cometh in the morning. (Psalm 30:5)

Too often we find ourselves looking backward into the night instead of marching forward into the morning. Too often we find ourselves willing to endure darkness rather than declaring, *no more night* in our lives. It is time for us to start living in the light of day. It is time for us to start living where the atmosphere of expectancy, drenched with the moisture from heaven, rains down, soaking the soil of hope and creating a breeding ground for miracles.

There is no time like the dawning. No matter how sultry the night has been, no matter how dark, "Joy cometh in the morning" (Psalm 30:5).

You may be walking through the driest, darkest, most desperate situation of your life, but hold on—joy comes in the morning. Remember, weeping lasts only for a night. The army of God goes forth and marches under the banner of light. Leave your night behind. Raise high the banner of Christ and march with the army of light.

_____

_____

_____

_____

_____

_____

_____

_____

_____

_____

"No matter how dark your night, Jesus will bring you joy in the morning."

Shine With His Light Today

In him was life; and the life was the light of men. (John 1:4)

Our Commander Himself declares, "I am the light of the world" (John 9:5). We march under the banner of light. Christ as the true light invades the darkness, and darkness cannot overcome His light. The Word proclaims, "In him [Christ] was life; and the life was the light of men. And the light shineth in darkness; and the darkness comprehended it not" (John 1:4-5).

Go forward with a church which gets up with the morning light and experiences the former and latter rains of God. Remember, no matter how hot the night has been, the dawn is always accompanied by a cool, moist breeze. A fresh breeze of God's Spirit is issuing forth today over the sapphire sill of heaven's gate for those who raise high the standard of Jesus Christ. Those under His banner are rejoicing every morning as they rise up saying, "This is the day which the Lord hath made; we will rejoice and be glad in it" (Psalm 118:24). The greatest day, the greatest dawn, the greatest morning that the church has ever seen lies straight ahead.

The church marches into the new millennium under Christ's banner of light, dispelling darkness wherever she goes and establishing His revolutionary kingdom of light. Today, dispel all darkness with the light of Christ wherever you go.

_____

_____

_____

_____

_____

_____

_____

_____

_____

"Darkness flees when you march under Christ's banner of light."

Reflect Christ's Light

Praise ye him, sun and moon: praise him, all ye stars of light. (Psalm 148:3)

In Palestine I've seen the moon hanging in the sky while the sun is still dawning. Both sun and moon share celestial beauty. The moon is significant only as she fulfills her purpose in reflecting the light, energy and glory of the sun. As we march under Christ's banner, we reflect His light and glory. This is how the world sees Christ reflected in us.

Genesis 1:27 declares that God created us in His own image. The word *image* refers to "a reflection." We are the moon to the Son of light. The moon has no ability to shine on her own. Those under His banner have no persona, no personality, no ability, no talent and no power of their own to dispel the darkness. Like Moses, we must go to the mountain of God to receive the light of His glory. His face shone with God's glory, not his own (see Exodus 34:29-35).

God is able as our banner (or standard) to do exceedingly abundantly in us above all that we can imagine or think (see Ephesians 3:20). The anointing of the bride—the church—is to go forth as the morning and to be like the moon—reflecting the awesome light and glory of the Bridegroom, Jesus Christ.

"Reflect His light wherever you go."

From Glory to Glory

But we all, with open face beholding as in a glass the glory of the Lord, are changed into the same image from glory to glory, even as by the Spirit of the Lord. (2 Corinthians 3:18)

Plant yourself under the standard of the true light of Jesus Christ. Be what the Bible ordains you to become: "But we all, with open face beholding as in a glass the glory of the Lord, are changed into the same image from glory to glory, even as by the Spirit of the Lord" (2 Corinthians 3:18).

God miraculously changes all those who march under His banner. His standard transforms and refreshes all those who raise it. Raise the standard and be changed! Radically surrender and be transformed from glory to glory.

Like the moon reflects the sun, you are to mirror the Son, Jesus Christ, and drive away all darkness. An old proverb says we must "light a candle to curse the darkness." Shelve that saying! Rather, burn with the blazing banner of Christ and chase the darkness back into the shadows of night.

_____

_____

_____

_____

_____

_____

_____

_____

_____

_____

_____

"When you radically surrender to Christ, His glory transforms you."

Point to the Spot!

But as one was felling a beam, the ax head fell into the water: and he cried, and said, Alas, master! for it was borrowed. And the man of God said, Where fell it?" (2 Kings 6:5-6a)

Are you an effective warrior for Christ? You may be like the man cutting wood when his ax broke and the ax head fell into the water. He cried out, "Alas, Master!" When you have lost your spiritual cutting edge, you are no longer able to do the work.

Looking into the murky waters of your past, ask the Holy Spirit to show you the spot where it happened. You may be bound by past sin. Point to the spot now and confess:

- Right there is where I surrendered to sin.
- Right there is where I started drinking from old wells of religious tradition.
- Right there is where I stopped praying and praising Him.
- Right there is where I stopped reading my Bible.
- Right there is where I compromised the truth.
- Right there is where impurity stained my purity.
- Right there is where I stopped confessing God's Word.

Now, stop pointing to the sin and start pointing to the Savior. Stop crawling around in the pigpen and start washing in the living water of Jesus. Cry out, "Here I am, God, standing in the need of prayer. Here I am, God, standing in need of You!"

The time has come for you to come clean with God. Get washed by the blood. Become transparent before Him and He will shine through you. Your spiritual weaponry will be restored, your anointing will increase and you will become a victorious warrior in the end time church!

"Point to the spot of your sin and come clean with God."

God Is Your Banner

And Moses [put your name in his stead] built an altar, and called the name of it Jehovah-nissi [God is my Banner]. (Exodus 17:15)

I am challenging you right now to build an altar where you live, work or worship. Stop what you are doing. Build an altar. If you have left His banner unattended, put that sin on the altar. Cover yourself and your altar with the banner of His love, crying out for His mercy and forgiveness. Read aloud this verse, "And Moses [put your name in his stead] built an altar, and called the name of it Jehovah Nissi [God is my *Banner*]" (Exodus 17:15).

Come out of the desert and into the living waters of God. Become a standard bearer today. Your past isn't important. What matters is your radical desire to surrender totally to Jehovah Nissi as your commander.

Standard bearers never audition for a role or present their past experiences and credentials as if being hired as mercenaries. Standard bearers refuse to drink stagnant waters from old wells. Standard bearers are birthed by the anointing of the Holy Spirit at the altar of Jehovah Nissi. Take your place of destiny as His standard bearer.

_____

_____

_____

_____

_____

_____

_____

_____

_____

_____

_____

"March boldly into battle under the banner of Jehovah Nissi."

Repent and Be Refreshed

Repent ye therefore, and be converted, that your sins may be blotted out, when the times of refreshing shall come from the presence of the Lord. (Acts 3:19)

Every fresh, new move of God in human history has been preceded by the devotion and righteous passion of one or more individuals who knew their God and knew where they were going.

In a day when the foundations of our society are no longer built on the solid rock of Christ but on the sinking sand of worldly relativism . . . God's people must come to the forefront and become what has been lacking in the body of Christ. We need godly, anointed standard bearers to raise the standards of physical purity, moral integrity and spiritual intensity.

God is equipping, preparing and anointing His church to be His standard bearers—a mighty army that repairs and restores the foundation of Bible truths.

As we count down to a new millennium, God is searching for a people, a remnant church, a revolutionary church, that is repentant, refreshed, restored *and* eagerly expecting the return of Jesus Christ. Have you repented of all sin and received refreshing from the presence of the Lord?

_____

_____

_____

_____

_____

_____

_____

_____

"Join the ranks of the remnant church today!"

Be a Conqueror Through Christ

Nay, in all these things we are more than conquerors through him that loved us. For I am persuaded, that neither death, nor life, nor angels, nor principalities, nor powers, nor things present, nor things to come, Nor height, nor depth, nor any other creature, shall be able to separate us from the love of God, which is in Christ Jesus our Lord. (Romans 8:37-39)

Are you ready to have restored to you everything the enemy has stolen and to take back what rightfully belongs to you? Are you willing to dig new wells and receive what God wants to do in your life?

Possibly you are fed up with trying to live on the emotional charge of weekly church services which leave you powerless to combat the driving forces of darkness during the week.

Your banner may seem full of holes, and from a distance your standard may appear tarnished. Your well may be obstructed so that no water is flowing forth. But let me remind you that you are the head and not the tail (see Deuteronomy 28:13)! You are above and not beneath. You are the victor and not the victim! His living water continually refreshes you.

Living water is flowing from the fountains of the Holy Spirit within you and you can never be separated from God's love and power. Live restored and renewed. Remove every obstruction of sin in your life and let His water flow through you so that you refresh others with His Spirit.

_____

_____

_____

_____

_____

_____

"Conquerors are refreshed by His living water."

Repent! God's Kingdom is at Hand

From that time Jesus began to preach, and to say, Repent: for the kingdom of heaven is at hand. (Matthew 4:17)

Sin is what caused our Kinsman-Redeemer, our High Priest, the Word from before the foundation of the world, to leave His eternal throne and invade earth through a lowly manger. Sin brought Jesus from heaven's majesty to a disgraceful, shameful death on a cross so that He could reconcile, revive, refresh and restore the body of Christ to the Father's side.

But the initial call you must obey was first uttered by the Savior and has been echoed by His standard bearers throughout history: "Repent!"

Without repentance, the next phases—refreshing, revival and restoration—cannot come (Acts 3:19). "*Repent,* and be baptized every one of you in the name of Jesus Christ for the remission of sins, and ye shall receive the gift of the Holy Ghost" (Acts 2:38, italics added).

"Obey Christ's call to repent."

Draw Near to God

Let us draw near with a true heart in full assurance of faith, having our hearts sprinkled from an evil conscience, and our bodies washed with pure water. (Hebrews 10:22)

Drawing near to God involves physical purity and moral integrity. We cannot live mired in immorality and then expect God to show up whenever we call upon His name. Nor can we have an evil conscience and expect our minds to be transformed into the mind of Christ.

Paul urges us, "Having therefore these promises, dearly beloved, let us cleanse ourselves from all filthiness of the flesh and spirit, perfecting holiness in the fear of God" (2 Corinthians 7:1). Begin today. Put away all unclean thoughts and acts. Present yourself as a holy sacrifice and approach His throne with the full assurance of His grace.

Draw near to God without pride and in full humility. Examine your heart and be washed and restored by the blood of Christ. Write down a self-examination and confess every sin that separates you from God.

_____

_____

_____

_____

_____

_____

_____

_____

_____

_____

_____

_____

"Boldly draw near to God with a pure heart."

Sorrow is Not Repentance

For godly sorrow worketh repentance to salvation. (2 Corinthians 7:10)

The Bible says that the "wages of sin is death" (Romans 6:23). Take a step back and examine your life for evidence of death. Ask these questions:

- Are you in a dry season?
- Are your relationships dying?
- Do you feel parched and empty?
- Is your joy dying?
- Are your plans and hopes dying?
- Is anything or everything that you touch dying?

The only way to turn away from the desert and death is to repent. No, I am not talking about just being sorry or sad about your sin. Sorrow is not repentance. I have seen people fall all over the altar on Sunday, consumed with tears and shaking with remorse, only to leave the altar and go about sinning all week. The next Sunday they come to the altar again, crying and expecting to feel something from God.

Sorrow may accompany repentance but sorrow is not repentance.

Repentance is change! Change your season . . . Change your mind . . . Change your actions . . . Change your direction . . . Change your character.

Repentance involves a total change of life. Get radical and give permission to Jesus Christ to change you from the inside out!

_____

_____

_____

_____

_____

_____

_____

"True repentance demands total surrender and radical change."

Thy Will Not Mine Be Done

I am the LORD thy God, which have brought thee out of the land of Egypt, out of the house of bondage. Thou shalt have no other gods before me. Thou shalt not make unto thee any graven image, or any likeness of any thing that is in heaven above, or that is in the earth beneath, or that is in the water under the earth: Thou shalt not bow down thyself to them, nor serve them: for I the LORD thy God am a jealous God, visiting the iniquity of the fathers upon the children unto the third and fourth generation of them that hate me; And shewing mercy unto thousands of them that love me, and keep my commandments. (Exodus 20:2-6)

In the kingdom of heaven you don't presume to tell God anything. You simply bow your head in reverence to the King of kings. No longer do you pray for what *you* want. Rather, the kingdom prayer is: "*Thy* kingdom come. *Thy* will be done, in earth as it is in heaven" (Matthew 6:10, italics added).

Jesus established the heavenly order on earth. God's kingdom is His right to govern every minute molecule of human existence. God's kingdom is His right of lordship, authority, power and law. God declares who shall be exalted and who shall be brought low. He shows mercy to whom He decides to show mercy. His say is final and absolute in our lives, marriages, families, vocations and church. He is King and we are not!

God will not share His throne with anyone or anything else. The ancient Israelites tried to make God just a *part* of their lives. They desired to worship God, but also to worship Baal and Molech. But God is a jealous God. We are to have no other gods before Him (Exodus 20:3).

_____

_____

_____

_____

_____

"Seek to do His will in your life daily."

Rend Your Heart Before God

All *have sinned and fallen short of the glory of God!* (Romans 3:23)

To march in His army and to raise His standard, we must humble ourselves, pray, seek God's face and *turn from our wicked ways.* That's repentance. Only after repentance does God hear from heaven, forgive us and heal our land.

It's time to put on sackcloth, sit in the ashes of repentance and cry out to God for His forgiving mercy through Christ Jesus. Perhaps you have read these words but believe yourself to be exempt from Jesus' call of repentance. You may think you are living a good life and are free from sin. But the convicting words of God confront you: "If we say that we have no sin, we deceive ourselves, and the truth is not in us" (1 John 1:8).

The truth steps on our toes, shouts in our faces and spotlights the darkness in our hearts that is filled with unrighteousness. "*All* have sinned, and come short of the glory of God!" (Romans 3:23, italics added, NIV).

The first step toward becoming God's soldier is repentance—putting on sackcloth and rending our hearts before God.

_____

_____

_____

_____

_____

_____

_____

_____

_____

_____

_____

"Put on sackcloth and turn from your wicked ways."

Are You Ready?

If we confess our sins, he is faithful and just to forgive us our sins, and to cleanse us from all unrighteousness." (1 John 1:9)

We need to repent of both sins of commission and sins of omission. God is holding us accountable for doing the things we shouldn't do, and for not doing the things we should. Now is the time to repent. Are you ready?

- Are you ready to stop doing that thing you know not to do? God can deliver you from the addiction of sin.
- Are you ready to do what you know is right? God can empower you to walk in righteousness.
- Are you ready to change your mind? If so, God can renew your mind.
- Are you ready to turn from sin and wickedness? If so, God can forgive you.
- Are you ready to admit your helplessness and hopelessness? If so, God can restore you.
- Are you ready for the dry season to end? If so, Christ will bring forth living water from your life.
- Are you ready to enthrone the exiled King? If so, Christ will establish His throne on the seat of your heart.
- Are you ready to ascribe to His lordship? If so, Christ will be Lord over all your life.

_____

_____

_____

_____

_____

_____

_____

_____

"If you are ready, God is faithful to forgive and renew you."

Be Refreshed and Restored

And I will restore to you the years that the locust hath eaten, the cankerworm, and the caterpillar, and the palmerworm, my great army which I sent among you. And ye shall eat in plenty, and be satisfied, and praise the name of the LORD your God, that hath dealt wondrously with you: and my people shall never be ashamed. (Joel 2:25-26)

It's time to raise the standard in the church. It's time for the church to launch out into the proverbial deep waters where it cannot stand by its own strength and efforts and where it must be sustained by the river and wind of the Holy Spirit.

Once we repent of our mediocrity and once we start desiring the refreshing of God, we will see God's wind begin to fill our sails. In Acts 3:19, we see that after repentance and conversion come the times of refreshing in God's presence.

I want you to know that God is in the refreshing business. He is in the restoration business. God is going to lean over the pavilions of glory and the sapphire sill of heaven's gate. He is going to draw in a breath of eternal air and begin to blow a blast, a whirlwind from heaven, that will refresh all of His people. A wind is starting to blow in the church. The sounds of God's refreshing wind and rain are moving the church beyond the status quo which we have known for so long. God is ready to refresh and revive your life.

_____

_____

_____

_____

_____

_____

_____

"Ask God to refresh and restore your life."

Live In Spiritual Expectancy

Arise, shine; for thy light is come, and the glory of the Lord is risen upon thee. (Isaiah 60:1)

What is the end time, revolutionary church like? She is not just an ordinary church. She is a church being blown by the wind of God. She is a revived, refreshed church marked by moral integrity, physical purity, spiritual intensity, personal devotion and holiness unto the Lord. She lives for His righteousness' sake and raises high His standard.

A church filled with repentant standard bearers is no longer content with empty pews or, worse yet, pew-sitters. She is a church breaking forth as the morning. Isaiah 60:1 describes such a church, "Arise, shine; for thy light is come, and the glory of the Lord is risen upon thee."

A church who looks forth as the morning will live in the spiritual atmosphere of expectancy with a leadership who refuses to move until God moves and refuses to give up until they receive all God wants to give them.

"Live in end time, spiritual expectancy."

Leaders, Repent

Therefore, O ye shepherds, hear the word of the LORD; Thus saith the Lord GOD; Behold, I am against the shepherds; and I will require my flock at their hand, and cause them to cease from feeding the flock; neither shall the shepherds feed themselves any more; for I will deliver my flock from their mouth, that they may not be meat for them. (Ezekiel 34:9,10)

What kind of leadership do we need in the revived and refreshed church of God's people? We need leaders who are willing to stay up all night in sackcloth seeking God and crying out, "More of You and less of me." We need leaders more concerned for the lost than for how the world views them.

We need priests so thirsty for a drink of living water from the river of God that they will pray the floodgates of heaven open. We need priests who have totally left the night behind and are willing to look forth into the morning.

We need church leaders who are repentant before God. And we need church members who will pray for their leaders instead of judging and criticizing them.

Pray for your pastor and church leadership. Ask God's Spirit to convict them and bring a spirit of repentance upon their lives. Thank the Lord for the living waters that flow from your leaders. Ask Him to make you a priest with a broken and contrite heart.

_____

_____

_____

_____

_____

_____

_____

_____

_____

"Pray for pastors and church leaders."

God's Wind Is Blowing

Then the Lord answered Job out of the whirlwind. (Job 38:1)

Prepare for the wind to blow in your life. Watch out! I'm not talking about a gentle breeze to refresh you. God is a whirlwind, a mighty tornado of eternal proportions; and He is ready to release His life into you as He did into Job, "Then the Lord answered Job out of the whirlwind" (Job 38:1).

God always distinguishes Himself by a wind. In the wind God sends provision. Remember how God propelled the Red Sea with a strong east wind so that dry ground appeared? Remember how God provided the wind to deliver the children of Israel, allowing them to cross the Red Sea and escape the pursuing armies of Pharaoh (Exodus 14:21)? Remember how God passed by Elijah with a great and strong wind (1 Kings 19:11)?

From the very beginning, God's wind and breath have been a propulsion for us. God breathed the wind of His breath into us and we became living souls (Genesis 2:7). We were propelled from clay into living bodies and provided with His breath so that life might be sustained in our earthen vessels.

God's wind of refreshing needs to blow in your life. His wind sweeps away all ritualism, legalism, religiosity and vain attempts to please man. His wind brings genuine Pentecostal power.

_____

_____

_____

_____

_____

_____

_____

_____

"Pray for the wind of God's Spirit to blow in your life."

Pray Passionately

Elias was a man subject to like passions as we are, and he prayed earnestly that it might not rain: and it rained not on the earth by the space of three years and six months. And he prayed again, and the heaven gave rain, and the earth brought forth her fruit. (James 5:17,18)

You have prayed until your tongue is swollen and completely dry. You have used every confession book until the pages are worn, torn and falling out. The dry heat of battle brings sweat to your brow. You throw your spiritual windows open hoping to feel a little breeze and to see a small cloud on the horizon foretelling a coming rain. God demands that you pray with passion for His rain. When you pray, always pray expecting the answer . . .

For the atmosphere of expectancy is the breeding ground for miracles. It doesn't matter what you are going through. It doesn't matter how dark your circumstances are. You are going to make it all the way to the other side. Remember God's promise, "When thou passest through the waters, I will be with thee; and through the rivers, they shall not overflow thee" (Isaiah 43:2). You will make it to the other side. He will see you through to the times of refreshing.

"Pray passionately for rain from heaven."

Baptized With Fire

I indeed baptize you with water unto repentance: but he that cometh after me is mightier than I, whose shoes I am not worthy to bear: he shall baptize you with the Holy Ghost, and with fire. (Matthew 3:11)

John's prophetic statement doesn't end with the baptism of fire. He also speaks of a purging, devouring, cleansing and an unquenchable fire that comes through Christ. He says, "Whose fan is in his hand, and he will thoroughly purge his floor, and gather his wheat into the garner; but he will burn up the chaff with unquenchable fire" (Matthew 3:12).

An Old Testament parallel or counterpart to this text speaks of the fire that devours and purges. Isaiah 33:10-12 reveals, "Now will I rise, saith the Lord; now will I be exalted; now will I lift up myself. Ye shall conceive chaff, ye shall bring forth stubble: your breath, as fire, shall devour you. And the people shall be as the burnings of lime: as thorns cut up shall they be burned in the fire."

When the fire of revival falls upon the church, God's fire burns, purges and cleanses sinners in the camp. Yes, there are sinners in the church. Isaiah 33:14 declares, "The sinners in Zion are afraid." Some stand in dire need of repentance. Jeremiah observed that God's people had become so indifferent to sin that they couldn't even blush at the sight of their shame (Jeremiah 6:15). That is happening in the church today. How we need God's fire in the church! The revival fire that sweeps through the church will be twofold: a devouring fire and an everlasting, baptizing fire.

_____

_____

_____

_____

_____

_____

_____

"Jesus, baptize your church with Holy Ghost fire."

God Is a Consuming Fire

For our God is a consuming fire. (Hebrews 12:29)

Do you resist the work of God? Do you try to disobey the voice of God in your life?

If you want revival and refreshing, you must be prepared for the fire. Ananias and Sapphira were drawn to the baptizing fire but lacked the fear of God needed for His devouring fire. They fought the fire. They wanted the blessing but thought that they could lie to the Holy Spirit. Both were destroyed by God's fire; the chaff was burned, and they lost their lives (see Acts 5:1-10).

Yes, God's revival fire will burn the chaff right out of you, your household, your family, your workplace and your church. All of us need that purging fire which prepares us to receive the eternal fire we need to burn in our spirits. The same fire that baptizes also burns, purges, cleanses and prepares us to live a holy life.

We are to burn as clear as the sun. Fire is heat, light and passion. Jesus said that He is the light of the world. That's fire! Jesus also embodied the love of the Father. That's passion. The baptizing fire and passion burning within Jesus explodes in our midst as a consuming fire. God in our midst is "a consuming fire" (Hebrews 12:29).

_____

_____

_____

_____

_____

_____

_____

_____

"Let God's fire consume all in you that is unholy and impure."

Forged in Fire

He that walketh righteously, and speaketh uprightly; he that despiseth the gain of oppressions, that shaketh his hands from holding of bribes, that stoppeth his ears from hearing of blood, and shutteth his eyes from seeing evil; He shall dwell on high: his place of defense shall be the munitions of rocks: bread shall be given him; his waters shall be sure. (Isaiah 33:15,16)

Once purged and baptized by fire, what is the anointed standard bearer of Jesus Christ like? He walks in righteousness. He speaks truth. He hates injustice. He keeps evil from his ears and eyes. He dwells in God's presence, knowing that the source for all his physical and spiritual needs is God and God alone.

That army of Christ welcomes the purging, devouring fire of the Holy Spirit for purification and the power to go boldly into the world.

God's people cry out, "Oh Lord, please send the fire!" With the wind, rain and fire comes His power! His refreshing fills us with power! Be forged in His fire and become His standard bearer of truth and righteousness.

_____

_____

_____

_____

_____

_____

_____

_____

_____

_____

_____

"Forged in fire, you will become the standard bearer of the Lord."

Walk in God's Power

And what is the exceeding greatness of his power to usward who believe, according to the working of his mighty power, which he wrought in Christ, when he raised him from the dead, and set him at his own right hand in the heavenly places. (Ephesians 1:19, 20)

Power is the prerogative of God alone. All true and lasting power resides in Him. One Greek word for power is *dunamis,* from which we get the English word *dynamite.* Within that one word resides the meaning of miracle-working power, authoritative power and awesome, mighty power. All power belongs to God. "God hath spoken once; twice have I heard this; that power belongeth unto God" (Psalm 62:11).

God's power both resides and is manifested in the trinity. God's creative power brought the heavens and the earth into being. Without the Son, who is the Word of God "was not anything made that was made" (John 1:3). By Him all things consist and hold together" (Colossians 1:17). Through the Holy Spirit, God's power is manifested in miracles, signs, wonders and gifts.

The refreshing of God will be marked by His power. The same power that created the universe and conceived the Savior will reside in us, bringing resurrection power into our daily lives. Are you ready for the refreshing, for the revival and for the resurrection power that will come into your life after repentance and conversion? Hear the promise of God: "But ye shall receive power, after that the Holy Ghost is come upon you" (Acts 1:8).

_____

_____

_____

_____

_____

_____

"Walk boldly in the power of God."

Lift Up a Standard

When the enemy shall come in like a flood, the spirit of the Lord shall lift up a standard against him. (Isaiah 59:19b)

When irritation levels are high and patience is low, Satan comes to you in great wrath to destroy your life. He presents you with a multitude of inordinate fears and grotesque images that flash and burn in your imagination, draining you from peaceful and restful sleep. The enemy clouds your countenance with a dark cloud of oppression, leaving you more and more confused and disoriented.

When you see these things come to pass, know that spiritual wickedness in high places has come to destroy your life. It is time for your repentance; and time for God's refreshing and restoration in your life. True repentance involves a change of mind and a change of heart about God and toward God.

So this is the change you need: Repent of sin. Come out of the desert. Leave behind the status quo. Lift high the standard of Christ against the enemy.

Remember, the Bible says, "When the enemy shall come in like a flood, the spirit of the Lord shall *lift up a standard* against him" (Isaiah 59:19b, italics added). As you count down to the new millennium, determine to lift up your standard against the enemy daily.

_____

_____

_____

_____

_____

_____

_____

_____

_____

"Raise up the Lord's standard against the enemy."

Corn, Oil and Joy

Behold, I will send you corn, and wine, and oil, and ye shall be satisfied therewith: and I will no more make you a reproach among the heathen.
(Joel 2:19)

There is a new day dawning just over the horizon! In the past the church has been looked upon with scorn and disdain because she lacked the power and spiritual armor to withstand even the smallest onslaught of Satanic attack. But this verse says that our corn, wine and oil will be restored.

- **Corn represents the Word of God.**

With the banner of God's Word we, the church, will once again blaze the trail of Gospel truth and march to the forefront in His strength and power to recover our ministry and authority.

- **Oil represents the Holy Spirit.**

The wind, fire, power and anointing of the Holy Spirit will be manifested in our churches and in our lives, producing mighty miracles and pointing to the cross of Calvary. We will again be known as a body which is ready to walk under the command of Jesus.

- **Wine represents joy.**

The wine or joy of the Gospel will be returned to us. Things in this world are not getting better; they are getting worse. Our only hope is in living for, trusting in and obeying God and His Word. He will give us a song to sing at midnight when trouble seems to be closing in all around. Nothing shall be able rob us of our joy in Christ (John 16:22).

Wine, oil and corn do not flow and grow in dry land. They are the fruits of the fresh rain of God falling on the prepared soil of God's people. Plow the dry land. Pray in the rain. Cultivate the wine, oil and corn. Bring in an abundant harvest from the Lord.

"Enjoy the end time harvest of corn, oil and joy."

Blessed By Your Enemies

And the Egyptians were urgent upon the people, that they might send them out of the land in haste; for they said, We be all dead men. And the children of Israel did according to the word of Moses; and they borrowed [demanded] of the Egyptians jewels of silver, and jewels of gold, and raiment: And the Lord gave the people favour in the sight of the Egyptians, so that they lent unto them such things as they required. And they spoiled the Egyptians. (Exodus 12:33,35,36)

The Hebrew word for *borrowed* in verse 35 means *demanded.* The Israelites turned the tables on Pharaoh and basically told him, "If you want us to leave so bad, you are going to have to give us something. You are going to have to restore some things to us. Give us back our children, give us back our flocks and herds, give us some clothes, and don't forget to give us some money!" So Pharaoh loaded them up, sent them on their way and asked them to bless him before they left.

Wouldn't that be something—your enemies asking you to bless them! Before the return of Jesus, God is going to give you favor. He is going to cause your enemies to be at peace with you. Those who have cursed you, He will cause to bless you. Psalm 5:12 says, "For thou, Lord, wilt bless the righteous; with favour wilt thou compass him as with a shield." Those who have betrayed you, laughed at you and mocked you are going to bow their knees at the spout where the glory of God comes out of your life. God will prepare a table before you in the presence of your enemies and make them provide the food too!

_____

_____

_____

_____

_____

_____

"The Lord prepares a table for you in the presence of your enemies."

God Will Restore Your Health

He brought them forth also with silver and gold: and there was not one feeble person among their tribes. (Psalm 105:37)

God is going to restore health to your body as He did to the bodies of the Israelites. Psalm 105:37 reveals, "He brought them forth also with silver and gold: and there was not one feeble person among their tribes."

Do you notice what God did? He healed every person. I know it is hard to comprehend. Perhaps your body has been wracked with pain, arthritis or disease for many years. But the Bible says they were *all* restored to health.

There weren't any eyeglasses, hearing aids, canes, wheelchairs or walkers. There wasn't any heart disease; there were no tumors or cancer.

God healed every earache, every headache and every backache. Before Jesus splits the eastern sky and comes in His magnificent magnitude, I believe every single person in the church is going to be healed.

_____

_____

_____

_____

_____

_____

_____

_____

_____

_____

_____

_____

"By His stripes, you are healed."

God Will Supply all Your Needs

But my God shall supply all your need according to his riches in glory by Christ Jesus. (Philippians 4:19)

We will recover wealth. The church of Jesus Christ is not going to leave this planet deprived and full of debt! In order to fulfill the Great Commission we must have money. In order to preach the Gospel through the medium of television and short-wave radio to lost and hurting people around the world, we must have more than just a few crumpled-up one-dollar bills.

Before you can pay for your children's Christian education, your mortgage or your doctor bills, you need money. God will supply your needs according to His riches in glory!

And as the Egyptians did to the Israelites, the world is going to heap on us, the church, so much wealth that we are going to be able to dig out of debt and have money left over to spread the Gospel message! "The wealth of the sinner is laid up for the just" (Proverb 13:22).

"Trust the Lord to supply all your needs."

Heed the Call!

Then said Jesus unto his disciples, If any man will come after me, let him deny himself, and take up his cross, and follow me. For whosoever will save his life shall lose it: and whosoever will lose his life for my sake shall find it. (Matthew 16:24, 25)

Across the misty plains of time, a voice reaches from the shores of Galilee to this land. The voice sounds as a trumpet, rings as a carillon, roars as the thunder and crashes as towering breakers along a jagged, rocky shore.

Unmistakable . . . that voice. With a word, that voice brought galaxies into being; raised corpses from the dead; pronounced healing to all who listened; spoke judgment to every two-faced hypocrite and comforted the lost and distraught.

Now, that same voice comes as a still, small voice; as the sound of rushing rivers; as the balm of Gilead; as the conviction of the deepest truth and as the command for countless legions. Hear that voice: "Take up your cross and follow me."

Out of nail-pierced hands, spike-punctured feet and a dagger-torn side flowed the cleansing stream of Emmanuel's blood. What we freely receive, cost Jesus dearly. Receive all you need today, and follow Him.

_____

_____

_____

_____

_____

_____

_____

_____

_____

_____

_____

"Heed the call of Christ. Follow Him wherever He leads."

Echo the Master's Word

When the Message we preached came to you, it wasn't just words. Something happened in you. The Holy Spirit put steel in your convictions. You paid careful attention to the way we lived among you . . . you imitated the Master. Although great trouble accompanied the Word, you were able to take great joy from the Holy Spirit!—taking the trouble with the joy, the joy with the trouble . . . Your lives are echoing the Master's Word, not only in the provinces but all over the place. The news of your faith in God is out. We don't even have to say anything anymore—you're the message! (1 Thessalonians 1:5-8 TMB)

A separation is coming for the church and her standard bearers. We are to separate ourselves from worldliness unto holiness.

The standard bearer cannot be of the world. Yes, we live in the world for the purpose of being salt, light and a fire blazing for Christ. Still, we live lives separate from the world's standard. We raise high the standard of Christ, not the standard of MTV or Wall Street or Main Street. We do not reverberate the message coming out of Washington. We echo the Master's Word.

Paul is not talking about the work that the Thessalonians were doing as a result of faith. He is speaking about the work of faith which caused them to become regenerated, born-again believers. That work of faith caused them to leave their dead idols.

Righteousness is not what you do. It is the work of faith in you that takes place after God has resurrected Himself on the inside of you. He deposits His holiness in you after burning out and purging from you every past idol. His consuming fire destroys your idols. That's the work of faith within you.

_____

_____

_____

_____

_____

_____

"Destroy every idol. Let faith work in you to accomplish His will."

Your Labor of Love

Remembering without ceasing your work of faith, and labour of love, and patience of hope in our Lord Jesus Christ, in the sight of God and our Father. (1 Thessalonians 1:3)

If you are to heed His call to wholeness, the work of faith will cause you to leave every idol. For what? For your labor of love. What is that labor of love? Service. No longer will the world's principle of 20/80 apply to the church. In the world 20 percent of the people in an organization do all the giving and all the work while 80 percent sit around watching the rest serve. This should not be so in God's terrible army which goes forth as the morning under Christ's banner.

God's response to the work of faith in you is to produce His labor of love through you.

As you leave idols, separate yourself from the world and live righteously, God responds by releasing His life and His living waters in you. His life is love, and that love is the inspiration for our labor, work and service in the kingdom of God.

I labor for Christ because I love Him. That love isn't something I have produced. Rather, the love in me is a fruit of the Holy Spirit (Galatians 5:22). God's life flowing out of me produces the love I need to labor effectively for Him. God's life in me is not a hate life or a critical life. In fact, His love flowing out of me into others becomes a well of refreshing for them. Are you refreshing others with your labor of love?

_____

_____

_____

_____

_____

_____

"The mark of a revolutionary church is God's love."

Faith Worketh by Love

For in Jesus Christ neither circumcision availeth any thing, nor uncircumcision; but faith which worketh by love. (Galatians 5:6)

It's time for the church not only to accept the unlovable who come to her, but also to go out seeking the unlovely. We need to find people to love! Everyone can see that we are loved and are walking in love.

Start in your own family. Love that husband or wife who at times is hard to love. Love that teenager who seems distant and rebellious. Love somebody; care about somebody; hurt for somebody!

I pray that the time comes when the saints heed the call of love to such a degree that we wake up in the middle of the night with someone on our hearts and begin to intercede. I pray that we begin fasting meals and giving the money we would have spent on the meals to feed hungry and starving people. I pray that we will get up early on Sunday morning to pick up someone who cannot drive and who desires to go to church.

We are to love God with all that we are, and then to love our neighbors as ourselves. Who is our neighbor? The word for *neighbor* comes from two words meaning "dwelling" and "near." Anyone dwelling near you is your neighbor. He may be living in a shack or a penthouse. He may be an alcoholic or a drug dealer. He may be from the inner city or the suburbs.

In others words, faith doesn't find its expression in religious acts but in acts of love. James 2:8 declares, "If ye fulfill the royal law according to the scripture, thou shalt love thy neighbour as thyself, ye do well."

"Express your faith by loving others, starting with your own family."

Loving God Daily

Jesus said unto him, Thou shalt love the Lord thy God with all thy heart, and with all thy soul, and with all thy mind. This is the first and great commandment. (Matthew 22:37, 38)

How is your prayer life? When was the last time you stayed alone in prayer until you were not alone anymore? How in love are you with God's Word?

Our relationship with God must grow continually. Prayer, loving the Word, confession and speaking forth the things of God are ways of allowing our lives to be permeated with love for Him. We must fall in love and stay in love with Jesus. He is our first love.

The three keys to building our vertical love relationship with God are prayer, the Word and worship. A church service cannot be the only time during the week when we express our love to God. When prayer, the Word and worship are expressed in a daily love relationship with the Father, then our church worship as a body will explode with praise and power. Powerless worship reflects powerless lives lived daily without God.

Too many church people live lives as practical atheists. They dance, sing, shout and pray in tongues in the church building, but their lives are nothing more than vacant tabernacles. You will never minister to God in corporate worship until you begin ministering to Him daily through personal worship, prayer and time in the Word.

_____

_____

_____

_____

_____

_____

_____

"Spend time today loving God in prayer, worship and the Word."

Express Love by Patience

But the fruit of the Spirit is love, joy, peace, longsuffering, gentleness, goodness, faith, meekness, temperance: against such there is no law. (Galatians 5:22, 23)

Patience is not a passive word; *patience* is an active word. We are going to wait. How are we going to wait? Reaping. We will expend our energies winning others to Christ in the time we have left on this planet. God can use us to reach out to those who are going to hell if we have the patience to wait on Him.

Patience does not mean sitting around polishing our armor and repairing our weapons. We are here to win the lost to Jesus Christ. He is our hope— the only hope we have to share with a lost and dying world. Take an unsaved family member to dinner. Serve that person. Love and minister the grace of God to that person. Echo Christ's love in your life to the lost. When we are patient until the coming of the Lord, working to bring in the harvest, revival will explode in our midst.

_____

_____

_____

_____

_____

_____

_____

_____

_____

_____

_____

"Loving others means being patient with them."

Agree in Prayer

Behold, how good and how pleasant it is for brethren to dwell together in unity . . . For there the Lord commanded the blessing, even life for evermore. (Psalm 133:1,3)

When two agree in prayer, heaven is moved. One chases a thousand, but two put ten thousand to flight (Deuteronomy 32:30). Jesus instructs us to be in unity and agreement when we pray, "Again I say unto you, that if two of you shall agree on earth as touching any thing that they shall ask, it shall be done for them of my Father which is in heaven" (Matthew 18:19).

God worked mighty signs and wonders through the early church because they were in one accord (Acts 2:1,46). They had one mind and heart. Unity commands the blessing from God. God's call to wholeness and unity will be heeded by his children who desire the Giver more than the gifts and the Servant more than being served.

Find a partner and pray together in agreement. That partner may be a spouse, family member, or another believer at church or at work. Set a time to pray regularly together. Use the space below to write a prayer asking God's Spirit to help you. Pray daily in agreement with another prayer partner.

_____

_____

_____

_____

_____

_____

_____

_____

_____

_____

_____

_____

"Pray in agreement with another believer today!"

It's Time for War

Put on the whole armour of God, that ye may be able to stand against the wiles of the devil. For we wrestle not against flesh and blood, but against principalities, against powers, against the rulers of the darkness of this world, against spiritual wickedness in high places. Wherefore take unto you the whole armour of God, that ye may be able to withstand in the evil day, and having done all, to stand. (Ephesians 6:11-13)

I want you to understand that we will have a season of war before a season of peace. We are Christ's army invading enemy territory and winning the peace in the name of Christ. We are in the battle. We face the Goliaths and the spiritual Saddam Husseins and drive them out of our Kuwaits, our homes, our streets and our towns. We say to every evil principality and power, "This is the season for war. Devil, I'm not just drawing a line in the sand; I am storming the beach!"

We are not fighting alone; God is always with us. He is in the desert trenches right beside us. The land may be dry and parched, with not a cloud in the desert's sky, but as we march into the new millennium we are looking for His refreshing rain. In the middle of the battle a downpour is going to fall and drown our adversary!

It's time for war. The time for talk is over! All our discussions and rhetoric have reached the apex of their ability to inspire us and change our situations. We don't come to the table to negotiate with the enemy. We come to a table of victory spread before the enemy by our God. It's time to raise the standard, put the enemy to flight and heed God's call to win.

_____

_____

_____

_____

_____

"In this countdown to the new millennium, prepare for war."

Become Radical for Christ

These shall make war with the Lamb, and the Lamb shall overcome them: for he is Lord of lords, and King of kings: and they that are with him are called, and chosen, and faithful. (Revelation 17:14)

In the twinkling of an eye, the King will ride into history. Jesus will span the expanse of eternity and time. He will ride on a white stallion, cracking a whip that will sound like a thousand cannons. The Lion of Judah, the King of kings and Lord of lords, the Word of God will usher in the kingdom of God and throw Satan into the pit of hell, bound for a thousand years.

But wait, there is a problem. We're not there yet. The Bible says that in that day the lion shall lie down with the lamb. Take a lion. Don't feed it for a week and put a lamb in its cage. If the lion lays down with the lamb (Isaiah 11:6), then the millennium is here. If the lion devours the lamb, Jesus has not yet returned. Jesus is coming, but until He rides we are still God's army invading the enemy's territory under the name of Jesus.

God is calling His church to win. His call takes us to a level beyond the status quo, beyond normalcy. We've stood on the sidelines too long, tolerating a society where right is wrong and righteousness is regarded as abnormal. It's time to become radical for Jesus Christ.

"Get off the sidelines. Get in the battle. Become radical for Christ."

Greater is He That is in You

Greater is he that is in you, than he that is in the world. (1 John 4:4)

We excuse sin in America with euphemisms. Immorality is called simply an "alternative lifestyle." Liars are merely extroverts with lively imaginations. Alcoholics are seen not as addicts but as victims of society. Murderers are now called the unfortunate victims of their environment. Our society tries to justify a son's killing of his parents by claiming that he is emotionally damaged and abused. Children can now divorce their parents.

The demonic forces of darkness are on the offensive. The devil has one thought in mind: to steal, kill and destroy (John 10:10).

There's only one thing that our enemy understands: somebody with a bigger stick than his. Listen to God's promise to us whom He has called to win: "Greater is he that is in you, than he that is in the world" (1 John 4:4).

It's time for war. It's time to get in the devil's face and let him know that his invasion of your mind, your body, your emotions, your finances and your church will not be tolerated. Not only will you resist him, but you will also overcome him by the Word of God and drive him back by the blood of the Lamb. Write down your testimony and the Scripture that sustains you.

_____

_____

_____

_____

_____

_____

_____

"Stand your ground. Christ in you will destroy the devil's works."

The Sword of the Spirit

Above all, taking the shield of faith, wherewith ye shall be able to quench all the fiery darts of the wicked. And take the helmet of salvation, and the sword of the Spirit, which is the word of God.
(Ephesians 6:16, 17)

I envision an army of God so equipped with the Word of God that they live with it, eat with it, sleep with it and use it every moment of every day. We have the weapon. It's time to use it constantly. With three simple words from the Bible, Jesus defeated the devil in the wilderness. He said simply, "It is written" (Luke 4:4).

It is time for war. The battle is raging. The devil is telling you, "You will always be in the desert." But you are God's child. Know and use the Word.

Let me warn you. The time will come when the flaming missiles of the adversary will be sailing all around you. You will not have time to reason, to think and to work through what you must do. But if you have the Word of God in you and give the Holy Spirit free reign, He will take over. The Word is the sword of the Spirit. He will put words in your mouth when you don't know what to say (Luke 21:15). God's Spirit in you will blaze forth, devastating the enemy with the Word.

"Defeat the enemy with the sword of the Spirit."

The Witness of Your Faith

And they overcame him by the blood of the Lamb, and by the word of their testimony; and they loved not their lives unto the death. (Revelation 12:11)

Having a supply line for the troops is so important in battle. Faith is part of our supply line in the church. The testimony of others builds up my faith. Your healing encourages me to pray for my healing and the healing of others in the body of Christ. Sharing with me about your miracles builds my faith to trust God for my miracles.

Don't keep your prayers to yourself. Pray for others in faith. The prayer of a righteous man will avail much in God's army. Build others up in the Lord.

Satan is defeated by the blood of the Lamb and the word of our testimony (Revelation 12:11).

Listen to Paul's encouragement in 1 Thessalonians 5:14,15, "Gently encourage the stragglers, and reach out for the exhausted, pulling them to their feet. Be patient with each person, attentive to individual needs. And be careful that when you get on each other's nerves you don't snap at each other. Look for the best in each other, and always do your best to bring it out" (*TMB*). Encouraging others is a mighty witness to your faith in Christ.

"Break through the silence. Witness boldly of your faith in Christ."

Set Armed Guards

Keep thy heart with all diligence; for out of it are the issues of life. (Proverb 4:23)

Set armed guards around your mind and your emotions. Guard your eyes and ears. Be careful what you watch on television or listen to on the radio. Don't bring an immoral video, book or magazine into your home. Stay away from anything that will pollute your mind.

Remember that to permit is to participate. You may not commit adultery, murder or steal, but if you allow sinful behavior into your house through different forms of so-called entertainment, it is the same as if you were committing the very act yourself.

Guard your heart. "Be careful [anxious] for nothing; but in every thing by prayer and supplication with thanksgiving let your requests be made known unto God. And the peace of God, which passeth all understanding, shall keep [guard] your hearts and minds through Christ Jesus" (Philippians 4:6,7).

_____

_____

_____

_____

_____

_____

_____

_____

_____

_____

_____

"What steps have you taken today to guard your heart?"

Offer the Sacrifice of Praise

By him therefore let us offer the sacrifice of praise to God continually, that is, the fruit of our lips giving thanks to his name. (Hebrews 13:15)

Anybody can offer God the sacrifice of praise on a clear day in the midst of a season of plenty (Hebrews 13:15). Anyone can sing a tune in the noonday sun. But God gives His people a song to sing at the midnight hour when trouble is closing in and darkness surrounds. Defeat the enemy with a shout of praise.

Don't clap your hands in worship because everyone else is clapping or the music is upbeat. We are a kingdom of priests called to clap our hands in praise of almighty God. "O clap your hands, all ye people; shout unto God with the voice of triumph" (Psalm 47:1). There is victory in praise.

The Bible says that we are to lift up holy hands in praise of God (Psalm 63:4; 134:2; Lamentations 3:41; 1 Timothy 2:8). Put the enemy on the defensive with an outgoing attack of praise.

Have you seen in sports what uplifted hands mean? It signifies scoring, making an offensive goal and winning. Lift up your hands in worship and praise. You have heeded the call to win, and you are more than a conqueror in Christ Jesus.

_____

_____

_____

_____

_____

_____

_____

_____

_____

"Are you facing difficulties? Then offer God the sacrifice of praise."

Pray in the Spirit

Praying always with all prayer and supplication in the Spirit, and watching thereunto with all perseverance and supplication for all saints. (Ephesians 6:18)

Romans 8:26 reminds us that "We know not what we should pray for as we ought: but the Spirit itself maketh intercession for us with groanings which cannot be uttered."

When I think of warfare and praying in the Spirit, the picture of a stealth bomber comes to mind. In Desert Storm the stealth bomber looked like a big, black stingray. It flew hundreds of missions and never even got a scratch from the enemy. Do you know why? Enemy radar could not detect it.

The same is true of praying in the Spirit. When we pray in tongues we slip right by the enemy, through enemy-held territory, and the devil doesn't know a thing. We won the Gulf War with air superiority.

Praying in the Spirit gives us spiritual superiority over the enemy. He cannot touch us.

_____

_____

_____

_____

_____

_____

_____

_____

_____

_____

_____

_____

_____

"Stop praying in your own strength. Pray in the Spirit."

Be Confident in the Lord

For the LORD shall be thy confidence, and shall keep thy foot from being taken.
(Proverb 3:26)

Far exceeding the plans of any human commander are the plans of the King of kings and Lord of lords. He has a winning strategy and more. He has already won through His death and resurrection. Our risen Lord declared, "All power is given unto me in heaven and earth. Go ye therefore, and teach all nations, baptizing them in the name of the Father, and of the Son, and of the Holy Ghost: Teaching them to observe all things whatsoever I have commanded you: and, lo, I am with you always, even unto the end of the world" (Matthew 28:18-20).

You can have confidence in the delegated authority and power of Jesus. When He sends us, we go with His power.

Heed the call to win. Be confident. "For we are made partakers of Christ, if we hold the beginning of our confidence steadfast unto the end" (Hebrews 3:14). The battle has already been won at the cross, but we must step out in faith to claim His victory in our own lives. We have not confidence in our own strength, but we have all assurance in His strength.

_____

_____

_____

_____

_____

_____

_____

_____

_____

"Make certain that your confidence is in the Lord, not in man."

Give Thanks

O give thanks unto the LORD; call upon his name: make known his deeds among the people. Sing unto him, sing psalms unto him: talk ye of all his wondrous works. Glory ye in his holy name: let the heart of them rejoice that seek the LORD.
(Psalm 105:1-3)

Giving thanks means counting our blessings. I was told the story of a man who owned a small estate and wished to sell it. He contacted a real estate agent and asked the agent to write an ad for the house and place it in the newspaper.

When the ad was ready, the agent took it to the owner for approval before he printed it.

The man read it over. The real estate agent slid the contract to list the house on the market across the table for him to sign, but he said, "I can't sign this."

The agent said, "Why not? You called me here. I have written the ad. I thought you wanted to sell your house."

He said, "Well, I did, but when I started reading what you said about my place, I realized I have been looking for a place like this for years!"

We need to be more thankful. Count your blessings. Start thanking God by asking Him to open your eyes to see what you already have in Christ Jesus. Have an attitude of gratitude. Thank the Lord for all He has done in your life.

_____

_____

_____

_____

_____

_____

"What are you thankful for today?"

Praise Opens Doors

And at midnight Paul and Silas prayed, and sang praises unto God: and the prisoners heard them. And suddenly there was a great earthquake, so that the foundations of the prison were shaken: and immediately all the doors were opened, and every one's bands were loosed. (Acts 16:25,26)

Paul and Silas had something to sing about even though they had been falsely accused, beaten with rods and locked in stocks in a Philippian jail (see Acts 16:23,24). We might ask, "Why were they so happy?" It was because their consciousness was not of prison but of God. Though they were physically bound in stocks, their souls were free to praise. Their songs were born not of burden, but of gladness.

They were God's messengers taking the Gospel to the world. They did not understand the meaning of imprisonment because they sang praises at midnight and trusted God's ways, not man's. Those who sing in prison can never truly be bound.

Those who sing God's praises continually will never cease to fulfill their destiny. Paul's and Silas' praise not only opened prison doors but also led a jailer and his family to Christ (see Acts 16:26-34). Praise changes you and your circumstances. Praise is the hinge upon which the door of worship swings open.

_____

_____

_____

_____

_____

_____

_____

_____

"Do you need a door opened? Begin praising God."

Everything to God's Glory

Whether therefore ye eat, or drink, or whatsoever ye do, do all to the glory of God. (1 Corinthians 10:31)

One of the greatest hindrances to worship in our lives is the separation between the religious and the real. We think that religion consists of prayer, reading the Bible, worship and Christian service. Our real life, on the other hand, involves eating, sleeping, cleaning the house, working, grocery shopping and the like. In God's kingdom there is no separation. The saint who lifts high the standard of Christ does *everything* in life to the glory of God.

"Whether therefore ye eat, or drink, or whatsoever ye do, do all to the glory of God" (1 Corinthians 10:31).

What does this verse mean? If Jesus has come to tabernacle with us, He never leaves us. We can worship Him any time and any place, no matter what else we are doing.

Paul, an apostle of Jesus Christ, was a tentmaker, but he also wrote two-thirds of the New Testament. Both his tentmaking and his writing were received by God as equal to his worship. When my wife, Joni, does the dishes or fixes dinner, God receives her activity as a humble act of worship. God receives even our eating and sleeping as worship if we do these things unto Him.

We must practice living to the glory of God so that daily labors become acts of worship. Every simple act of your day today can become a priestly act offered to God.

_____

_____

_____

_____

_____

_____

"Let every act in life be to the glory of God."

You Are a Tabernacle

What? know ye not that your body is the temple of the Holy Ghost which is in you, which ye have of God, and ye are not your own? For ye are bought with a price: therefore glorify God in your body, and in your spirit, which are God's.
(1 Corinthians 6:19, 20)

When the Holy Spirit came to indwell you, a consuming fire purified the crucible of your heart, making it an ark. The blood of Christ cleansed you of every sin, washing over your life and preparing a mercy seat for the ark of your heart. At the depths of your being is a tent, a tabernacle, a holy of holies for your worship and meeting with God. Jesus made it all possible.

"The Word became flesh and dwelt among us" (John 1:14). The word *dwelt* means "tabernacled." Jesus tabernacled among us. This is where God met with man and man met with God. Jesus Christ has become your mediator, your meeting place with God. He has given you the Holy Spirit. Because of Christ, the holy of holies now resides in your heart. Enter in, worship and meet with God.

Every moment of every day can be a time of worship. As you fulfill God's calling and purpose in your life, you are worshiping Him. When fulfilling the purpose of God, then all of life becomes a sanctuary dedicated to the worship of God.

_____

_____

_____

_____

_____

_____

_____

_____

"Worship the Lord in the tabernacle of your life."

The Final Generation

And from the days of John the Baptist until now the kingdom of heaven suffereth violence, and the violent take it by force. (Matthew 11:12)

We are the final generation lifting high the standard today. We are destined for the experiential manifestation of the glory of God. We are destined to experience a perpetual rain and harvest in our lives. The revolution has begun. The wind of God is stirring His people.

The remnant, revolutionary church expects to use spiritual force to topple the kingdom of darkness. We are not pew sitters. We are prophets and priests exercising dominion over the earth. By His power and force, we declare what belongs to the King and take back what the enemy has stolen.

God is raising up warriors who sound the warning: Jesus Christ is coming soon! Repent! Be refreshed through the wind, rain, fire and power of the Holy Spirit. Restore to the kingdom what has been lost. Take back today what the locust has eaten and feast at the table of the King!

"The revolutionary church is establishing God's kingdom in our age."

Come Quickly, Lord Jesus

He which testifieth these things saith, Surely I come quickly. Amen. Even so, come, Lord Jesus. (Revelation 22:20)

Jesus is coming. He is coming for a church who is eagerly looking for His appearing. Faster than the fastest hoof that ever struck pavement . . . faster than the quickest bolt of lightning ever struck out of a dark-throated storm cloud, Jesus is coming.

Those chariots which haven't ridden the winds since Elijah are getting ready to carry the Son of God across eternity's skies to meet His bride. Jesus is preparing for His second advent on this planet. He is coming for a church who is patiently waiting for, watching for and expecting Him.

The curtain on this final drama of humanity is not coming down; it is going up. The stage has been set, and we are the players. The last great revival is not coming; it is here! God has saved the best for last, and that includes you!

Jesus is coming soon! Comfort one another by proclaiming His imminent return (1 Thessalonians 5:1-11; Matthew 25:31). Take the Gospel into all the world (Matthew 28:18-20; Mark 16:15).

Declare Christ's righteousness and judgment. Serve the "least of these" in His name (Matthew 25:34-40). Tread upon serpents and take authority over the enemy (Mark 16:17,18; Luke 9:1; 10:19,20).

"Pray that Jesus comes quickly."

Time is Accelerating

Behold, the days come, saith the Lord, that the plowman shall overtake the reaper, and the treader of grapes him that soweth seed; and the mountains shall drop sweet wine, and all the hills shall melt. (Amos 9:13)

Do you see it? The sower will overtake the reaper. God's promised harvest is that sowing and reaping will happen at the same time. The harvest of souls and abundance of the saints is coming quicker than we can preach, or sow. Time is caught up in an accelerated process. "Then shalt thou call, and the Lord shall answer; thou shalt cry, and he shall say, Here I am" (Isaiah 58:9a). Notice the immediacy of God's response. God responds suddenly when we cry out as Elijah did.

The closer we get to the end of the age and the imminent return of Jesus, the shorter time becomes. The time is coming when there will only be seed time and harvest. In fact, the time is coming when seed time and harvest will be at the same time.

Not only will we reap suddenly what we sow, but God will also give seed to the sowers and multiply their seed. "Now he that ministereth seed to the sower both minister bread for your food, and multiply your seed sown, and increase the fruits of your righteousness" (2 Corinthians 9:10). That means that whenever we sow seed, God comes behind us and sows more.

So when we begin to harvest, we are not just harvesting what we have sown, but also what God has sown as well. He brings such multiplication and increase to our sowing that before our seed can hit the ground, we are reaping a harvest.

_____

_____

_____

_____

_____

_____

"In the new millennium, prepare to reap and sow in the same season."

What are You Sowing?

Be not deceived; God is not mocked: for whatsoever a man soweth, that shall he also reap. For he that soweth to his flesh shall of the flesh reap corruption; but he that soweth to the Spirit shall of the Spirit reap life everlasting.
(Galatians 6:7,8)

What are we to sow? We are to sow joy into the life of someone filled with sorrow. We are to sow hope into the middle of a hopeless situation. We should bless someone who needs a blessing without any expectation of their gratitude or giving back to us. We need to sow money into the good soil of God's work, knowing that He will bring a great harvest of souls.

We should not only sow in good times, but also in times of famine, so that we may reap a bountiful harvest. The widow sowed in famine and saw God provide a perpetual harvest. Elijah sowed in the midst of a drought and saw God bring forth a great rain. Are you sowing in your famine as well as in your abundance?

It is God's will that His saints prosper. John 10:10 proclaims, "The thief cometh not, but for to steal, and to kill, and to destroy: I am come that they might have life, and that they might have it more abundantly."

_____

_____

_____

_____

_____

_____

_____

_____

_____

"Sowing today will bring a bountiful future harvest."

False Evidence Appearing Real

Fear thou not; for I am with thee; be not dismayed; for I am thy God: I will strengthen thee; yea, I will help thee; yea, I will uphold thee with the right hand of my righteousness. (Isaiah 41:10)

We might call fear: *False Evidence that Appears Real.* In others words, fear springs from the lies of the enemy and the world. Fear is a mirage from Satan. He attacks us with difficult circumstances that we feel, in the natural, we can never get through.

But the Bible says, "For we walk by faith and not by sight" (2 Corinthians 5:7). We must not react to our circumstances. Instead, we should respond to every circumstance with faith, being content in what God is doing in and through us. Paul wrote about the attitude that we need: "I know both how to be abased, and I know how to abound; everywhere and in all things I am instructed both to be full and to be hungry, both to abound and to suffer need" (Philippians 4:12).

We do not fear because God is with us (Isaiah 41:10). We are not to be moved to fear by what we see or feel. We fix our eyes on Jesus. We do not look at false evidence that appears to be real; instead, we stand on the Word of God. So, when our body screams that we are sick, we scream back that we are well. When our finances say that we don't have a cent to our name, we declare that we will sow in famine, expecting a bountiful harvest in the new millennium.

"Walk by faith not by fear."

Fear and Faith Are Opposites

For God hath not given us the spirit of fear; but of power, and of love, and of a sound mind. (2 Timothy 1:7)

Fear and faith are opposites. They cannot live in the same heart. One will destroy the other. Perfect love casts out all fear. "There is no fear in love; but perfect love casteth out fear" (1 John 4:18a). So love and fear cannot abide in us at the same time.

Fearful thoughts have no place in our minds. So we must take every fearful thought captive (2 Corinthians 10:5). In the power of His Spirit, we can cast out every fear and replace it with confidence and assurance.

Don't worry about tomorrow. Do not become anxious about what you will need. Sow today as God gives you seed and opportunity. Cast out fear. Say, "Spirit of fear, in the name of Jesus, I cast you out. I refuse to be controlled by fear and doubt."

"Replace all doubt with faith in Jesus."

Give and it Will be Given to You

Give, and it shall be given unto you; good measure, pressed down, and shaken together, and running over, shall men give into your bosom. For with the same measure that ye mete withal it shall be measured to you again. (Luke 6:38)

If we are afraid to let go of what is in our hand, we will never reap a harvest. Jesus declares in Luke 6:38, "Give and it shall be given unto you."

We can never receive until we give. We can never reap a harvest until we sow. There must be the process of exchange. When He tells us in Malachi 3 that we should tithe and He will rebuke the devourer, that is exactly what we must do with His money. Greed not only says, "What's mine belongs to me." Greed goes further by saying, What's yours is mine."

When you take from God, you end up owing Him both what you stole and 20 percent on top of that! "And if a man will at all redeem ought of his tithes, he shall add thereto the fifth part thereof" (Leviticus 27:31). Your greed will cost you heavily. As you bind fear and greed, and allow love to motivate your giving, you will receive a bountiful harvest.

_____

_____

_____

_____

_____

_____

_____

_____

_____

_____

_____

"Bind fear and greed in your life by trusting God and giving."

Sow Even in Tough Times

And there was a famine in the land, beside the first famine that was in the days of Abraham. And Isaac went unto Abimelech king of the Philistines unto Gerar. And the Lord appeared unto him, and said, "Go not down into Egypt; dwell in the land which I shall tell thee of. Sojourn in the land, and I will be with thee, and will bless thee; for unto thee, and unto thy seed, I will give all these countries, and I will perform the oath which I sware unto Abraham thy father." . . . Then Isaac sowed in that land, and received in the same year an hundredfold: and the Lord blessed him. (Genesis 26:1-3,12)

Sow when times are tough. We can learn from Isaac the principle of standing and sowing in the midst of famine and our present circumstances.

Our natural tendency is to hold on tight to what we have when lack attacks. But the wise steward knows that there will be no harvest without first sowing. If we refuse to give in our lack, we will never experience the promised harvest. The truth of sowing and reaping remains constant in abundance and in scarcity.

Whatever we sow, we will reap (Galatians 6:9). If we sow to famine, we will reap a famine. If we sow to abundance, then we will reap a bountiful harvest.

_____

_____

_____

_____

_____

_____

_____

"Dare to sow in tough times."

Don't Eat Your Seed

And she said, As the Lord thy God liveth, I have not a cake, but an handful of meal in a barrel, and a little oil in a cruse: and behold, I am gathering two sticks, that I may go in and dress it for me and my son, that we may eat it, and die. (1 Kings 17:12)

Do you remember the story about the widow in Zarephath? She knew that if she and her son decided to eat the last of their oil and meal, they would then die.

But she had another option. She could sow her seed instead of eating it. She could make a loaf of bread for the man of God, Elijah, and then see the promised harvest from God. Her obedience to God's command, through Elijah, brought her a perpetual and promised harvest.

When Elijah asked her for a cake, at first the poor widow claimed that she didn't have it. But God never asks you for what you don't have. He only asks you for what you want to keep for yourself.

Remember, if what is in your hand is not big enough to be your harvest, then it is your seed. Elijah rebuked the fear in the woman and told her to give what she had. In return, God supplied what she needed—a promised harvest of ever-increasing grain and oil.

_____

_____

_____

_____

_____

_____

_____

_____

_____

"If what's in your hand isn't your harvest, then it is your seed."

Don't Give Up!

And Joseph dreamed a dream, and he told it his brethren: and they hated him yet the more. (Genesis 37:5)

What God promises, He always does. God promises us that when we give, we receive back "good measure, pressed down, and shaken together, and running over, shall men give into your bosom. For with the same measure that ye mete withal it shall be measured to you again" (Luke 6:38).

In Genesis 37-51, we read the story of Jacob and Joseph. God promised His provision, privilege, and harvest to Joseph in a dream. But Joseph had to wait many years to receive his inheritance. Through slavery, false accusations, prison, and repeated disappointment, Joseph never gave up. Why? Because he had a Word from the Lord. He laid hold of that promise and would not let go. He persevered. That means he refused to give up. You have God's Word for a promised harvest. Don't give up!

Jacob also had God's Word to supply all of his needs through the covenant the Lord had made with his grandfather, Abraham. The day came that Joseph's promise from God was fulfilled. Pharaoh made Joseph second in command over all of Egypt and entrusted him to build storehouses for grain during the seven good years to prepare for the coming seven years of famine.

So Jacob, during the years of terrible famine, sent his sons into Egypt to find food. Joseph disguised himself and met with his brothers. He sent wagons laden with food for his father, Jacob. Jacob had sent empty wagons to Egypt, but because of God's covenant with him, they returned full. Your wagons are coming. Don't give up!

"When God gives you a dream, don't give up!"

Lay Hold of God's Word

And in the fourth watch of the night Jesus went unto them, walking on the sea. And when the disciples saw him walking on the sea, they were troubled, saying, It is a spirit; and they cried out for fear. But straightway Jesus spake unto them, saying, Be of good cheer; it is I; be not afraid. And Peter answered him and said, Lord, if it be thou, bid me come unto thee on the water. And he said, Come. And when Peter was come down out of the ship, he walked on the water, to go to Jesus. (Matthew 14:25-29)

On a word from the Lord, Peter stepped over the side of a boat tossing in a storm on the Sea of Galilee, and he began walking on water toward Jesus. But when he saw the wind and the waves, he became afraid and started to sink. At first, faith had silenced all fear and doubt. But then Peter took His eyes off of the Word and started listening to his own fearful voices that spoke False Evidence that Appeared Real. So Peter sank. He had forgotten God's Word. Now, is it any harder to walk on water in a storm than in the sunshine? Of course not! What made it hard to walk on water was Peter's fear.

Remember to apply God's Word, no matter what your situation or circumstance. Refuse to take your eyes off His promise and don't be afraid to look again. Let this be the straight path of moving into God's purpose for you.

- Do not doubt the Word of God.
- Do not listen to the opinions of men.
- Do not believe the lies of the devil.
- Do not look at the storms—only the Savior.
- Guard what your ears hear.
- Speak words of faith rooted in the Word.

_____

_____

_____

_____

"When facing the storms of life, lay hold of God's Word."

Prepare for Rain!

Thus saith the Lord, Make this valley full of ditches. For thus saith the Lord, Ye shall not see wind, neither shall ye see rain; yet that valley shall be filled with water, that ye may drink, both ye, and your cattle, and your beasts. (2 Kings 3:16,17)

When God promises rain, then get ready. Even when the kings of Israel did not see rain coming, they were told to get ready by the man of God. You must prepare for rain—the outpouring of God's Spirit and blessing—even when you cannot see it in the natural.

Prepare for rain even when there's not a cloud in the sky. Prepare for rain even when you feel nothing but doubt. Prepare for rain even when the stench of dryness and death is surrounding you. Your crops may be wasting in the field. Dust storms may be filling your nostrils. Wind may be cracking your lips and parching your soul. Nonetheless, prepare for rain!

_____

_____

_____

_____

_____

_____

_____

_____

_____

_____

_____

_____

_____

_____

"When God promises rain, prepare for rain!"

Hold on to God's "Yes!"

For all the promises of God in him are yea, and in him Amen, unto the glory of God by us. (2 Corinthians 1:20)

Victory belongs to those who will not take "No" for an answer. Why? Because the promises of God in Christ are "Yes" and "Amen."

God had promised Elijah that it would rain. So Elijah sent his servant six times to look for rain, and Elijah's servant had returned to him six times with the observation, "There is nothing" (1 Kings 18:43). But Elijah refused to take "No" for an answer. He continued in prayer on his knees with his face buried between his legs.

When faith faces a lack of evidence, it refuses to allow the report to be final. If there is no cloud on your horizon, fall to your knees. Cry out to God. Don't let your lack shape your prayers. Let God's promise define your prayer and praise.

Refuse to accept "No" as the final answer. Pray through to your breakthrough. God has already said, "Yes." He has given His Word. Nothing else is needed to believe. Hold on to God's Word even when evidence and past experience is lacking. Stop looking for fleeces and signs . . . look to the promise of God.

_____

_____

_____

_____

_____

_____

_____

_____

_____

"When evidence is lacking, hold on to the Yes of God."

Send Forth Angels

But to which of the angels said he at any time, Sit on my right hand, until I make thine enemies thy footstool? Are they not all ministering spirits, sent forth to minister for them who shall be heirs of salvation?
(Hebrews 1:13,14)

We have the authority to send forth ministering spirits into the harvest. When was the last time you exercised your authority in faith, and when was the last time you sent forth ministering spirits into the harvest to get what belongs to you?

Isaiah 55:11 declares, "So shall my word be that goeth forth out of my mouth: it shall not return unto me void, but it shall accomplish that which I please, and it shall prosper in the thing whereto I sent it."

When was the last time that you spent time declaring God's Word of provision, perpetual privilege, and promised harvest in your life?

Psalm 103:20 declares, "Bless the Lord, ye his angels, that excel in strength, that do his commandments, hearkening unto the voice of his word." When the Word of the Lord goes forth—the written, prophetic or proclaimed Word—you must decide immediately whether you will speak and walk in His word or ignore it.

Every day you can declare under the anointing of the Holy Spirit, "In the power of the Spirit and under the authority and inspiration of the Word, I declare that the holy angels go forth now and become reapers in the fields that I have sown, which are white unto harvest." Do not wait until tomorrow to begin your declaration. Go forth and declare your harvest today and say, "I bind every hindering spirit on my life. I release the anointing of God with His angelic hosts to bring in my harvest."

Stop sitting around looking for someone to call and waiting for something to do. Stop watching your harvest rot in the field. Go get the harvest. Send forth ministering angels.

_____

_____

_____

_____

"Send forth ministering angels to bring in your harvest."

You Cannot Bankrupt God

And when he came to himself, he said, How many hired servants of my father's have bread enough and to spare, and I perish with hunger! I will arise and go to my father, and will say unto him, Father, I have sinned against heaven, and before thee. (Luke 15:17,18)

You may bankrupt yourself, but you can never bankrupt God. You can lose everything you have, but you can never lose everything God has. You can run away from God, but God will never run away from you. You can lose your love for yourself and God, but you can never make God stop loving you. God says to His children, "Yea, I have loved thee with an everlasting love; therefore, with loving-kindness have I drawn thee" (Jeremiah 31:3).

In the parable of the Prodigal Son, the fact that the younger son ran away didn't cause the father to stop loving him. The same is true in our relationship with God. David describes God's loving presence that abides with us in this way: "Whither shall I go from thy Spirit? Or whither shall I flee from thy presence? If I ascend up into heaven, thou art there: if I make my bed in hell, behold thou art there" (Psalm 139:7, 8).

Think about these truths:

- God always answers the prayers of His children.
- God always gives us what we ask in His will.
- The inheritance given to us by God in Christ belongs to us now.
- A child may fail, mess up or run from the Father, but he can never hide from Him.
- God's inheritance for us is a gift—it cannot be earned or lost.
- His love for us is unconditional—nothing we do can make Him stop loving us.

_____

_____

_____

_____

"God has everything you need. Return now to the Father."

Slave or Waiter?

Henceforth I call you not servants; for the servant knoweth not what his lord doeth: but I have called you friends; for all things that I have heard of my Father I have made known unto you" (John 15:15).

Are you a slave or a waiter? A slave serves out of necessity and obligation. However, a waiter serves his customer's table willingly. He wants the job. He enjoys the benefits. And his sole desire is to please the one whom he serves. He knows an inheritance is his. He understands that the one upon whom he waits pays the bills, keeps him in a job and rewards him—the customer actually serves his needs by contributing to his salary and his tip.

Now, no analogy is perfect. We can find places where this analogy doesn't fit and falls short of depicting our relationship with God. But taken on the surface, we can learn much about the difference between serving as a slave versus serving as a waiter.

Are you a slave or a waiter before God? Slaves always expect God to do something for them. They are always complaining about their workload and lack of adequate recognition. But waiters love just hanging out with the Lord. Being in His presence is reward enough for waiting upon Him. Their attitude is one of gratitude. Instead of always whining, they are always worshiping. They understand the paradoxes of servanthood:

- The servant is actually being served (Luke 12:37).
- The last are always first (Luke 22:26; Mark 10:43–45; Matthew 23:10–12).
- Those at the foot of the table always go to the head of the table (Luke 14:8–10).
- Rewards are never earned but are always given (Matthew 20:1–16).

Jesus did not come to be served but to serve. We are to follow His example.

_____

_____

_____

_____

_____

"Are you a slave or a waiter?"

Come Home to the Father

And he arose, and came to his father. But when he was yet a great way off, his father saw him, and had compassion, and ran, and fell on his neck, and kissed him. (Luke 15:20)

Search the Gospels. Nowhere will you find a person who was ever refused anything from Jesus. At times, He gave conditions to test the hearts of those who wanted something from him, such as the rich young ruler (Luke 19). He could have received the eternal life which he sought, but Jesus told him to first let go of his idol—money. Once he had sold everything and given it to the poor, he could follow Jesus and receive the abundant life he desired.

Jesus healed the leper, the blind man, the woman with the issue of blood, and the paralytic. He restored the man with the withered hand and raised Jarius' daughter and Lazarus from the dead. Why? Because Jesus was just like His Father. He was a giver and a lover. He was the Father with hands and feet. He was Word that became flesh and dwelt among us (John 1:14).

God touched human life through a man—Jesus. He came not to be served but to serve. Like the father who waited for his prodigal son to come home, the Father waits for an eternity for us to come home, back into His arms. After waiting and waiting, God could wait no more. Love seeks out that which is loved. Before we could ever turn back toward home, He came to us through His Son, Jesus. He gave us everything we asked for and more. Before we asked, He died for us, offering us His eternal gift of love—everlasting life. He wants us to live forever with Him!

_____

_____

_____

_____

_____

_____

"Receive eternal life with God, through Jesus."

Resolve to Break Through

For my flesh is meat indeed, and my blood is drink indeed. He that eateth my flesh, and drinketh my blood, dwelleth in me, and I in him. As the living Father hath sent me, and I live by the Father: so he that eateth me, even he shall live by me. (John 6:55-57)

Before the breakthrough comes the vision of what God can and will do if you will act in faith. Notice this: it's not vision we lack but resolve.

Breaking through requires much of us. God has done his part. He has issued the invitation, Come to My table. Eat of my flesh. Drink of my blood. Dwell in me and I will dwell in you (John 6).

All the elements needed for a breakthrough have been provided for you. The breakthrough for your harvest is here. The breakthrough for your healing is here. The breakthrough for your prosperity is here. The breakthrough for your inheritance is here. But will you leave your present bondage with the resolve and perseverance to break through every obstacle and stronghold in order to realize God's vision for you?

God's vision for you is Christ indwelling you with every bondage broken, and you living in complete liberty.

Will you break through?

_____

_____

_____

_____

_____

_____

_____

_____

_____

"You have the vision. You have all you need to break through."

Move Beyond Complacency

And I say unto thee, Arise, and take up thy bed, and go thy way into thine house.
(Mark 2:11)

Your breakthrough lies on the other side of your complacency. You will never have a breakthrough if you sit around doing nothing and expecting God to do everything. The truth is that God has already done all He needs to do. His Son died on the cross, saving you from sin and healing you by His stripes.

God has already provided your inheritance for abundant life now and eternal life forever. He has set before you a vision of doing even greater things than Christ did (John 14:12). The greatest obstacle holding you back is complacency.

With complacency you trade in your armor of God for a harmless garment of comfort. So take up your bed and walk. Stop laying around waiting for God to move. Move to God . . . repent, stand up and walk!

The Spirit of God is quenched. The fire that waxed in your bones has grown lukewarm, and the gifts of the Spirit that once stirred within you lay dormant.

What must you do? Repent! (Acts 2:38; 2 Corinthians 7:9–10). Turn away from the sin of lazy comfort and languishing in past memories. Refuse to pick up old sin, offenses and failures.

_____

_____

_____

_____

_____

_____

_____

_____

"Stop sitting around complacently this year. Take up your bed and walk."

You Are Royalty

But ye are a chosen generation, a royal priesthood, an holy nation, a peculiar people; that ye should show forth the praises of him who hath called you out of darkness into his marvellous light.
(1 Peter 2:9)

Not only are we priests and kings—a holy nation—we are also friends with Christ. Jesus tells us, "Henceforth I call you not servants; for the servant knoweth not what his lord doeth: but I have called you friends; for all things that I have heard of my Father I have made known unto you" (John 15:15).

We are blood-bought and Holy Ghost-filled. That makes us blood brothers and sisters with Jesus Christ. He sealed the covenant of our restoration with His blood just as blood covenants of the ancient world were sealed. We are in the family of the King. We are princes of the King of kings and lords under subjection to the Lord of lords.

"And hath raised us up together, and made us sit together in heavenly places in Christ Jesus" (Ephesians 2:6). You are no longer under the table sweeping for crumbs. You are at the table of Christ drinking from His cup and eating of His bread. Jesus has set for you a position of honor at His table. He has restored you completely and brought you from shame to honor, guilt to forgiveness, lack to abundance, and from sickness to health.

_____

_____

_____

_____

_____

_____

_____

_____

"As royalty, you can sit with the King at His table."

Restored by the Master

He restoreth my soul. (Psalm 23:3)

When an antique furniture dealer buys an old table at a garage sale, no one understands its value. The veneer is chipped. The finish is worn. The legs may be broken and the supports may be wobbly, but the dealer knows its intrinsic value. He takes the old table back to his shop and begins to patiently restore it. The old finish is removed, and the table is freshly stained. The veneer, legs and supports are repaired. Old things are passing away. Everything about the table is becoming new (2 Corinthians 5:17).

What was a worthless piece of junk at the garage sale now takes the honored place in the show window of the dealer's shop. Everyone who passes by marvels at the fine, restored piece of furniture. Its value has been restored. The table's beauty, usefulness and worth have all been restored by the master craftsman.

So it is with our lives. We are old, worn, useless and worthless. Sin has aged us and ruined our shine and luster. Our only worth is to be cast into the fire and used for kindling. But Jesus sees through our old nature and values us. He buys us from the junk heap and restores our image and worth. We become brand new through Him, and His restoration gives us an honored position at His table. With praise and joy, we exclaim with David, "He restoreth my soul" (Psalm 23:3).

_____

_____

_____

_____

_____

_____

_____

"Be restored by the Master."

Slay Your Giants

Then said David to the Philistine, Thou comest to me with a sword, and with a spear, and with a shield: but I come to thee in the name of the LORD of hosts, the God of the armies of Israel, whom thou hast defied. This day will the LORD deliver thee into mine hand; and I will smite thee, and take thine head from thee; and I will give the carcases of the host of the Philistines this day unto the fowls of the air, and to the wild beasts of the earth; that all the earth may know that there is a God in Israel. And all this assembly shall know that the LORD saveth not with sword and spear: for the battle is the LORD's, and he will give you into our hands. (1 Samuel 17:45-47)

Now the time has come to lay down our instruments of praise and pick up our weapons of attack. God has given us the word of restoration. He has returned what the enemy has stolen and the locusts have eaten. Now God wants us to attack the giants and possess the land.

There came a time when the shouting had to stop and the battle had to be joined. David did not stand on the sidelines and listen to Goliath's threats. He went forth into battle to slay the giant.

"But Pastor Parsley," you may protest, "I'm just waiting on God. Some day my ship will come in, or maybe I'll win the sweepstakes or the lottery. Then I will claim my provision from God. Then I will mount the attack."

Please understand that God's provision has already been given to us through the cross and resurrection of Jesus Christ. His provision of abundant life is for now. His provision of eternal life is our everlasting inheritance. So what are you waiting for? Attack!

Attack and slay your giants.

_____

_____

_____

_____

_____

"This is the year to slay your giants."

Be Persistent in Prayer

And all things, whatever ye shall ask in prayer, believing, ye shall receive. (Matthew 21:22).

Be persistent in prayer (Luke 18:1–8) and diligently seek the Lord (Hebrews 11:6). As we pray through to God's vision of provision, the vision is clear, the virtue is mighty, and the victory is assured. God has given us the weapon of prayer to pull down the enemy's strongholds and to possess the land. The whole life of the believer is prayer—every act, thought, word and wish. Our types of prayer weapons include:

- Praying with the authority to bind and loose (Matthew 16:19).
- Praying in agreement (Matthew 18:19).
- Praying to petition God (Mark 11:22–24).
- Praying with thanksgiving and praise(2 Chronicles 20).
- Praying to commit, dedicate, and consecrate (Philippians 4:6,7).
- Praying in intercession (Romans 8:26).
- Praying in the Spirit; building up ourselves in the Holy Spirit (1 Corinthians 14; Jude 20).

_____

_____

_____

_____

_____

_____

_____

_____

_____

_____

"Will you persist in prayer today?"

Take the Battle to the Enemy

Then shall the King say unto them on his right hand, Come, ye blessed of my Father, inherit the kingdom prepared for you from the foundation of the world: For I was an hungered, and ye gave me meat: I was thirsty, and ye gave me drink: I was a stranger, and ye took me in: Naked, and ye clothed me: I was sick, and ye visited me: I was in prison, and ye came unto me. (Matthew 25:34-36)

Take the battle to the enemy. Invade his territory. Feed the hungry, clothe the naked, visit the lonely and imprisoned and minister to the sick as unto Jesus (Matthew 25).

The anointing of God's Spirit is upon you to preach good news in the enemy's camp; to bind up the brokenhearted; to proclaim liberty to the captives; and to open up the prisons for those who are bound (Isaiah 61:1).

Take the weapon of your good works and march right into the enemy's camp, boldly proclaiming Jesus' name. Set the captives free. Bring God glory and take back what the enemy has stolen. "Let your light so shine before men, that they may see your good works, and glorify your Father, which is in heaven" (Matthew 6:16).

_____

_____

_____

_____

_____

_____

_____

_____

_____

_____

"As you march toward the millennium, take the battle to the enemy."

The River of God

And he shewed me a pure river of water of life, clear as crystal, proceeding out of the throne of God and of the Lamb. In the midst of the street of it, and on either side of the river, was there the tree of life, which bare twelve manner of fruits, and yielded her fruit every month: and the leaves of the tree were for the healing of the nations. (Revelation 22:1,2)

The outpouring of God's Spirit upon our generation is beginning to flow from the throne of God through us and into our world. The river of God brings His abundant harvest. At first in Ezekiel 47:3, the river was only ankle deep. The spiritual walk of God's people was touched, but much in their lives needed refreshing. "Repent, therefore, and be converted, that your sins may be blotted out, when the times of refreshing shall come from the presence of the Lord" (Acts 3:19). Those times of refreshing are flowing through us, but there is more!

Then the river of God flows up to our knees (Ezekiel 47:4). Our prayer lives are beginning to explode with authority and intercession. God's hand is being moved by our prayers (Acts 10:1–4). We are seeking corporate prayer by the body of Christ to shake our churches out of their complacency; to shake our preachers out of laziness and man's traditions and to shake God's people, bringing them to their knees in prayer and intercession. We need the Lord to shake our communities, bringing a new hunger and thirst for God throughout our land. The fields are ripe to harvest! Pray!

Then the river of God flows waist deep (Ezekiel 47:4) inspiring us to gird up our loins, to run the race with patience, to fix our eyes on Jesus, and to minister in His name with signs and wonders.

We have witnessed the river touching our ankles, our knees, and our waists. But now there is more. The river is so deep and wide that we cannot leave anything in our lives untouched by God's Spirit. We must swim in the river (Ezekiel 47:5). Are you in the river of God?

_____

_____

_____

_____

"Are you swimming in the river of God?"

Jesus Is Our Jubilee

And ye shall hallow the fiftieth year, and proclaim liberty throughout all the land unto all the inhabitants thereof: it shall be a jubilee unto you; and ye shall return every man unto his possession, and ye shall return every man unto his family. (Leviticus 25:10)

The fiftieth year sabbatical was a significant and momentous occasion for every Jewish person. Jubilee was a time of liberation, freedom and celebration. In Jesus we possess eternal Jubilee. He is our Jubilee!

To the slave Jubilee meant release for him and his family from their taskmasters and a return to their own land. Jesus sets us free.

To every person Jubilee also signified a year when oppression from their adversaries ceased. Jesus breaks the yoke of oppression.

To those held captive to debt, it was a year when all debts were canceled. Most importantly, the Year of Jubilee was a year when God Himself provided the harvest. It was a year when everything went back to God! Jesus has paid the debt of our sin on the cross and given us abundant life.

Refuse to enter the new millennium in bondage or a captive to anyone or anything. Declare Jesus to be your Jubilee.

"Jesus will set you free!"

The Transforming Anointing

Then shall we know, if we follow on to know the LORD: his going forth is prepared as the morning; and he shall come unto us as the rain, as the latter and former rain unto the earth. (Hosea 6:3)

There are literally hundreds of ways one could describe the anointing of God. As a river travels across a terrain, trickling down rocks and crevices while leaving its mark by tracing out an intricate trail of its own, so is the anointing of God. When purposefully harnessed and released through your life, the anointing can cool the fevered brow of an infant child.

The anointing can calm the cries of parents waiting for a call from a runaway teenager. It can still the tempest storms of trials and tribulations which Satan uses to assault your life.

Ezekiel described this potential power as waters steadily rising, first around the ankles, then around the waist, until eventually its depth could not be measured for the magnitude of its manifestation (Ezekiel 47).

The prophet Hosea proclaimed that it was like rain coming down out of heaven (Hosea 6:3).

The Psalmist eloquently painted a panoramic picture of this yoke-destroying, burden-removing, tangible substance as a river which makes glad the city of God. (Psalm 46:4.)

John, the Beloved, illustrated it as an unction or special endowment from the Holy One. (1 John 2:20).

The anointing will cause that which was once dead to live again! It is the life force of Almighty God!

_____

_____

_____

_____

_____

_____

_____

"The anointing transforms existence into life."

The Anointing Destroys the Yoke

And it shall come to pass in that day, that his burden shall be taken away from off thy shoulder, and his yoke from off thy neck, and the yoke shall be destroyed because of the anointing. (Isaiah 10:27)

There is a difference between break and destroy. When you break something it implies it can be put together again. However, when something is destroyed, it means to "cause it to cease to be as though it never existed."

For instance, take an expensive, beautiful vase, drop it and watch it break in two; it can be fixed again. Take that same vase, strike it with a hammer and shatter it into a million pieces. With glass lying like dust upon the floor, it is beyond any hope of being repaired. You are unable to tell a vase ever existed! That's what the anointing will do in your life! It will destroy the oppression of the adversary beyond restoration!

The yoke is any bondage that tries to oppress or take lordship, or authority, in any area of your life. If there is anything other than Jesus that has authority in your life, then there is a yoke upon you. But, the good news is, you can be delivered by the anointing that destroys every yoke!

_____

_____

_____

_____

_____

_____

_____

_____

_____

_____

*"Is there a bondage in your life
that needs to be destroyed by the anointing?"*

Cross the Line

And if it seem evil unto you to serve the LORD, choose you this day whom ye will serve; whether the gods which your fathers served that were on the other side of the flood, or the gods of the Amorites, in whose land ye dwell: but as for me and my house, we will serve the LORD. (Joshua 24:15)

In this year before the millennium, we're at a strategic inflection point. We are at a point where a decision must be made and I'm going to grab you by the spiritual nape of the neck and I'm going to throw you up against the wall of decision. Today we remember Jesus on the cross. It's decision time!

You must choose. The cross points in two directions. And you may deny the cross. You may spit upon the cross. You may bury the cross or you may overlay it with gold and sit it in a sanctuary of worship, but there's one thing you cannot do with that cross; you cannot ignore it! It demands for the human soul to deal with it!

You must choose to follow Christ or the world. You've hit the proverbial wall. You cannot go on any longer as you have been going. God is stepping flat in the middle of your pathway of life and demanding that you make a choice!

Something's going on! A fault line is developing in the body of Christ. A polarization is going on, a separation, a standard shift. There's something rumbling under our feet we cannot deny.

You are called to be part of a radical, revolutionary choice and when you cross the line, there's no turning back.

_____

_____

_____

_____

_____

_____

"Cross the line. Never go back to the world."

Laying on of Hands

Therefore leaving the principles of the doctrine of Christ, let us go on unto perfection; not laying again the foundation of repentance from dead works, and of faith toward God, of the doctrine of baptisms, and of laying on of hands, and of resurrection of the dead, and of eternal judgment. (Hebrews 6:1,2)

These are the foundational doctrines of the Christian faith. The laying on of hands is one of the major doctrines of our faith. If you are hooked up with a church that does not practice these doctrines, you are not hooked up with a New Testament church. You may be hooked up with a religious organization, but if they are not obeying the basic doctrines and tenets of the Christian faith, then they are not a New Testament church.

There is a reason and a purpose for the laying on of hands. Something happens when hands are laid upon you. That is the reason the Bible says to lay hands on no man suddenly, because during the laying on of hands there is a transference of the anointing of God. It is a tangible thing, and I want to make this profound statement: it is housed within your body.

The anointing is not floating around out there somewhere. Jesus didn't say the anointing is hanging around. Jesus didn't say the anointing is a kind of pseudo-spiritual cosmic thought. He said that the Spirit of the Lord was upon Him. Likewise, as sons of God (John 1:12), we have the Spirit of the Lord upon us as well. One way that you receive and impart the anointing is through the laying on of hands.

_____

_____

_____

_____

_____

_____

_____

"The laying on of hands imparts the anointing of God."

Resurrection Anointing

That I may know him, and the power of his resurrection, and the fellowship of his sufferings, being made conformable unto his death; if by any means I might attain unto the resurrection of the dead. (Philippians 3:10,11)

There is an anointing you and I can experience, the anointing of resurrection, which walked into the borrowed tomb of Joseph of Arimathea and raised the three-day dead body of the Prince of God.

The anointing of resurrection is one of the greatest anointings available to the body of Christ. This is because it reaches all the way to the last foe, Death, who is cloaked in blackness and sitting upon a throne of skull and bones.

It was into a scene of death that Jesus walked, in John chapter 11, where the Bible records these words: "Jesus saith unto her, Thy brother shall rise again. Martha saith unto him, I know that he shall rise again in the resurrection at the last day" (vv. 23,24). Did you notice what Martha said? She said, "I know he will rise again at the last day." She was looking toward the future and not expecting a miracle then.

So many, in the body of Christ, view miracles in the future tense rather than believing right now for Jesus to meet their need. I call it the someday syndrome. It is more captivating than the twilight zone. The people who live there are always looking for something down the road. The mountain of their problem has eclipsed the radiance of God's power. But Jesus came to declare resurrection anointing today! Now is the appointed time!

Picture Jesus turning His eyes toward Martha and fastening His gaze upon her as if to say, "I am the resurrection, and the life: he that believeth in me, though he were dead, yet shall he live" (vs. 25).

Once you find the anointing of the resurrection, it does not matter where death lurks! It must bow its knee, and resurrection power will make that which was dead in your life to live again!

_____

_____

_____

_____

"Live in the resurrection anointing."

Golden Goblets

Thou art weighed in the balances, and art found wanting. (Daniel 5:27)

Belshazzar, the king of Babylon, threw a party for a thousand of his nobles. Suddenly he decided he wanted to use the golden goblets from the house of the Lord. In his own pride and arrogance, He thought he had a right to use that which had been sanctified unto the Almighty for use in the temple of the Lord alone.

As Belshazzar lifted one of the glasses and began to drink, the judgment of God came swiftly. Upon the wall a hand wrote the sentence of his destruction.

Scripture records that very same night his enemies invaded the land and he was slain. Those things that are sanctified to the Lord take on a significance far greater than the physical elements they possess. What are the sanctified things, the golden goblets, that God has entrusted to your keeping?

_____

_____

_____

_____

_____

_____

_____

_____

_____

_____

_____

"Never profane the sacred, sanctified things of God."

Hope in His Plan

For I know the thoughts and plans that I have for you, says the Lord, thoughts and plans for welfare and peace and not for evil, to give you hope in your final outcome. (Jeremiah 29:11 AMP)

There is hope in Jesus. When you are painted with the anointing of the Lord, you are infused with hope for your final outcome. Regardless of the situation or what the circumstances surrounding your life look like, you can have steadfast confidence and assurance that everything is going to be all right.

What is hope? It is favorable and confident expectation to do with the unseen and future happy anticipation of good. Hebrews 11:1 says, "Now faith is the substance of things hoped for, the evidence of things not seen."

The anointing comes to give you hope in your final outcome! The anointing of God will make you see things differently than anyone else sees them.

When the doctors look at you and say you have to die and cannot live, faith will answer the door and drive out fear. When mourning for a lost loved one surpasses the hope for a better day, God will give you the garment of praise. You can stand in the face of the adversary and say, "It is well!"

_____

_____

_____

_____

_____

_____

_____

_____

"March into this new millennium with hope!"

Sow in Times of Lack

Isaac sowed in that land, and received in the same year an hundredfold: and the LORD blessed him. (Genesis 26:12)

Genesis tells us of a drought that came upon the land, leaving nothing but parched and dusty ground. The famine it caused was so severe, Isaac and his family were ready to flee to Egypt. But the Lord had another plan and appeared to Isaac, saying, "Dwell in the land which I shall tell thee of" (Genesis 26:2).

Isaac obeyed, tilling the soil and planting his meager seed. God blessed his obedience and faithfulness with a harvest that continued until he became extremely wealthy.

"He that observeth the wind shall not sow; and he that regardeth the clouds shall not reap" (Ecclesiastes 11:4). Those who dwell on the wind instead of the Word clutch their seed, afraid to sow. Your situation may seem hopeless, but you serve a God who created man from the dust of the ground! Trust in Him with all your might. Sow in your times of famine and reap a king's reward.

_____

_____

_____

_____

_____

_____

_____

_____

_____

"Sowing in lack brings a harvest of abundance."

Possess the Provision Promised to You

The Spirit of the Lord is upon me, because he has anointed me to preach the gospel to the poor; he hath sent me to heal the brokenhearted, to preach deliverance to the captives, and recovering of sight to the blind, to set at liberty them that are bruised, to preach the acceptable year of the Lord.
(Luke 4:18,19)

Nearly 2,000 years ago, our Canaan King, before the Spirit of the Lord anointed Him with power and majesty, fasted for 40 days in the wilderness. He was tempted, tested and tried, and successfully subdued the prince of the power of the air, Satan himself, with the penetrating statement, "It is written!"

Full of the Holy Spirit, this strong Galilean then proceeded to Nazareth. As was His custom, the Bible says He entered the synagogue on the Sabbath day. The magnitude of the moment was signified by the silence among the masses, as the Savior stood up to read. Our Canaan King boldly proclaimed:
Jesus became our Jubilee, our Great Liberator! Though it was not depicted by a day on the calendar, Jesus declared, "This is the acceptable day or the day when My free favors profusely abound!"

This year God has already made the provision for us to possess our promised land! You can walk in God's favor and acceptance today. Write down how you have experienced His favor in your life.

_____

_____

_____

_____

_____

_____

_____

"You can possess the provision of His favor."

Are You Willing to Fast?

And he said unto them, This kind can come forth by nothing, but by prayer and fasting. (Mark 9:29)

You can fast without praying and it has an effect. You can pray without fasting and it has an effect. But when you combine praying and fasting, you then target your need with the greatest spiritual strength available to you.

Faith needs prayer for growth and development, and prayer needs fasting for growth and development. Fasting means to abstain from something, and it does not necessarily have to be food. Adam and Eve were commanded to abstain from the tree of the knowledge of good and evil.

The reason so many in the body of Christ are not the spiritual giants they want to be is because they give their body everything it wants! Instead, many fast the wrong man. We fast our spirit man, only allowing it to eat during Sunday and midweek church services, while we feed our body three meals a day plus dessert.

The more God blesses you, the more you need to check your flesh. The quickest way to access the spirit world is to deny your flesh. Romans 8:13 declares, "Mortify the deeds of the body." What deeds of the flesh do you need to mortify today? List them and determine to keep an abiding fast from them.

_____

_____

_____

_____

_____

_____

_____

_____

_____

"What will you pray and fast for today?"

Tradition Blocks the Anointing

Making the word of God of none effect through your tradition, which ye have delivered: and many such like things do ye. (Mark 7:13)

Tradition is an adversary which will stop the flow of God's anointing in your life. In Mark 7 the Pharisees were questioning Jesus and His disciples for not walking after the custom, or tradition, of the elders.

But Jesus' response to them was, "This people honoureth me with their lips but their heart is far from me" (vs. 6). He accused them of rejecting the commandments of God in order to fulfill their own man-made traditions. So Jesus said to them, "You have made the word of God of none effect through your tradition, which ye have delivered: and many such like things do ye."

How often we in the church go about with our man-made doctrines and philosophies because it is what generation after generation has done all along! The sad statistics verify that this will stunt our spiritual growth because there is no real power in our methods!

You cannot manufacture an anointing, nor do you have to. If you are a child of God, the Spirit of the Lord is upon you and He has anointed you!

_____

_____

_____

_____

_____

_____

_____

_____

_____

_____

_____

"What traditions are coming between you and the power of God?"

Today is the Day

For he saith, I have heard thee in a time accepted, and in the day of salvation have I succoured thee: behold, now is the accepted time; behold, now is the day of salvation. (2 Corinthians 6:2)

Today is the day of the favor of the Lord in your life. You have been marked for your miracle, but Satan desires to stop you any way he can. The Bible says, however, to begin to walk in His supernatural favor and anointing.

The very moment you realize that the God in Christ has become the Christ in you and you know who you are in Him, you have begun to walk in God's favor.

Tomorrow is but a dream, and yesterday is but a memory, but right now today, the Bible declares, is the day of salvation; now is the appointed time (2 Corinthians 6:2).

Today, it is your time . . . for your thing . . . from your God, because it is God's time for His thing from you!!!

The Psalmist said it so well when speaking of the release of the children of Israel from Egyptian bondage:

"When the Lord brought back the captives to Zion, we were like those who dream. [It seemed so unreal!] Turn to freedom our captivity and restore our fortunes, O Lord, as the streams in the South. He who goes forth bearing seed and weeping shall doubtless come again with rejoicing, bringing his sheaves with him" (Psalm 126:1,4,6, AMP).

The man or woman who comes to God in the power of the anointing will not leave His presence empty handed! They will leave with a greater miracle harvest than was in their hand! Today, you are anointed and marked for a miracle!

_____

_____

_____

_____

_____

"Walk in God's favor today."

Yield to the Spirit

Then was Jesus led up of the spirit into the wilderness to be tempted of the devil. (Matthew 4:1)

Surrendering to the Holy Spirit is not a one-time occurrence that happens when we are born again. We must surrender daily, moment by moment.

It is easy to spot those who are yielding to the Holy Spirit and those who are not. A believer who is led by the Spirit will have victory over sin (Galatians 6:15); power to witness (Acts 1:8) and will possess the fruit of the Holy Spirit; love, joy, peace, patience, kindness, goodness, faithfulness gentleness and self-control.

A Spirit-controlled life does not happen overnight; it takes practice. It requires obedience, and it demands confession of our sins.

Today and every day, give your life back to God as a living sacrifice and surrender your life to the Holy Spirit's guidance and control.

_____

_____

_____

_____

_____

_____

_____

_____

_____

_____

_____

"Yielded to the Spirit, you will bear His fruit."

Touch the Hem of His Garment

When she had heard of Jesus, came in the press behind, and touched his garment. For she said, If I may touch but his clothes, I shall be whole. (Mark 5:27,28)

Do you remember the woman with the issue of blood? What was the first thing she did? She heard Jesus was in town. This woman had possibly heard the stories of the multitudes Jesus had healed from town to town. Perhaps she heard the story of blind Bartimaeus. Maybe one of her relatives shared with her the wonderful display of compassion and deliverance toward the young child who often cast himself into the fire. Something so stirred her to the very depths of her spirit to believe this man, the carpenter's Son, could heal her also.

Secondly, she spoke to herself. Faith will cause you to talk to yourself. There are two hinges of faith found in Romans 10:10 which says, "For with the heart man believeth unto righteousness; and with the mouth confession is made unto salvation."

Third, she then touched the hem of His garment. The word touch here is the Greek word "hepto," or to take hold of. Like Jacob wrestling with the angel at the brook at Jabbock all night, this woman grabbed hold of Jesus with "pit bull" faith.

Fourth, she felt healing come in and sickness go out! Once she touched the hem of Jesus' garment she was immediately set free! How wonderful one touch can be! Many were in the crowd that day and thronged Him. They were familiar with the outward signs of a Carpenter whose face was weather beaten and whose hands were calloused. But this woman grasped hold of the Anointed One and His anointing.

Jesus has the anointing without measure. It does not matter what your need is. His anointing is not limited and His power is perpetual. He will meet you at the point of your greatest need!

_____

_____

_____

_____

"By faith reach out and touch Jesus."

Victory Through Christ

O death, where is thy sting? O grave, where is thy victory? The sting of death is sin; and the strength of sin is the law. But thanks be to God, which giveth us the victory through our Lord Jesus Christ.
(1 Corinthians 15:55,56)

Consider a rejected carpenter's son. Don't let the Jerusalem Post write their headline on Friday, lest they have to print a retraction on Sunday. Let the ringing of the hammer be heard. Let nails part sinew and flesh. Watch His nerves jerk and quiver. Watch His body shake up again and down again. See Him wheezing with blood spewing from His mouth with every breath.

Watch death prancing back and forth at the base of a place called "The Skull." How could victory ever come to a place called death? Women are screaming, men are paralyzed and the earth turns black as sackcloth.

Dig that cross up out of the ground in the torrent of thundering rain and lightning. Let it fall in the mud with the body of the Prince of God. His blood has soaked the earth. Since the beginning, creation had groaned for redemption. Now the first taste of a new order has brought heaven and earth together in His blood. Wrap Him in grave clothes.

A few faithful bury Him in a borrowed tomb. But, don't count Him out; He's the Anointed One. And on the third day watch Him defeat death and be the first begotten of many.

Death could not stop Him. Now it cannot stop you. His resurrection has been birthed in you by the Holy Ghost. Death has no claim on you. You have nothing to fear. So live boldly for Christ in this last day before eternity!

_____

_____

_____

_____

_____

_____

_____

"Death has no hold on you. Fear nothing. Live boldly for Christ."

Faith Follows Through

Ye see then how that by works a man is justified, and not by faith only. (James 2:24)

The Bible says by your works shall you be justified. Well now wait a minute. Here's a paradox. Here's the seeming contradiction, because the Bible also says that salvation is by grace, through faith, not of works lest any man perish. So what is He saying? He's saying that your eternal salvation swings upon the hinge of the provisionary work of the blood of Jesus Christ on Calvary, nothing more, nothing less.

Then what does it mean when the Bible comes right along side of faith and says that you shall be justified by your works? It means that true faith isn't just lip service to the truth, it's living the truth.

The radical Christian in the new millennium will not only talk about what he believes, he will live it!

_____

_____

_____

_____

_____

_____

_____

_____

_____

_____

_____

_____

"Faith is more than lip service. It's following through with the works of faith."

Your Life Source

But we have this treasure in earthen vessels, that the excellency of the power may be of God, and not of us. (2 Corinthians 4:7)

There is something at work within you. There is something producing motion against satanic resistance in your life. It is the anointing. What is that treasure? It is the Holy Ghost.

The Holy Ghost is alive on the inside of you now, and He is bigger than you. Not only is He bigger than you, but He is also bigger than all your problems. He is bigger than any mountain that you can or cannot see.

John 7:38 says, "He that believeth on me, as the scripture hath said, out of his belly shall flow rivers of living water."

Your spirit becomes the generator that takes the Word of God and changes it into the fuel the Holy Ghost uses to produce the anointing in your life.

The anointing becomes your life source.

_____

_____

_____

_____

_____

_____

_____

_____

_____

_____

_____

_____

"The anointing will become your life source of power and strength."

The Spirit Lives in You

Go not down into Egypt; dwell in the land which I shall tell thee of: Sojourn in this land, and I will be with thee, and will bless thee; for unto thee, and unto thy seed, I will give all these countries, and I will perform the oath which I sware unto Abraham thy father.
(Genesis 26:2,3)

The Bible records that Isaac pitched his tent in the valley of Gerar. While there, he found great favor with Abimelech, King of the Philistines, and he began to dig the wells which this very group of people had stopped up. When he began to dig, he found a well of "springing" water. The Hebrew word for springing in this passage actually means living.

Isaac had such favor that those from without the covenant were not able to stop the life source of God from flowing in his life. This is the way it is with the devil. When you walk in the anointing God has placed in your life, the adversary is unable to get to the source of that anointing on the inside of you!

But notice what happened next. The herdsman of Gerar strove with Isaac over the water but were unable to overcome him there!

Proverb 4:23 admonishes us to, "Keep thy heart with all diligence; for out of it are the issues of life," because the devil will try to steal your fountain of power. Satan will try to stop up your well, but the Spirit of the Lord will raise up a standard against him!" (Isaiah 59:19)

If you are born again, there is an anointing on the inside of you. The Spirit whom Jesus spoke of when He stood up in the synagogue to read from the Book of Isaiah and announced, "The Spirit of the Lord is upon me because he has anointed me," is the same Spirit which dwells in you.

_____

_____

_____

_____

_____

_____

"The anointing of the Holy Spirit will destory every bondage."

Power from Above

But ye shall receive power, after that the Holy Ghost is come upon you: and ye shall be witnesses unto me both in Jerusalem, and in all Judaea, and in Samaria, and unto the uttermost part of the earth. (Acts 1:8)

Maybe you don't feel like the Holy Spirit is resident in you now. Perhaps you have never understood what it means to allow the life force of God to reside in you through the baptism of the Holy Spirit, and to walk in the anointing. Right in the middle of reading this book you can, by praying this simple prayer:

Heavenly Father, I believe your Word which says you would not leave me comfortless, but give unto me the Comforter in the person of the Holy Spirit. I ask you now to baptize me in the Holy Spirit and infuse me with power beyond myself.

Give me power to stand against the attacks of the devil and power to be a witness of your mighty acts, bearing your name in all that I say and do. I receive this power from on high now.

I receive the anointing in my life, as a result of this fresh baptism of fire and power, to liberate the captives, heal the brokenhearted and release all who are oppressed. I thank you for it, Lord, in the precious name of Jesus. Amen.

"Ask the Holy Spirit to baptize you now with power."

Know Him

And I will take you to me for a people, and I will be to you a God: and ye shall know that I am the LORD your God, which bringeth you out from under the burdens of the Egyptians. (Exodus 6:7)

Every fresh, new golden era of human history has always been preceded by the devotion and righteous passion of one or more individuals who:

1) *knew* their God and,
2) *knew* where they were going.

I did not say they knew about Him. I said they knew Him. They were not casually acquainted. They were intimately involved with Him—not His organization, not His philosophy, not His doctrine, not His personality, but His person.

Somebody said, "I found the Lord." You didn't know where to look. It was God who went looking for Moses and found him at Midian. It was God who went searching for Jacob and found him at Bethel. It was God who looked for Saul and found him on the road to Damascus. God is seeking you out that you may *know Him.*

_____

_____

_____

_____

_____

_____

_____

_____

_____

_____

_____

"God desires that you know Him, not just that you know about Him."

It Is Written

And there was delivered unto him the book of the prophet Esaias. And when he had opened the book, he found the place where it was written, The Spirit of the Lord is upon me. (Luke 4:17,18a)

Jesus having been tempted 40 days and 40 nights while fasting in the mountain wilderness, defeated the devil on three fronts: his spirit man, his soulish man and his body. He responded to the attack of the adversary with these words: "It is written." Why? Because what is written is anointed. He came down out of that mountain and went to Sunday morning church service.

It was delivered unto Him the book of the prophet Isaiah, chapter 61, and He stood up and began to read, "The spirit of the Lord is upon me," and they all looked at Him like "Who do you think you are?" He looked right back at them as if to say, "I know exactly who I am. The spirit of the Lord is upon me; for He hath anointed me to preach the gospel to the poor; to heal the brokenhearted, to preach deliverance to the captives, the recovering of sight to the blind, and to set at liberty them that are bruised; to preach the acceptable year of the Lord."

He then closed the book because He was done. All that He is doing now in your life has already been done, finished, and completed in His perfect will. Do you need healing? Done. Do you need financial blessing? Done. Do you need restoration? Done. Do you need revival? Done. Most of all, do you need Him? Done. He's with you until the end of the age.

_____

_____

_____

_____

_____

_____

_____

"Has the Spirit of the Lord done what He desires in your heart?"

Invite Change

Behold, I shew you a mystery; We shall not all sleep, but we shall all be changed.
(1 Corinthians 15:51)

Have you ever noticed God never stops? He is continually making all things new. He only finishes one thing to begin something else. He only stops to start again. He only lets midnight be black because joy comes in the morning. God is constantly initiating change.

But we don't like change! We resist it at every opportunity. We don't like things to change.

A wife asked, "Honey, will you love me if I dye my hair red?" Her husband replied, "I've loved you through five other colors. I don't know what difference that is." Is the change in your life superficial and cosmetic or are you willing to allow Christ to change and conform you to His image?

What new thing is the Lord doing in your life today? Are you resisting His change?

_____

_____

_____

_____

_____

_____

_____

_____

_____

_____

_____

_____

"Lord, change me to be like you."

Don't Be Religious, Be Radical

Having a form of godliness, but denying the power thereof: from such turn away.
(2 Timothy 3:5)

Religious Christians are satisfied with appearances. They appear at church on holidays and special occasions so that they might look spiritual. They appear at religious events and go through the rituals so that others will think them to be spiritual. But religion isn't spiritual. Being radical is spiritual!

Radical Christians join together in revolutionary churches not for the sake of appearances because of change. Religious Christians only change outward appearances but radical Christians have been changed by the Holy Ghost.

Religion portrays a form of godliness but has no life-changing power. Are you religious or radical?

_____

_____

_____

_____

_____

_____

_____

_____

_____

_____

_____

_____

_____

"Refuse to be religious. Be radical!"

The Prize

Henceforth there is laid up for me a crown of righteousness, which the Lord, the righteous judge, shall give me at that day: and not to me only, but unto all them also that love his appearing. (2 Timothy 4:8)

The prize is not to the beginner. Everybody looks great at the starting line. If I'm going to know if you've really got it or not, I can't know at the starting line! I have got to get down the road somewhere. I must see if you can successfully navigate the temptations that will try your soul, the testing of the fiery furnace and the overflowing of waters! I have got to get down here somewhere and see if you're able. If you're running the race and I'm watching your progress, I must finally position myself at the finish line to know whether or not you will receive the prize.

The prize is not to the beginner, only to the finisher. If the prize was awarded at the beginning, heaven would be overpopulated; but to the finisher who refuses to be denied his position or delayed in the pursuit of His promise goes the crown of glory. On that crowning day when you meet Jesus face-to-face, you will be able to declare with Paul, "I have fought the good fight and have finished the race!"

_____

_____

_____

_____

_____

_____

_____

_____

_____

_____

"The crown only goes to those who finish the race."

Be Filled With the Spirit

And be not drunk with wine, wherein is excess; but be filled with the Spirit.
(Ephesians 5:18)

The only way to endure, the only way to last, the only way to feel the victory of the finish line tape being broken across your chest in this eternal game is to be willing to change. Andy Grove, the president of the Intel Corporation (second wealthiest computer mogul that has ever lived, second only to Bill Gates whose combined personal wealth is larger than that of most third world countries), released a little book on paranoia.

Grove said that when change and unexpected crises happen, they will crush you if you're not prepared to face them. But for those who are prepared, when a new wind blows, they adjust their sails. Instead of being crushed, they will be propelled at the pinnacle of that wave into something that they never even knew existed.

So it is with the wind of God's Spirit. He stirs the oceans of our lives and new waves sweep into our lives. Are you ready to ride the wave of His Spirit in this countdown to the new millennium?

_____

_____

_____

_____

_____

_____

_____

_____

_____

_____

_____

_____

"Let the wind of the Spirit fill your sails and propel you forward."

Spirit Outpouring

And it shall come to pass afterward, that I will pour out my spirit upon all flesh; and your sons and your daughters shall prophesy, your old men shall dream dreams, your young men shall see visions: and also upon the servants and upon the handmaids in those days will I pour out my spirit.
(Joel 2:28,29)

We are living in an hour when the last, greatest move of the Spirit of God is about to be unleashed throughout the earth. You are now living in the outpouring of God's Spirit which brings His blessing and favor.

Etched upon the heart of every Christian is the emblem of a child of God. You and I have been chosen by the Lord to bear His mark of sonship and to go forth in the unction of the Holy Spirit, to be partakers of all the blessings of Christ!

The Spirit of the Lord is upon you to enable you not only to live in the acceptable day of the favor of the Lord, but also to transcend above every onslaught of Satan. You have the Spirit of God to receive whatever you need from the Lord. If you need a healing, it is yours to claim. If you need deliverance, it too can be yours. Everything you need is available to you now!

_____

_____

_____

_____

_____

_____

_____

_____

_____

_____

"You can live in God's favor and abundance."

How Hot Are You?

I know thy works, that thou art neither cold nor hot: I would thou wert cold or hot. So then because thou art lukewarm, and neither cold nor hot, I will spue thee out of my mouth. (Revelation 3:15,16)

We are no longer divided over racial lines. We are no longer divided over sexual lines. Thank God for it. I'm a Baptist boy who was saved in a Pentecostal service with a woman preaching, and we did not believe in women preachers.

We're no longer divided over denominational walls. They're all coming down. But there is a *spiritual* dividing line. Jesus said it this way: "I would that you were hot or cold. For if you're lukewarm I'll spew you out of my mouth." What divides us is a thermometer. It's a temperature dividing line. The degree that you are on fire for Jesus really matters in the kingdom of God.

Here's the separation! The hot are getting hotter and the cold are getting colder.

"Are you hot for Jesus?"

Have You Noticed?

For I am come to set a man at variance against his father, and the daughter against her mother, and the daughter in law against her mother in law. And a man's foes shall be they of his own household. He that loveth father or mother more than me is not worthy of me: and he that loveth son or daughter more than me is not worthy of me. And he that taketh not his cross, and followeth after me, is not worthy of me. (Matthew 10:35-38)

Have you noticed that some people who used to begin to check the time at 15 minutes before the service ended are now checking 15 minutes after the service starts? Others have decided that watch watching isn't a part of worship and they have left their watches at home.

Have you noticed that folks you used to hang with, you can't hang with any more? Have you noticed that God is forming new alliances and that steel is sharpening steel? There's something going on. People who used to lift up one little hand in praise have now been seen sitting on it. But others who never raised a hand in worship now raise both hands, while shouting and dancing at the same time. Have you noticed a separation going on?

Some people who used to miss Sunday night service have now been seen staying home on Sunday morning, too. But right on the other side of the fault line we've got these crazy Christians who are pounding the pastor's door down saying, "Can we have a prayer meeting? Can we have more Bible study? Can we call on the lost?" The gap is widening. The church is getting radical for Jesus. List the ways you are becoming radical for Jesus:

_____

_____

_____

_____

_____

_____

_____

"Have you noticed that it's time to get radical for Jesus?"

Die to Self

I am crucified with Christ: nevertheless I live; yet not I, but Christ liveth in me: and the life which I now live in the flesh I live by the faith of the Son of God, who loved me, and gave himself for me. (Galatians 2:20)

Chickens cluck. Dogs bark. Cows moo. Birds fly. Fish swim and hogs grunt.

You can take a hog and baptize it in $150 an ounce perfume, paint its toenails, wrap a mink stole around its body, and carry it into your parlor. We've got a lot of pigs in the parlor. You an prop it up in a luxury recliner and give it a remote control to a 52-inch TV set. But don't turn your back on your pig, because just as soon as you do, he's coming out of that parlor and going right to the mud hole. Why? Because he's a hog, once a hog always a hog.

The time has come and is now over for you to stop masquerading as something you are not and to conform to the One you are supposed to imitate—Christ. Pretense is past tense. Perfection is present tense, and the only way to get from the pig pen to the Prince's parlor is through the Cross.

Are you ready to die to self and be raised to a new life in Christ Jesus?

_____

_____

_____

_____

_____

_____

_____

_____

_____

_____

"Live today in the newness of Jesus Christ"

The Power of Praise

I will praise thee, O LORD, with my whole heart; I will show forth all thy marvellous works. I will be glad and rejoice in thee: I will sing praise to thy name, O thou most High.
(Psalm 9:1,2)

The anointing is manifest to destroy the yoke! What is the yoke of this generation? The yoke of this generation is sinners masquerading like they're happy and church folk masquerading like they're dead!

Did you wake up today with a "Hallelujah" on your lips and in your heart? Do you believe that the same Spirit that invaded the borrowed tomb of Joseph of Arimathea and raised to life again the three-day dead body of the Prince of God lives in you?

Do you know that the same Spirit that empowered Jesus to walk on the water, stopped the woman's issue of blood, wiped the blindness from Bartimaeus' eyes and found money in a fish's mouth is now living on the inside of you? If you really believe that and cannot muster a "Hallelujah" today then the yoke hasn't been broken in your life.

Stand up right now. Declare with a shout, "Hallelujah!" Let your praise spring forth from the anointing on your life so that every yoke that would bind you is broken in Jesus' name.

"Begin each day with praise. Shout to the Lord, 'Hallelujah!'"

God's Party

For this my son was dead, and is alive again; he was lost, and is found. And they began to be merry. (Luke 15:24)

Parties have punctuated our heritage and become the exclamation point of the loose-living, sin- infected society in which we live.

Take for example a young Nazarite named Samson, seduced by sin, laid his head in the lap of Delilah, told her the secret of his power. Belshazzar, intoxicated with his own glory, threw himself a party. Herod threw a party for his adulteress wife. Drunken and yielding to the seductions of her young virgin daughter as she danced scantily clad before him, he cried out, "Whatever you want up to the half of my kingdom shall be yours!"

Today tens of thousands of Americans are duped by the party spirit from the ballroom of the White House to the bridge night at the neighbor's house. It really doesn't matter if the drinks of choice are a fine wine sipped from crystal glasses or cheap beer slurped from a paper cup. It doesn't matter if the attire is black tie or blue jeans, or if the drug of choice is prescription Valium or crack cocaine, the *results* are the same.

The Kingdom of God is the only lasting, real party in town. All the rest is counterfeit. Come to God's party and rejoice today with the Father.

_____

_____

_____

_____

_____

_____

_____

_____

_____

_____

"God is celebrating that once you were lost but now you are found. Come to His party."

Radiate Joy!

And ye now therefore have sorrow: but I will see you again, and your heart shall rejoice, and your joy no man taketh from you.
(John 16:22)

The X-generation, so-called because of their seeming lack of direction and destiny, search their peer groups to find acceptance and a solid foundation. Instead they receive only partial satisfaction in smoke-filled, drug-infested parties that mask their pain and camouflage their cravings.

The world today looks to the church with hunger in its eyes and a hole in its heart. The world looks to the church and often, to its chagrin, they find no love, no life, no laughter, no hope, no help and no happiness. They see only a church whose garments are tainted, tattered and torn. They stand up and exclaim, "Why would I want to be a part of that bunch? They're obviously more miserable than me." And it's true, isn't it? The most excitement most church folk ever see is a Saturday night bingo game or an occasional spaghetti dinner.

Are you radiating the joy of the Lord today? Are people attracted to Jesus because of the overflowing joy that bubbles out of you? Would they know just by being with you, that you have a joy that no man can take? Put on the garment of praise and reflect His joy today.

_____

_____

_____

_____

_____

_____

_____

_____

_____

"Let everyone see your joy in Christ."

Be Salt and Light

Ye are the salt of the earth: but if the salt have lost his savour, wherewith shall it be salted? it is thenceforth good for nothing, but to be cast out, and to be trodden under foot of men. Ye are the light of the world. A city that is set on an hill cannot be hid. (Matthew 5:13-14)

Today is your opportunity to penetrate your world as salt and light for Jesus Christ. You can be salty enough to make others thirsty for the living water that only Jesus offers. Jesus tells us, "But whosoever drinketh of the water that I shall give him shall never thirst; but the water that I shall give him shall be in him a well of water springing up into everlasting life (John 4:14).

How will you be salt today? In what ways will Jesus' living water flow out of you into the lives of others?

Be light in your world today. Where there is darkness, shine with the light of His truth and love. Remember, light overcomes darkness. You have nothing to fear from the dark. You are a child of light!

List people with whom you will share living water and to whom you will be a source of light to, today. Begin praying for them now and write down how you will reach out to them in Jesus' name.

_____

_____

_____

_____

_____

_____

_____

_____

_____

_____

"As the millennium approaches live your life to draw others to Jesus."

What is too Much?

But thou shalt remember the Lord thy God: for it is he that giveth thee power to get wealth, that he may establish his covenant which he sware unto thy fathers, as it is this day. (Deuteronomy 8:18)

How much is too much? Is enough ever really enough? Will there ever be too many people who give their lives to God? Wouldn't it sound strange if I were to say we should put a limit on the number of people who can receive salvation? But, unfortunately, when it comes to the majority of people in the body of Christ to believe for perpetual abundance in their lives, they shrug it off as religious piety and settle for a poverty mentality.

The Lord not only wants us to be blessed in our individual lives, but for us to be a blessing. Decide to bless someone today.

"Be God's instrument of blessing today in the lives of others."

Drunk on New Wine

And be not drunk with wine, wherein is excess; but be filled with the Spirit. (Ephesians 5:18).

I'm looking for some drinking buddies. I'm looking for somebody who wants to get drunk on new wine! I'm looking for somebody somewhere who is tired of what you've had, tired of the status quo and tired of dead, cold religion.

I'm looking for those who want to stand up with me and at the top of their lungs shout, "It's my time to receive all that God has for me." I'm tired of no anointing! I'm tired of going through the motions! You can't tell me I can't come in when He's already sent me an invitation and set a place for me at his banqueting table!

I'm tired of a world acting like they're having fun and a church acting like they're in a funeral service. There's only one reason to have a body and that's to express the life of God that's within it! Shout, "The party's here! The party's now!"

"Tell others that they are invited to the party of the ages with the King of kings."

What's That Scent?

For we are unto God a sweet savour of Christ, in them that are saved, and in them that perish. (2 Corinthians 2:15).

Drop a bottle of perfume in a room and days later, the room is still filled with the sweet aroma of the perfume's scent. In fact, one may walk through the room and just by being in the presence of the sweet perfume, others can sense the fragrance on that person's clothing, hair and skin.

When we are in the presence of God, His sweet aroma lingers on us—our speech, actions and attitudes. Not only can other Christians sense His presence on us when we are with Him, the unsaved can also sense that something is different about us.

When was the last time an unsaved person commented, "There's something different about you. I can sense it. What is it?" In what ways does your life exude the sweet perfume of being in His presence?

_____

_____

_____

_____

_____

_____

_____

_____

_____

_____

_____

_____

_____

_____

"Let the sweet perfume of Jesus' life flow through you to others."

Put Away Unbelief

And he did not many mighty works there because of their unbelief. (Matthew 13:58)

Something's missing. It's faith untainted by doubt. Where is the faith for miracles, signs and wonders in the church today that was so evident in the book of Acts? When you pass a poor, homeless person on the street, their stench might be so strong that you would faint. While you know that they stink, they have grown accustomed to their own stench and it doesn't bother them. Likewise, our stench of unbelief doesn't bother us. We have grown accustomed to the stench of unbelief corporately and individually.

We have also become accustomed to the stench of "Gospel entertainment"! We have substituted performance for power. We have become accustomed to praying with no results! I don't know where this doctrine came from, "We'll pray for it and believe it'll happen some day." God's Spirit told me, "Go to the New Testament. Open up Matthew, Mark, Luke and John and find me a place where healing was tentative, where a miracle was ever wishful or where a someday, *hope so* theology is taught."

Stop postponing and procrastinating. Put away unbelief. Instead of putting off believing for God's miracles until tomorrow, believe now without doubt!

_____

_____

_____

_____

_____

_____

_____

_____

_____

*"The stench of unbelief needs to be replaced
in your life by the aroma of faith."*

Bold Preaching

But we preach Christ crucified, unto the Jews a stumblingblock, and unto the Greeks foolishness; But unto them which are called, both Jews and Greeks, Christ the power of God, and the wisdom of God. (1 Corinthians 1:23,24)

It's time to stop empty preaching and to begin preaching the Gospel with boldness and power. Empty preaching uses vain clichés to communicate tired messages from powerless pulpits.

But powerful preaching is a life focused on the cross of Jesus Christ. Radical Christians cannot get the cross out of their minds or speech. They constantly think and talk boldly about Jesus—crucified and raised from the dead.

The radical Christians that God is calling forth for the new millennium know that the time is short and the season is *now* to preach in the boldness of God's power. Where are you preaching? Is your pulpit at work, home or on the streets? Where the sermon of your life is preached make certain that your proclamation boldly exalts Jesus Christ.

"Is your life a radical, bold sermon proclaiming Christ."

Learn of Christ

Take my yoke upon you, and learn of me; for I am meek and lowly in heart: and ye shall find rest unto your souls. For my yoke is easy, and my burden is light. (Matthew 11:29,30)

In a dead church, praise has to be taught. For those alive, praise is as natural as breathing. For those seeking the gifts and not the Giver, we must teach the scriptural foundation for tongues, dancing and shouting (1 Corinthians 12-14; Psalms 132:9, 149:3).

Instead of teaching the Word of God, many are we have found ourselves teaching how to react to His Word. In that, there is no life, no unction, no power and no joy.

The radical, revolutionary church of the new millennium will be focused on learning about Jesus instead of learning about how to be the church.

We need a life-changing, radical experience, face-to-face encounter with Jesus Christ.

"Ask the Holy Spirit to empower you to learn of Christ."

Prefer the Power of God

That your faith should not stand in the wisdom of men, but in the power of God.
(1 Corinthians 2:5)

If you use the book of Acts as your example and the rest of the New Testament simply to define and explain what transpired in that book, you will come away from Scripture with the stunning realization that I have come to: the church has been miscarrying. Twentieth century Christianity has aborted the Gospel. Too often we prefer the wisdom of men instead of the power of God.

We have many powerful pulpiteers but few are power-filled preachers. We have planted vineyards and trees that are miscarrying and bearing no fruit. We're losing a generation who wants no part of the institutional church. They are looking for someone who is radical for Jesus.

Are you pretending to follow Jesus or are you truly filled with the Spirit, drunk on new wine, overflowing with the anointing, and ready to march against all hell with a heavenly cause and under the banner of the King of kings?

_____

_____

_____

_____

_____

_____

_____

_____

_____

_____

_____

"Choose the power of God over the wisdom of men."

You Must See Jesus

Looking unto Jesus the author and finisher of our faith; who for the joy that was set before him endured the cross, despising the shame, and is set down at the right hand of the throne of God. (Hebrews 12:2)

Let me see Him. I must see Jesus. For whom are you looking? Are you going to church hoping to see a man—a preacher, a teacher or a prophet of God. Are you looking to a person to inspire, motivate and educate you? If so, you will never see Jesus.

If you can see Him, cancer can melt out of your body. If you can see Him, you won't have to muster up a memorized shout!

If you can see Him, you won't have to worry about your baby being on crack cocaine. If you can get past all the religion and the ritual, then something will change in your life!

Stop looking to others or to something else and start *looking unto Jesus.* What you need in this countdown to the millennium is not more religion; you need a revelation of Jesus.

_____

_____

_____

_____

_____

_____

_____

_____

_____

_____

_____

"Stop looking for religion. Instead, look to Jesus."

The Real Jesus

And he that sat upon the throne said, Behold, I make all things new. And he said unto me, Write: for these words are true and faithful.
(Revelation 21:5)

We need to say to people on the sidelines of our churches: If you're not going to join us, please don't work against us. Please, please don't tell people that Jesus died for them while looking and acting so lethargic. In the radical church of the new millennium, we can never settle for a tired, pale representation of Jesus.

Settle for nothing less than the real, alive, resurrected, radical, revolutionary Jesus. The real Jesus makes all things new!

I'm tired of the world stealing our party. I'm tired of them smiling while the church is frowning. I'm tired of retreating while the world advances. I'm tired of the church losing instead of winning and of being the tail instead of the head. What are you tired of? Are you tired enough of the world that you're willing to be changed by Christ? The real Jesus will change you. Nothing and no one else will!

"Change my heart, O God. Make me all brand new!"

Our Hope

Looking for that blessed hope, and the glorious appearing of the great God and our Saviour Jesus Christ; Who gave himself for us, that he might redeem us from all iniquity, and purify unto himself a peculiar people, zealous of good works.
(Titus 2:13,14)

Hope is not in a bottle, not in a needle, not in a creed and not in a church. The church is not the answer. The church contains the answer, which is Jesus! For the drug addict, Jesus! For the prostitute, Jesus! For the preacher, Jesus! For the backslider, Jesus! For the cancer patient, Jesus! For the homosexual, Jesus; for the White House, Jesus! For your house, Jesus!

Shout it from the highest mountain. He's the anointed one who destroys every yoke of bondage. He's the Lily of the Valley, the Staff of Life and Honey in a Rock. He's the I Am that I Am, the Alpha and Omega, the beginning and the end! He's at every start and stop in life and everywhere in between. His name is Jesus!

Say to yourself, "My hope is built on nothing less than Jesus' blood and righteousness!"

_____

_____

_____

_____

_____

_____

_____

_____

_____

_____

_____

"Today, put all of your faith, love and hope in Jesus."

No Pressure

This book of the law shall not depart out of thy mouth; but thou shalt meditate therein day and night, that thou mayest observe to do according to all that is written therein: for then thou shalt make thy way prosperous, and then thou shalt have good success. (Joshua 1:8)

I refuse to live under pressure one more moment. I don't have any pressure. I'm on this planet, not to be the recipient of pressure, but to put the pressure on the adversary. I will continually speak the Word of God so that I may live under prosperity not pressure.

With every shout, every hallelujah, every song and every wave, I'm going to exert pressure. And sooner or later the enemy will learn that if he dares to touch my stuff, I will not allow it. I refuse to be pressured or intimidated by the enemy.

I **will** be relentless. I **will** walk around my house and speak the Word of God until my tongue falls out, but I will not be delayed in the pursuit of my promise. I **will not** be denied.

Are you caving in to the pressure of the enemy? Are you reacting to what the devil is doing instead of acting out the Word of God? Either you live under pressure or you apply pressure. I choose to push back the kingdom of darkness and to pressure the enemy at every turn with the sword of the Spirit. What about you?

_____

_____

_____

_____

_____

_____

_____

_____

_____

*"Get out from under the enemy's pressure.
Apply the pressure of God's Word."*

Declare Victory Not Defeat

Declare his glory among the heathen; his marvellous works among all nations. For great is the LORD, and greatly to be praised: he also is to be feared above all gods.
(1 Chronicles 16:24,25)

I refuse to allow anything into my life that's not from God's Word. Is that your declaration today? If it's not from God's holy Word, then it's foreign to me. Your spiritual man will cast off failure like your body will cast off a virus. Decide to stand firm on the Word of God. Make a commitment to take possession of the land and take back from the enemy what he has stolen from you.

The devil may seek to destroy, steal and kill, but refuse to be intimidated. Choose to declare Christ's victory. Decide to speak the Word of God not the analysis, research and polling of man. Man's opinion or assessment of my predicament isn't reality. Circumstances do not determine the future, and the past does not determine the present.

Start declaring what God has done! Start speaking victory!

"Make Jesus' victory, not your defeat, the declaration of your mouth."

The Time of War

For though we walk in the flesh, we do not war after the flesh: (For the weapons of our warfare are not carnal, but mighty through God to the pulling down of strong holds;) Casting down imaginations, and every high thing that exalteth itself against the knowledge of God, and bringing into captivity every thought to the obedience of Christ; And having in a readiness to revenge all disobedience, when your obedience is fulfilled. (2 Corinthians 10:3-6)

Ecclesiastes 3:1 declares that to everything there is a season. There is a time of war and a time of peace. The problem with many Christians is that they don't understand *the law of first mention*. They don't understand that war precedes peace.

People have the misconception that we must labor in warfare. But 2 Corinthians 10:4,5 reveals that the weapons of our warfare are not carnal. They're not fleshly. They're mighty, through God, to the pulling down of strongholds and casting down of imaginations.

Before you can have the spiritual fruit of peace you will experience the spiritual warfare of pulling down strongholds. The price of peace is spiritual warfare. Begin today to pull down strongholds, not with your own strength, but in the might of the Lord.

_____

_____

_____

_____

_____

_____

_____

_____

_____

"Begin exercising your spiritual weapons to pull down strongholds."

Fight the Fight of Faith

That I may know him, and the power of his resurrection, and the fellowship of his sufferings, being made conformable unto his death.
(Philippians 3:10)

We fight the fight of faith. It is not passive but aggressive. We must learn to stop warring in the flesh and instead to fight in the Spirit.

Fighting in the flesh will frustrate, fatigue and anger you. Fighting in the flesh will steal your joy. Fighting in the flesh will take your peace. Trying to make it happen on your own will destroy the force of life that is within you.

What battles are you trying to fight in the flesh? Are you willing today to put on the armor of God and war with the Word of God? In the Spirit, the battle is already won. Stop trying to win and start trusting the victory that Christ has already won through His resurrection.

_____

_____

_____

_____

_____

_____

_____

_____

_____

_____

_____

_____

_____

_____

_____

"Let Christ win your battles through the power of His resurrection."

Praise Defeats the Enemy

Let the saints be joyful in glory: let them sing aloud upon their beds. Let the high praises of God be in their mouth, and a two-edged sword in their hand; To execute vengeance upon the heathen, and punishments upon the people; To bind their kings with chains, and their nobles with fetters of iron; To execute upon them the judgment written: this honour have all his saints. (Psalm 149:5-9)

Perhaps you have been spending your days cursing the devil and lamenting all the difficulties in your life. Stop cursing and complaining. The enemy is never defeated by your negativism; however, praise always destroys his schemes and plans.

Your lips of praise become the two-edged sword that cuts the chains and bondages that the enemy uses to discourage you. Instead of talking about what is wrong today, redeem your time with praise. Instead of magnifying the devil's evil, exalt the Lord.

Fill your day with praise and the enemy will be defeated at every turn. For what will you praise God today?

_____

_____

_____

_____

_____

_____

_____

_____

_____

_____

_____

_____

"Use praise today to defeat the enemy's schemes."

Be Careful How You Ask

Call unto me, I will answer thee, and I will show thee great and mighty things which thou knowest not. (Jeremiah 33:3)

Are you confident that your prayers will be answered? If not, remember that your confidence does not rest in yourself or your ability to pray effectively. Rather, your assurance rests in the one who answers your prayers—Jesus. Jesus tells us to ask, and it shall be given . . . seek and ye shall find . . . knock and it will be opened.

1 John 5:14 reads, "And this is the confidence that we have in him, that, if we ask any thing according to his will, he heareth us." Because He hears us, we know with steadfast confidence and assurance that we have granted to us, for our present possession, those things whatsoever we requisitioned Him for. We need to ask. . .

- In His will
- In His way
- In His timing
- In agreement with His Word.

Are you praying with confidence in Christ? Pray confidently knowing that as you pray in His will, He will answer your every need.

_____

_____

_____

_____

_____

_____

_____

_____

_____

_____

"Pray confidently for His will in your life."

Anticipation Is Confident Expectation

Being confident of this very thing, that he which hath begun a good work in you will perform it until the day of Jesus Christ: (Philippians 1:6)

Hope is a favorable, confident expectation that God will act. Something good is about to happen. How do I know that? Because God is a good God and the devil is a bad devil. So I have a confident anticipation.

A critical element of hope is anticipation. Hope anticipates that God will fulfill every promise and plan that He has made. Hope anticipates that God will meet us at our deepest point of need. Hope anticipates that upon encountering difficulties and trials, God will walk us through to victory. Hope anticipates meeting Jesus at the end of time and rejoicing in Him as Lord and Savior.

What are you anticipating this year that God will complete in you? Are you trusting Him for all your needs? Hope in confident anticipation that something good is about to happen.

_____

_____

_____

_____

_____

_____

_____

_____

_____

_____

_____

_____

"The world expects the worse to happen. Hope expects God's best."

Faith Sees

Howbeit when he, the Spirit of truth, is come, he will guide you into all truth: for he shall not speak of himself; but whatsoever he shall hear, that shall he speak: and he will shew you things to come. He shall glorify me: for he shall receive of mine, and shall shew it unto you. All things that the Father hath are mine: therefore said I, that he shall take of mine, and shall shew it unto you. (John 16:13-15)

Faith sees by the Spirit what can't be seen in the natural, and faith knows what cannot otherwise be known. Why? Because faith deals with the Holy Ghost . . . and the Holy Ghost goes where you can't go, hears what you can't hear, comes back and brings you a message you could never know.

The Holy Ghost has access into both realms—the natural and the supernatural. How do I know something? The Holy Ghost told me. How does He know? He went where I couldn't go. He heard something I couldn't hear, and He came back and gave me a report about something that otherwise I could never know.

He has been where I cannot go and revealed what I could never know. So, my faith is not in myself but in Christ. By His Spirit, know that your tomorrow and the next millennium is in His hands. You can never know all that tomorrow holds, but you know confidently who holds tomorrow!

_____

_____

_____

_____

_____

_____

_____

_____

_____

_____

"Listen to the Spirit as He reveals tomorrow to you."

Repentance and Refreshing

Repent ye therefore, and be converted, that your sins may be blotted out, when the times of refreshing shall come from the presence of the Lord. (Acts 3:19)

I have good news for you: repentance is flowing through the body of Christ. Moreover, it is the goodness of God that leads to repentance. True biblical repentance leads to refreshing.

We stand on the precipice of the greatest outpouring of the Holy Ghost in the world. When it comes, it will blow the props out from under you. What you've been depending on you're not going to be able to depend on anymore because God's going to do a brand new thing. And by doing so, He's going to return each of us to the discarded biblical values of the past.

Examine yourself and repent of the sins of commission (doing what I know is wrong) and omission (failing to do what is right). Decide that coming clean with God is the only way to live as you approach the new millennium.

_____

_____

_____

_____

_____

_____

_____

_____

_____

_____

_____

"Repent and be refreshed."

MILLENNIUM JOURNAL

DAY 224 SATURDAY   **MAY 22**

Begin Again

Is there any thing whereof it may be said, See, this is new? it hath been already of old time, which was before us. (Ecclesiastes 1:10)

The book of Ecclesiastes said that which was shall be again. I'm looking forward to that day because I can go back past the epistles, and I can go back to the way it was in the book of Acts and begin again.

After denying Christ three times, Peter was able to begin again through Jesus' forgiveness. The disciples and believers waiting in the upper room "began again" in following Jesus in the baptism of the Holy Ghost and with power. Saul got to begin again as Paul. The people of God were able to begin again in history as the church of the living Christ. Perhaps it's time for you to begin again with Jesus as well.

This year before the millennium is a year of beginnings. Write down all the new beginnings you are making and are willing to make.

_____

_____

_____

_____

_____

_____

_____

_____

_____

_____

_____

_____

_____

*"Are you willing to begin again and
become radical like the early Christians?"*

Christ Is Returning!

Then we which are alive and remain shall be caught up together with them in the clouds, to meet the Lord in the air: and so shall we ever be with the Lord. (1 Thessalonians 4:17)

If we truly believe that we're living in the last days, then we must believe this: Upon the return of Jesus of Nazareth, on the wild wings of glory, we will leap off this planet like a magnet leaping in the air. We will be drawn into the presence of the Lord.

In a twinkling of an eye, Jesus will slide His long, lean Galilean leg over that steamy white stallion and the crack of His long whip will billow out like the crash of a thousand cannons. And just before the magnificent magnitude of His perfect person sweeps out from north to south and east to west, the trumpet of the archangel will sound and we will join Him in the sky.

Are you ready for the return of Jesus? Write down what you need to do spiritually to get ready for His return.

_____

_____

_____

_____

_____

_____

_____

_____

_____

_____

_____

_____

"Start preparing for Jesus' return today."

Stop Sitting Around

Therefore let us not sleep, as do others; but let us watch and be sober. For they that sleep sleep in the night; and they that be drunken are drunken in the night. But let us, who are of the day, be sober, putting on the breastplate of faith and love; and for an helmet, the hope of salvation.
(1 Thessalonians 5:6-8)

I don't know how you sit around in silence when the graves are going to burst open, the sky is going to be rent in two, and the Lord shall descend from heaven with a shout in the voice of the archangel and the trump of God. The dead in Christ shall rise first and then we which are alive will be caught up in the air with Him. I intend on being alive in Christ and to be caught up in the air with Him.

Stop sitting around, and start telling somebody about Jesus: tell your neighbor, tell your colleagues at work, tell friends and strangers because Jesus is coming back.

In this countdown toward the new millennium, are you alive in Christ, actively serving Him, or are you just sitting around—comfortable in your salvation? Describe how you will tell someone about Jesus today:

_____

_____

_____

_____

_____

_____

_____

_____

_____

_____

"Don't just sit there. Get up and serve the King of kings."

Restoration Is Happening!

And I will restore to you the years that the locust hath eaten, the cankerworm, and the caterpiller, and the palmerworm, my great army which I sent among you. (Joel 2:25)

A lady once said to me, "Pastor, when we get to heaven we'll have victory over the devil."

I said, "That's a lie."

You won't need victory over the devil in heaven; he's not there. Down here is where you need victory over the devil.

Here and now the devil must give back what he has stolen. What is he going to give back? Your finances must be returned. Your health will be restored. Your seed will bring forth a bountiful harvest. All that has been bound will be set free.

The Spirit is restoring all that the enemy has stolen. But you must be ready to receive what is returned. Open your hands this year and receive all that the Spirit has for you.

"Prepare this year to receive back all that the enemy has stolen."

This Year, Break Through

So they came up to Baal-perazim; and David smote them there. Then David said, God hath broken in upon mine enemies by mine hand like the breaking forth of waters: therefore they called the name of that place Baal-perazim.
(1 Chronicles 14:11)

Baal-perazim literally means, "Lord of the breakthrough." Because David sought God's direction first (v. 10), he knew it was God's victory. David acknowledged God as the One who brought about his victory. He said, "I couldn't have done it if God had not gone before me."

There will be many battles to fight this year, but realize that you are not standing alone. The God you serve is the repairer of the breach, and the battle is not yours, but it is His. When you seek God first in the matter, you can be assured of the victory.

The battle belongs to the Lord (1 Samuel 17:47). So, never defend yourself. Let Him be your strong tower, your defense, and your refuge. Are you trying to fight battles He has already won? Put on His armor and go forth in His Spirit, not your own might and power (Zechariah 4:6).

This is the year for you to break through the barriers that would hold you back from serving Christ in the new millennium.

_____

_____

_____

_____

_____

_____

_____

_____

_____

_____

"Are you ready for your breakthrough? If so, then surrender!"

It Is Settled

For ever, O LORD, thy word is settled in heaven.
(Psalm 119:89)

When Joshua led the children of Israel into the Promised Land, news of their conquests spread quickly. The terrified Gibeonites devised a plan to avoid being conquered. Several men approached the camp dressed in dirty, worn-out clothes, carrying old wine and moldy bread. They told Joshua they were ambassadors from a distant land and asked Israel to enter into a covenant with them, and he did (Joshua 9).

Later, when Joshua learned the truth, the Israelites murmured that the Gibeonites should not be spared (v. 19), but the covenant was absolutely binding. It had to be honored, even though they had been tricked!

How much more will God, whose Word is settled in heaven, honor His covenant with you! Your Word, O Lord, has settled my past, present and future. I trust Your Word for forgiveness of confessed sin. Your Word has prepared me to face my present and my future with victory

"Let God's Word settle the issues in your life once and for all."

God Has It All

For thou art an holy people unto the LORD thy God: the LORD thy God hath chosen thee to be a special people unto himself, above all people that are upon the face of the earth. (Deuteronomy 7:6)

We have nothing God needs. Our best works are as filthy rags before His holiness (Isaiah 64:6). God receives nothing from the covenant except the one thing He desires—a relationship with His children.

God chose you to be a partaker of His covenant. In Isaiah 41:9 He says, "I have chosen thee, and not cast thee away."

Give Him all you have—your desires, dreams, sorrows and needs—and allow Him to replace them with His abundant life. When you give Him all of you, you lose nothing of value.

_____

_____

_____

_____

_____

_____

_____

_____

_____

_____

_____

_____

_____

_____

_____

"Give all that you have to God."

The Covenant Sign

For we are the circumcision, which worship God in the spirit, and rejoice in Christ Jesus, and have no confidence in the flesh. (Philippians 3:3)

In biblical times and even today in many places, covenant partners symbolize their pledge by cutting into their flesh and making a blood covenant. The covenant partners then no longer lived for themselves but for their covenant partner.

When God entered into covenant with Abraham, he instituted a different kind of symbol. Throughout the history of Israel, male circumcision was the indelible sign of a covenant relationship with God. But the covenant sign changed in the New Testament from the physical to the spiritual.

The sign of the new covenant that Jesus instituted is the acceptance of His blood as the propitiation for our sin and then the indwelling of the Holy Spirit. We are recognized by the sign and seal of His Spirit within us (Acts 2:38, Ephesians 1:13).

Determine to display all the fruit of the Spirit: love, joy, peace, longsuffering, gentleness, goodness, faith, meekness, and temperance (Galatians 5:22–23). They reflect the very nature of Christ in you—the hope of glory (Colossians 1:27).

Boldly share the Gospel with those whom the Holy Spirit gives you the opportunity to share. As a Spirit-filled believer, allow your life to point to the Greater One. He must increase while you decrease (John 3:30).

_____

_____

_____

_____

_____

_____

_____

_____

"Does the covenant sign of Christ mark your life for all to see?"

His Spirit Will Guide You

But when the Comforter is come, whom I will send unto you from the Father, even the Spirit of truth, which proceedeth from the Father, he shall testify of me. (John 15:26)

"Jesus Christ the same yesterday, and to day, and for ever (Hebrews 13:8). Jesus does not change. He was not a different Jesus for John than He is for you today. When you see Him with spirit eyes, you will see the same Jesus John knew.

The Holy Spirit makes this possible, for He was sent to show us Jesus. Howbeit when He, the Spirit of truth, is come, he will guide you into all truth . . . He shall glorify me: "for he shall receive of mine, and shall shew it unto you (John 16:13, 14)."

The Holy Spirit was called alongside us to help. He is our comforter, our helper and our teacher, given to us to carry out God's part of the covenant! Welcome the Holy Spirit into your life and allow Him to lead you into all wisdom (1 Corinthians 2:7).

In this countdown to the new millennium, you need the Holy Spirit more than ever to teach, guide, comfort and direct you. Ask Him to be your guide today in every decision.

"You need the guidance of the Holy Spirit today."

God Remembers His Covenant

And God heard their groaning, and God remembered his covenant with Abraham, with Isaac, and with Jacob. (Exodus 2:24)

God knew the descendants of Abraham would suffer the bonds of the Egyptians for more than 400 years, and He even told Abraham about it when they established their blood covenant (Genesis 15:13-16).

God had a plan for Abraham's descendants before Abraham had any children. He looked forward through time and chose the land He would bring them to. He foresaw the results of idolatry, and in His perfect time brought forth a covenant people to establish a holy nation.

When the cry of Abraham's descendants reached God's ears, He was ready and He "remembered His covenant." Because of the everlasting promises He had made to Abraham, deliverance was on the way!

The promises of the covenant will never be broken. When you are in need, cry out to God. Your deliverance is on the way! God will remember His covenant with you in the new millennium.

"God will never forget His new covenant."

Diligently Seek Him

But without faith it is impossible to please him: for he that cometh to God must believe that he is, and that he is a rewarder of them that diligently seek him. (Hebrews 11:6)

This verse doesn't say that He is a rewarder of casual acquaintances or those who know something about Him. It says, "God rewards those that diligently seek Him."

If you are in a trial where the devil has stopped you in your tracks, don't become bitter or talk about it; that will only compound the problem. Find yourself a closet, climb into the mountain of God; and like Jacob, declare, "Lord, I will not let thee go unless thou bless me" (Genesis 32:26).

There is help to be found in the mountain of prayer. God said, "Call unto me, and I will answer thee and shew thee great and mighty things which thou knowest not" (Jeremiah 33:3).

The promises of God are *yea* and *amen* (2 Corinthians 1:20). God's promises will not fall to the ground powerless if you will fall to your knees in prayer, proclaiming God's Word with authority and speaking forth His promises.

_____

_____

_____

_____

_____

_____

_____

_____

_____

_____

_____

"When you seek Him, you will find Him."

God Is With You

But he [Shammah] stood in the midst of the ground, and defended it, and slew the Philistines: and the LORD wrought a great victory. (2 Samuel 23:12)

Every year, Shammah tilled his field and planned his harvest. Every year the Philistines took it from him. Shammah was again preparing to harvest his crop when he saw the Philistines coming.

This time something rose within him. He strode to the edge of his property and shouted, "Stop!" The chariots screeched to a halt as the jeering Philistines asked who this defiant man was.

When he declared, "I am Shammah!" they turned and headed back over the hills. They knew all about the God of the Israelites, who is not only Jehovah Nissi, our banner of victory, and Jehovah Jireh, the God who supplies all our needs . . . but He is also Jehovah Shammah, the God who is present in the midst of thee.

You are not alone. He is with you every step of the way.

_____

_____

_____

_____

_____

_____

_____

_____

_____

_____

_____

_____

_____

"God is with you. Pray that in the new millennium you will draw closer daily to Him."

Don't Believe a Lie

He chose David also his servant, and took him from the sheepfolds. (Psalm 78:70)

The devil likes to condemn us and keep us down by whispering in our ears, "Look at you trying to act as if you're somebody when you know you're nobody. You've come from nowhere, and you're going nowhere."

When he does, remember David was faced with a similar situation. His father didn't even call him from tending the sheep when Samuel came to choose a king (1 Samuel 16:11). His brothers were older, wiser, taller, more handsome and more experienced.

What David accomplished in his life for God had nothing to do with where he started and everything to do with the fact that God picked him out. Be not be dismayed. Regardless of your circumstances, God will take you out of wherever you are and bring you to wherever He wants you to be.

_____

_____

_____

_____

_____

_____

_____

_____

_____

_____

_____

_____

_____

"God declares that you are important to His plans today. "

Don't Go Back

And he said unto me, My grace is sufficient for thee: for my strength is made perfect in weakness. (2 Corinthians 12:9)

When the Israelites wanted to go back to Egypt, Moses said, "There isn't anything there for you any more. God's purpose and plan for you is straight ahead."

The future is unlimited in God. You don't have to feel bound by the things that once bound you. You have someone inside you who is greater than anything you will ever face.

One of the best things that can happen to you is to face an obstacle that is impossible to overcome by yourself. Then, when you are victorious, everyone must say, "It was God."

God is never in retreat. He is continually advancing His kingdom, moving forward in His divine plan and purpose. God wants to bring you all the way through, sustaining you in the midst of every trial. Rejoice, because blessing, strength and enabling power are straight ahead.

Don't dread the approaching millennium. Embrace the coming days as a set time for God to move mightily in your life.

"This year is God's set time to prepare you for the end time."

God Can Work In Your Weaknesses

Most gladly therefore will I rather glory in my infirmities, that the power of Christ may rest upon me. Therefore I take pleasure in infirmities, in reproaches, in necessities, in persecutions, in distresses for Christ's sake: for when I am weak, then am I strong.
(2 Corinthians 12:9,10)

A pastor who was accomplishing great things for God was asked the key to his success. Everyone thought he would respond with, "You need charisma," or "the ability to relate to people." They were astounded when, instead, he replied, "I have found the most important characteristic for anyone who wants to accomplish great things in the kingdom of God is weakness." Anything worthwhile ever done in God's kingdom hasn't been accomplished as a result of men's efforts. It is a result of God using individuals who cannot do things by themselves.

As you start your day, put God in charge. Ask Him to do what you cannot do through your own ability.

_____

_____

_____

_____

_____

_____

_____

_____

_____

_____

_____

"Ask God to manifest His strength in your weaknesses."

Recognize Your Weakness

. . . And he wist not that the Lord was departed from him. (Judges 16:20)

When God gives you a particular strength, gift or talent, guard against it becoming a weakness to you. You can reach the point where you say, "I can do this by myself. I don't need God."

Nebuchadnezzar made that statement and lost his kingdom. Sometimes we lose our direction or think we can do what God has called us to do without His anointing and His presence.

When Samson heard Delilah say, "Get up Samson, the Philistines are upon you," he thought, "I'll just get up and shake myself as other times." I believe what follows is one of the saddest verses in the Bible. It tells us the Spirit of God had departed from him . . . and he didn't even know it.

Only when we recognize our weakness can we recognize God's strength. Acknowledge the One who has made His overcoming power and wisdom available to you.

_____

_____

_____

_____

_____

_____

_____

_____

_____

_____

_____

_____

"Admit your weakness today before it becomes your snare."

God's Plan

. . . that ye may stand perfect and complete in all the will of God. (Colossians 4:12)

God is a faithful Father; He has a plan for you. Within that plan is the promise of provision. "Where there is no vision, the people cast off all restraint" (Proverb 29:18 ASV). The vision—the plan of the Father—sets the parameters for our provision, protection and peace. God will take care of you, as long as you stay in the vision.

When you step into your plan, you step out of His and the protection and provision it supplies. In Colossians 2:10 Paul said, "We are complete in Him." In Colossians 4:12, Paul prayed that we might stand perfect and complete in all the will of God.

If we become complete in the will of God, we march in His plan and provision—because He has, in eternity past, laid out our tomorrow, secured its borders and planted a victory flag in the middle of it. Defeat is not part of God's plan for you.

_____

_____

_____

_____

_____

_____

_____

_____

_____

_____

_____

"Step into His plan and out of yours."

The Struggle

. . . nevertheless not as I will, but as thou wilt.
(Matthew 26:39)

God will orchestrate circumstances to cause us to surrender our will to His. Surrender never comes without a struggle, and your soul—your mind, will and emotions—struggle with your spirit for control.

We struggle because we don't know tomorrow. We can only see today, but God knows and understands tomorrow the same way as we know and understand yesterday.

We struggle to resist our heavenly Father's plan, because in order to operate in that plan, we must live a Gethsemane lifestyle. Just as Jesus struggled in the Garden of Gethsemane, we too must come to the point where we are willing to say, "Not my will, but thine be done." We must come to the point of surrendering our will and acknowledging and accepting His will at work in our lives.

Have you bowed your knee in surrender, or are you still struggling for control of your tomorrow?

_____

_____

_____

_____

_____

_____

_____

_____

_____

_____

_____

"Surrender your will to His."

Radical Surrender

I beseech you therefore, brethren, by the mercies of God, that ye present your bodies a living sacrifice, holy, acceptable unto God, which is your reasonable service. (Romans 12:1)

When you are born again, you are not the person you used to be. You do not think the way you used to think or go where you used to go. No longer are you in the kingdom of this world; you have been promoted to a higher place. People like to talk about a new world order, but the best of all worlds is the one God has established in His Word! When you move into His divine realm, you are no longer bound by the world's restrictions.

It is not a one-way street, however. Proverb 3:5 says we are to trust in the Lord with ALL our hearts. Paul said, "I am crucified with Christ: nevertheless I live; yet not I, but Christ liveth in me" (Galatians 2:20).

Is your life partially given, or, like Paul's, fully surrendered to God? Do you say "yes" or "no" to your King? No limit living requires no limit giving! In radical faith, give your all—surrender all—to Jesus.

_____

_____

_____

_____

_____

_____

_____

_____

_____

_____

_____

"Radical faith requires radical surrender."

Upon His Wings

As an eagle stirreth up her nest, fluttereth over her young, spreadeth abroad her wings, taketh them, beareth them on her wings. (Deuteronomy 32:11,12)

God compares His relationship with Israel to that of the eagle who observes the feathers of its young to determine when they are ready to fly—and then deliberately disturbs them out of the nest.

Often we do not know when we are ready to step out in faith, but God does; and when we are, He will thrust us out. As in the manner of a young eagle soaring for the first time, we can also soar . . . because we know it is His timing and He is right there with us as we go forth.

As the eagle leads her young from the nest, she flies under them, guiding their journey. And if they become weary, she carries them home upon her wings. When we cannot go on any longer, He carries us to our destination. You can always count on His strength that will never let you fall.

_____

_____

_____

_____

_____

_____

_____

_____

_____

_____

_____

_____

_____

"Ride upon His wings today."

The Father's House

Destroy this temple, and in three days I will raise it up . . . he spake of the temple of his body.
(John 2:19,21)

Although death gripped mankind for thousands of years, the author of life trampled death and hell. When Jesus hung on the cross, suspended between heaven and earth, the sun was absent and the earth silent.

But on the third day, the angels watched as the resurrected Son arose with the keys of hell and death in His hands (Revelation 1:18).

Though hell comes and tempests rage, you have the assurance that regardless of whatever happens to you in this life, your eternal home awaits you. When your earthly body is finished, you are going to wing your way to the pavilions of God's glory and station yourself in a place called heaven, where the streets are not just paved with gold but are made of it.

Because you know your Redeemer lives (Job 19:25), you have the assurance that you are bound for the Father's house.

"In Christ, your place in eternity is secure."

Look Up!

Then took they Jeremiah and cast him into the dungeon of Malchiah the son of Hammelech, that was in the court of the prison: and they let down Jeremiah with cords. And in the dungeon there was no water, but mire: so Jeremiah sunk in the mire. (Jeremiah 38:6)

Jeremiah was persecuted and imprisoned on several occasions, and finally left to die in a dank, wet cistern. After years of faithfully preaching the Word of God, he was tossed into a pit of mud from which there was no escape. But God used an unlikely method to rescue him—an Ethiopian eunuch and some rotten rags (v.11).

When you feel like the enemy has overpowered you and the world is against you, always remember that God has not forgotten you. He has given us His Word that He will never leave us or forsake us (Deuteronomy 31:6).

You may be up to your neck in problems, and so deep in debt you cannot see the light of day, but get ready . . . your redemption draweth nigh.

"When buried beneath your problems, look up to the Lord."

Great Faith

He [Abraham] staggered not at the promise of God through unbelief; but was strong in faith, giving glory to God. (Romans 4:20)

Halfway across the Galilee, the disciples became frightened and woke Jesus, saying, "Don't you care that we perish?" Jesus stilled the storm and rebuked the disciples for not moving on in their faith (Matthew 8:25,26). How do we grow from the "little faith" of whiny Christians to the "great faith" of Christians who are strong in their faith?

Every day that your mind is renewed in the Word of God, your soul is brought up to a higher level of faith-filled living. God expects us to mature and become strong in our faith. The stronger we become, the more glory we give Him. Strengthen yourself in the Word; exercise your faith and go from whining in the boat to unwavering faith.

_____

_____

_____

_____

_____

_____

_____

_____

_____

_____

_____

"Stop complaining. Strengthen yourself today by confessing the Word of God."

Draw a Line

The thief cometh not, but for to steal, and to kill, and to destroy: I am come that they might have life, and that they might have it more abundantly.
(John 10:10)

With these words Jesus drew a line in the sand between the works of God and the works of the devil. God's work is life-giving, healing and uplifting. "Every good gift and every perfect gift is from above, and cometh down from the Father of lights" (James 1:17). Everything that steals, kills and destroys is the work of the devil. Sickness, disease and injury do not come from God.

Don't play around with salvation. You are either a child of the devil or a child of God; and the devil hates his own kids. He will use you, abuse you and destroy you, as long as you play around in his kingdom.

Draw close to God through prayer (Psalm 91:15), giving (Luke 6:38), fasting (Luke 2:37) and living right (Romans 6:13). Praise Him for your salvation that allows you to walk in victory.

"Draw a line and forbid the enemy to cross it, in Jesus' name."

You Are Accepted

I in them, and thou in me, that they may be made perfect in one; and that the world may know that thou hast sent me, and hast loved them, as thou hast loved me. (John 17:23)

Jesus prayed that we would know just how much our heavenly Father loves us. He loves us just as He loves Jesus! He loves us unconditionally. While we were still sinners, He sent His only Son to die in our place (Romans 5:8).

Order your thinking, your feelings and your ideas according to God's Word, for you are a child of God and precious in His eyes. If you see yourself as the expression of the love of God, there are things you will not do and places you will not go.

We do not serve God to gain His acceptance. We are accepted, so we serve God. We do not follow Him in order to be loved. We are loved, so we follow Him.

_____

_____

_____

_____

_____

_____

_____

_____

_____

_____

_____

_____

_____

"God's love accepts you where you are and refuses to let you stay there."

Follow Jesus to the Father

For my thoughts are not your thoughts, neither are your ways my ways, saith the Lord.
(Isaiah 55:8)

God's thoughts are not our thoughts; and His ways are not our ways. But He has revealed Himself to us through His Son, Jesus Christ, who said, He that hath seen me hath seen the Father . . . (John 14:9).

God has not only revealed Himself to us through His Word, but through the life and ministry of Jesus, who was the Word of God incarnate (John 1:1). As we read His words and observe His life—the mind, the heart and the ways of God are revealed to us.

Follow Jesus and let Him lead you to the Father. As you study and meditate on the life and ministry of Jesus in the Gospels, you will have a more intimate relationship with Him.

_____

_____

_____

_____

_____

_____

_____

_____

_____

_____

_____

_____

"Let go of your way so that He might have His way in you."

Shaped by the Potter

We have this treasure in earthen vessels, that the excellency of the power may be of God, and not of us. (2 Corinthians 4:7)

Once we grasp the purposeful will of God for our lives, we no longer desire to kick against the pricks. Instead, we will find ourselves free from fear, in humble submission to His will. But if we are not acquainted with His character, we have trouble releasing ourselves into His purpose.

The Potter takes the clay made from the dust of the ground, puts it on His wheel, and begins to shape and fashion it. Perhaps you have so many trials and tribulations in your life that you can't focus and you are losing your grip; you feel as if you can't hold on much longer. But the Potter never takes His loving eyes away from you. God is working His plan in your life.

You are not going to fall off the wheel; you are not going to perish in the depths of your trial. His eyes and His hands are upon you. You are that weak and perishable container being formed to radiate the glorious power and light of God.

_____

_____

_____

_____

_____

_____

_____

_____

_____

_____

_____

"On the Potter's wheel, you are shaped by His image."

Your Miracle Is Now

Behold, I and the children whom the LORD hath given me are for signs and for wonders in Israel from the LORD of hosts, which dwelleth in mount Zion. (Isaiah 8:18)

God wants to be identified as your God. And He wants to do it with the thundering "amen" of signs and wonders.

Once we were lost, without hope and far away from God; but now that we belong to Christ Jesus we have been brought very near to Him because of His blood (Ephesians 2:12,13). The Cross was the price of access into the presence, power, anointing and glory of God!

When you meet God and He meets you, the anointing that destroys every yoke is manifested, and your miracle is on its way as sure as the sun will come up tomorrow.

Welcome Him now and give Him free reign in every aspect of your life. . . and get ready for your miracle.

_____

_____

_____

_____

_____

_____

_____

_____

_____

_____

_____

"Are you ready for your miracle?"

He is the "I Am"

Jesus therefore, knowing all things that should come upon him, went forth, and said unto them, Whom seek ye? (John 18:4)

Jesus knew all that was to come. He asked the question not because He was wondering what was happening, but to reveal whom they sought. The soldiers came to arrest who they thought was a fleeing peasant but found themselves confronted by the Commander-in-chief of a heavenly army.

The Greek phrase, "I am He," comes from two Greek words. In Exodus 3:14 this phrase is expressed as "I AM who I AM" and is taken from the Word Yahweh, which means "Ever Present." Jesus declared His deity in John 8:58 when He said, "Before Abraham was, I AM" and again to the soldiers in the Garden of Gethsemane. The very power of the words, "I am He" hurled them backwards (v.6). The soldiers did not take Jesus captive any more than Jesus lost His life. He gave it willingly for all mankind.

Seek the ever-present God of the universe for who He is . . . not for what He can do for you. The "I am" is leading you into the new millennium.

_____

_____

_____

_____

_____

_____

_____

_____

_____

_____

_____

_____

"Ask the 'I Am' to lead you in every step of life."

Blessed Hope

And if Christ be not risen, then is our preaching vain, and your faith is also vain . . . But now is Christ risen from the dead, and become the firstfruits of them that slept.
(1 Corinthians 15:14,20)

All of Christianity rests on the fact that Christ is risen from the dead. Romans 1:4 says He was declared to be the Son of God with power, according to the spirit of holiness, by the resurrection from the dead.

Our hope lies in an empty tomb. What made Jesus God was not just His ability to lay down His Life, for many can lay down their lives, but Jesus is the only One who could pick it up again.

If Christ has not arisen, then there will be no sounding of the trumpet, and neither will we arise. But because we have been made one with Christ, one day we too will experience the resurrection power of the Holy Spirit.

He is risen. And they who are asleep in Christ along with those who remain will most surely arise to meet Him in the air.

This is our blessed hope. In spite of what the news media says, you are entering the new millennium in hope, not despair.

_____

_____

_____

_____

_____

_____

_____

_____

_____

_____

"Walk today in blessed hope. Rebuke all despair, heaviness and sorrow."

Give What You Have

And Elisha said unto her, "What shall I do for thee? tell me, what hast thou in the house? And she said, Thine handmaid hath not any thing in the house, save a pot of oil. (2 Kings 4:2)

A widow, deeply in debt, came to Elisha for help. Her creditors were ready to take her sons into slavery as payment. Elisha told her to gather as many vessels as she could and to fill them with the small amount of oil she owned.

She obeyed the prophet, and miraculously the oil flowed until she ran out of jars to pour it into. There was more than enough oil to sell and pay the debt, with plenty of money left over for herself and her children to live on.

God never asks you to give Him what you do not have. You may be like the widow with a pot of oil, facing a debt you cannot pay. You may be like Samson, holding nothing in your hand but a jawbone, watching a thousand Philistines advance. They offered God the little they had, and God turned what they had into a miracle.

Give God whatever you have today and He will create a miracle. List the things that you will give Him today:

_____

_____

_____

_____

_____

_____

_____

_____

_____

_____

_____

"Your miracle begins with giving what you have."

Cling to the Rock

From the end of the earth will I cry unto thee, when my heart is overwhelmed: lead me to the rock that is higher than I. (Psalm 61:2)

Sometimes faith is not much more than clinging to Christ with all your might. Charles Haddon Spurgeon tells of the limpet, a type of mollusk, that fastens itself to the rocks of the English seashore.

Those wanting to harvest these creatures can walk softly up to the rocks on which they are clinging, strike them a quick blow with a stick and off they will come. However, you have warned the limpet clinging next to it. He heard the blow you gave his neighbor, and now clings with all his might. It is impossible to pry him loose!

The limpet doesn't know much; he isn't acquainted with the geological formation of the rock. He only knows that he has found something to cling to for his security and salvation.

It is the limpet's life to cling to the rock, and it is ours to cling to Jesus with all our might. He is an immovable rock, strong and mighty.

How will you cling to the Rock today? Describe the many ways the Rock will sustain you in your march into the new millennium.

_____

_____

_____

_____

_____

_____

_____

_____

_____

_____

_____

"Are you clinging to the Rock today?"

Fire In Your Bones

Then I said, I will not make mention of him, nor speak any more in his name. But his word was in mine heart as a burning fire shut up in my bones, and I was weary with forbearing, and I could not stay. (Jeremiah 20:9)

Jeremiah spoke these words when opposition was at its height. Jeremiah lamented to the Lord for calling him into the ministry. The pressure seemed too great. But just when he thought life was over and he saw no hope, something sprung up within him.

Holy Spirit fire ignited when Jeremiah felt unable to continue. When he had come to the end of himself, Jeremiah was ready to quit but he could not as the fire of God burned within his spirit.

Fill yourself with the Word and when you think you are ready to quit, don't throw in the towel. Rest in God and watch as the Word begins to kindle in your heart, empowering you, refueling you, just as you are running out of steam. When the devil is bearing down on you the fire from heaven will burn brightly within your spirit. Write a prayer asking God to send the fire.

_____

_____

_____

_____

_____

_____

_____

_____

"Lord, fill me with your fire."

God Is All Sufficient

Nay, in all these things we are more than conquerors through him that loved us. (Romans 8:37)

Like Job, who lost everything, you may feel as though you are far from God's blessing. As he sat in the ashes of ruin, his wife urged him to curse God and die. But Job proclaimed, I know that my redeemer liveth! (Job 19:25).

Job kept his eyes on God and was completely restored. The same God who brought Job back from the jaws of death and destruction can touch your life. Everything you need is already available because our God is El Shaddai, "the One who is all sufficient."

God did not send the children of Israel into Canaan to be defeated, but to conquer. He wants your Promised Land to be conquered, and He wants to use you to conquer it. El Shaddai, who is all sufficient, has given you all you need to possess your land. It is time for you to tell the dethroned and defeated devil to, "Stand back! You have no authority. I am taking what is rightfully mine."

"Because He is all sufficient, you don't have to be."

God's Guidance

Howbeit when he, the Spirit of truth is come, he will guide you into all truth: for he shall not speak of himself; but whatsoever he shall hear, that shall he speak: and he will shew you things to come. (John 16:13)

Pilots of small aircraft are required to be "instrument rated." This means they can fly without depending on their vision. In a storm, pilots can lose all sense of direction. Their only hope is to lock onto their instruments and depend on the aircraft's guidance system to show them the way.

The Word of God is our spiritual guidance system. We must not depend on what we can see with our eyes or feel with our emotions. The devil attacks us in the realm of our senses, but the Holy Spirit guides us in our spirits (John 16:13).

The writer of Hebrews calls "faith" the substance of things hoped for, the evidence of things not seen (Hebrews 11:1). No matter what is happening around you, put your faith in the true, undeniable Word of the living God, and He will see you through.

Today may seem like a dark storm to you. Turn on the guidance system of God's Word to see you through. Write down some Scriptures that God is giving to see you through:

_____

_____

_____

_____

_____

_____

_____

_____

_____

"God's Word is your sure and absolute guide."

Renew Your Mind

The land, whither ye go to possess it, is a land of hills and valleys. (Deuteronomy 11:11)

God promised the children of Israel He would bring them into a new land, but the land was not all lush valleys. The settlers also had hills to contend with. They had to plow across inclines and deal with soil erosion when the rains came. Life in the Promised Land has many ups and downs.

Circumstances are part of God's process that brings us into His Promised Land. We are all going to experience both good times and bad.

Expect opposition, for it will surely come. Any farmer knows that after he plants his crop, the birds will be after his seed, the rabbits will be after the tender young leaves and both will be after the fruit of the vine.

Keep your mind renewed in what God has to say about your seed, and nothing will be able to threaten your harvest—not people, not opinions, not fear, not greed nor doubt. God says when we sow in faith, He will stand on the edge of our land and rebuke the devourer for our sakes. Sow abundantly, and trust God for your harvest.

_____

_____

_____

_____

_____

_____

_____

_____

_____

_____

*"Let the Spirit of God renew your mind so that
His thoughts are your thoughts."*

Raise Your Expectations

Having the same spirit of faith . . . I believed, and therefore have I spoken; we also believe, and therefore speak.
(2 Corinthians 4:13)

I have met people who believe the Bible teaches that whatever we ask we can have . . . with no strings attached. They obviously have not read 1 John 5:14: "And this is the confidence that we have in him, that, if we ask anything according to his will, he heareth us."

We can't ask outside the will of God and expect an answer. But when our request lines up with His will, we have the guarantee that He will not only hear us, but also that our answer is on the way.

Your hope and expectation will never rise above your level of confession. You will reap tomorrow the harvest of the words you sow today. Release your confession from a heart full of faith and belief in the God of the Word, and rest in confidence that He will hear and respond. What are you expecting today based on your confession? Write your confession down and then speak it all day.

_____

_____

_____

_____

_____

_____

_____

_____

_____

_____

_____

_____

"Let the level of your confession go from finite to infinite."

Faith Marches On!

And when he thus had spoken, he cried with a loud voice, Lazarus, come forth. (John 11:43)

Fear hinders, but faith marches into enemy territory. The only power the spirit of fear has is what we give to it. In the natural realm, the spirit of fear seems overwhelming. When we operate in the realm of the natural, fear leaves us vulnerable to the devil's tactics. We must supernaturally discern the tactics of the enemy.

When Jesus approached the grave of Lazarus, He saw the stone was firmly in place. His sense of smell told him the man was dead. He heard with His own ears the weeping mourners. He could taste the bitterness of His own tears. But Jesus did not let His senses lead Him away from the tomb. He was not looking at the situation with the eyes of man, but with the eyes of faith. He cried out, "Lazarus, come forth!" Death fled when Jesus looked past the natural and operated in the spiritual.

Never trust your feelings, "For we walk by faith, not by sight" (2 Corinthians 5:7). Put your trust in God alone.

_____

_____

_____

_____

_____

_____

_____

_____

_____

_____

_____

"Faith marches into the enemy's camp and sets the captives free."

Submit to God

I thank my God always on your behalf, for the grace of God which is given you by Jesus Christ; That in every thing ye are enriched by him, in all utterance, and in all knowledge.
(1 Corinthians 1:4,5)

When you submit your life to God and live by His rules, great things begin to happen.

Your income is changed: The wealth of the sinner is laid up for the just (Proverb 13:22). Your investments are changed: "Lend, hoping for nothing again; and your reward shall be great" (Luke 6:35). Your giving is changed: "Give, and it shall be given unto you; good measure, pressed down, and shaken together, and running over" (Luke 6:38). Your life is changed: "Therefore if any man be in Christ, he is a new creature: old things are passed away; behold, all things are become new" (2 Corinthians 5:17).

The kingdom of God is filled with abundance for those who allow Him to transform their lives.

Are you ready to be transformed?

_____

_____

_____

_____

_____

_____

_____

_____

_____

_____

_____

"Great things will happen when you turn everything over to God."

We Are Vessels

I have been young, and now am old; yet have I not seen the righteous forsaken, nor his seed begging bread. (Psalm 37:25)

The Lord takes pleasure in the success of His servants. Yet God's abundance is not granted so you can simply lavish it upon yourself. It is given to establish the kingdom of God throughout the earth (Deuteronomy 8:18).

We are created to be vessels through which He can pour out His abundance and blessing. God looses abundance in our lives so we, in turn, can deliver it unto the earth to help bring about His kingdom.

God uses vessels who are not contaminated by the ways of the world. The abundance of God overflows from vessels of gold, who have been purified by the Refiner's fire.

Set your heart and your mind on becoming a vessel unto honor, sanctified, and ready for the Master's use, and prepared unto every good work (2 Timothy 2:21).

_____

_____

_____

_____

_____

_____

_____

_____

_____

_____

_____

_____

"Ask God to use you as His vessel."

The Oil of Joy

To grant [consolation and joy] to those who mourn in Zion–to give them an ornament (a garland or diadem) of beauty instead of ashes, the oil of joy instead of mourning, the garment [expressive] of praise instead of a heavy, burdened, and failing spirit–that they may be called oaks of righteousness [lofty, strong, and magnificent, distinguished for uprightness, justice, and right standing with God], the planting of the Lord, that He may be glorified. (Isaiah 61:3 AMP)

The Lord wants to mark you with an anointing which will propel you through every line of Satan's defense. It is from Luke 4 that Jesus proclaims God's acceptance, but it is from the Book of Isaiah that He is actually reading.

One verse in particular, which He did not quote is Isaiah 61:3. The Lord wants to give you the oil of joy for mourning. He wants to anoint you with an anointing which will transcend every circumstance you may face. The Shunammite woman was anointed with the oil of joy, because the only words she could say when facing death itself were, "It is well!"

The Psalmist said of this oil, "Thou lovest righteousness, and hatest wickedness: therefore God, thy God, hath anointed thee with the oil of gladness above thy fellows" (Psalm 45:7).

What is the oil of joy? The actual translation is a shining forth of cheerful anticipation for mourning. In Isaiah 61, the Lord said He would give unto you the garment of praise for the spirit of heaviness. What is the garment of praise? It is a cover of celebration for the spirit of hopelessness. Hopelessness implies acceptance or resignation to the current situation with no future anticipation of change. Joy clothes the present with anticipation that God will change all heaviness into praise. Be clothed with His joy!

_____

_____

_____

_____

"Take off heaviness and put on the garment of praise and the oil of joy."

Speak Faith

And my tongue shall speak of thy righteousness and of thy praise all the day long. (Psalm 35:28)

Three important factors are at work in the process of possession.

Have faith. Jesus tells us to have faith in God (Mark 11:22). Speak faith into your spirit. Remind yourself of the promises of God. Remember, God "calleth those things which be not as though they were" (Romans 4:17).

Believe. "Whosoever shall say unto this mountain, Be thou removed, and be thou cast into the sea; and shall not doubt in his heart, but shall believe that those things which he saith shall come to pass; he shall have whatsoever he saith" (v.23).

Pray. "What things soever ye desire, when ye pray, believe that ye receive them, and ye shall have them" (v.24). When these elements are combined, they are more powerful than any weapon of war. You are no longer looking at what you have, but what you shall have.

_____

_____

_____

_____

_____

_____

_____

_____

_____

_____

_____

"Speak faith into every situation of your life."

Called as Priests

And He hast made us unto our God kings and priests; and we shall reign on the earth. (Revelation 5:10)

A literal translation renders this verse not "kings and priests" but rather "a kingdom of priests." Fifteen hundred years before Jesus ever came to the earth, God told His people they would be a kingdom of priests (Exodus 19:6).

But when Moses went into the mountain with God, the people rebelled, making a golden calf (Exodus 32:1-4). Upon seeing what they had done, Moses broke the tablets of God's law, saying, Who is on the Lord's side let him come unto me (v.26) . . . and only the Levites came.

God is now fulfilling His original plan through you and me—His church! Just as the priests of the Old Testament bore the ark on their shoulders, we are to bear His glory wherever we go—the malls, the streets, the workplace. We have all been called into His priesthood and anointed with the power of the Holy Spirit to minister the saving Gospel of Jesus Christ.

"Be a priest and minister in the name of Christ to someone today."

Be an Ambassador for Christ

Now then we are ambassadors for Christ, as though God did beseech you by us: we pray you in Christ's stead, be ye reconciled to God.
(2 Corinthians 5:20)

True fulfillment in life comes when you stop running to and fro, grasping for things to fulfill you, and begin to realize the marvelous plan God has for you.

Of the billions of people on this planet, you have the unique role of husband, father, wife, mother, son or daughter. God has positioned you to serve Him in whatever environment you find yourself. It is our responsibility to let a hurting world know that God, in His love, sacrificed His Son on the Cross for them.

God has ordained a special place of ministry for each of us. This isn't a choice on our part. God has commissioned every believer with the ministry of reconciliation. Reflect today on the roles you alone can fill and then determine to fulfill those roles to the very best of your God-given abilities.

_____

_____

_____

_____

_____

_____

_____

_____

_____

_____

_____

_____

"As His ambassador, usher in God's kingdom wherever you go."

Stay Committed

For the which cause I also suffer these things: nevertheless I am not ashamed: for I know in whom I have believed, and am persuaded that he is able to keep that which I have committed unto him against that day. (2 Timothy 1:12)

God is God, whether the answer to your prayer manifests or not. Shadrach, Meshach and Abednego looked death in the eye and said, "Our God is more than able to deliver us, but even if he doesn't we will still serve Him" (Daniel 3:16-18).

Settle it in your mind and in your spirit once and for all that you are committed to God and His ordinances. Determine that, come what may, you are going to serve Him in loving obedience.

We all know what to do when God is speaking to us. It is when He is silent that those who have not settled it begin to falter in their walk. You will stumble over every rock of adversity the devil tosses in your path, unless you can shout like Timothy with the conviction of knowing in whom you believe.

"Commmitment is anchored in God's Word as the final word."

The True Vine

I AM the true vine, and my Father is the husbandman. (John 15:1).

God will bring people into your life to perfect the fruit of His Spirit in you. When He does, if you say, "We have a personality conflict, and I am just going to have to get away from that person," you take the pruning shears of the Holy Spirit out of God's hands.

When He wants to cut off that which hinders your growth, you may respond, "No, God, I won't change there. I like that fruit. Don't change that, God. Get your pruning shears away from me." Don't resist God's pruning in your life.

God brings persons or situations into your life, because there is an area of your life only that person, that relationship or that situation can perfect in you. Notice the people God brings into your life, and you will begin to see the kind of person you are with God. He says, "Show that person the same love, compassion, forgiveness, patience and tolerance I have shown you." Write a prayer of thanksgiving for that person.

_____

_____

_____

_____

_____

_____

_____

_____

_____

_____

"Thank the Lord for all the people He is using to prune your life."

Focus on the Lord

But every man is tempted, when he is drawn away of his own lust, and enticed. Then when lust hath conceived, it bringeth forth sin; and sin . . . death. (James 1:14,15)

I have seen great ocean liners docked in the ports of Hong Kong, vessels weighing thousands of tons with mammoth engines that propel them across the oceans. But they will be docked in the bay, and a little old tug boat can hook a chain to one of the ocean liners and draw it away. It would be a different story if that ocean liner suddenly started its engines and threw its gears into reverse.

The same thing is true of believers. The devil cannot take you in tow unless your engines are shut down. 2 Timothy 2:26 says, "These are they that are taken captive of the devil at his will." Don't allow the devil to dry dock your spirit.

If you shut down your mind to the things of God, you will give in to your own lusts and passions, allowing the enemy to seduce you.

Keep your mind and heart focused on the Lord and resist the temptation to gaze at the things of this world.

"Stay focused on the things of the Lord."

Walk in the Word

My people are destroyed for lack of knowledge. (Hosea 4:6)

When you give in to temptation, it is because you have not secured your victory for one of two reasons. One, you are receiving His Word, but choosing not to walk in it. When you know what the Bible says about your situation and walk in the light of that knowledge, you will not fall into temptation. You will see the snares of the devil and avoid them.

The second reason so many fall into temptation is because they are uninformed of God's instructions. Just because you don't know the law doesn't mean you won't get arrested for disobeying it. People get into all kinds of sin, die of cancer and live in poverty—because they are ignorant of the power available to them.

Secure your victory by finding out what God has to say about your situation and then determine to do what He says to do about it. Apply God's Word to every decision as you march into the new millennium.

_____

_____

_____

_____

_____

_____

_____

_____

_____

_____

_____

_____

"Know God's Word and then obey it."

Stagger Not

He staggered not at the promise of God through unbelief; but was strong in faith, giving glory to God; and being fully persuaded that, what he had promised, he was able also to perform.
Romans 4:20,21)

The word stagger in Greek means to "doubt or hesitate." Abraham did not slide back and forth between faith and fear—two mutually exclusive expectations. You cannot have faith and fear in the same heart. One drives out the other. You do not have to rebuke fear or overcome fear. Have faith in God and fear not. Fear and faith cannot exist together.

Abraham was fully persuaded. Christians are not fully persuaded about anything—that their spouse is the right one, that their church is the right one or their choice for lunch is the right one.

Stop wading in the shallow flatlands of weak spiritual existence and launch out into the deep. Be fully persuaded that the God you serve is able to perform what He has promised!

_____

_____

_____

_____

_____

_____

_____

_____

_____

_____

_____

_____

"Stand firm in faith. Don't stagger or waver to the right or the left."

A Higher Standard

Therefore is the kingdom of heaven likened unto a certain king, which would take account of his servants. (Matthew 18:23)

Jesus used the parable of the king who wanted to settle accounts with his servants to explain one of the laws by which citizens of His kingdom are to abide.

He said, "I'm holding you to a higher standard—my standard." If Jesus could forgive you while you were still a sinner—cheating and stealing; running around on your spouse; lying to your friends and stealing from your employer—He expects you to be able to forgive just as fully and completely.

He goes on in verse 24 to say that if we don't settle our accounts by being forgiving, God will have a rough account to settle with us!

God is calling you and me to a higher standard as this millennium closes and a new one dawns. The way we were isn't good enough. We must move to a new level of holiness and purity.

On your countdown to the new millennium, decide to live up to the higher standard of Jesus Christ. Determine that you will walk the highway of holiness.

_____

_____

_____

_____

_____

_____

_____

_____

_____

_____

_____

_____

"Walk the highway of holiness living a pure and upright life."

Change the Channel

But we all, with open face beholding as in a glass the glory of the Lord, are changed into the same image from glory to glory, even as by the Spirit of the Lord. (2 Corinthians 3:18)

Life is like a television with a remote control. If you do not like the channel, change it. If you do not like the way life is treating you, change the way you treat life. If you do not like the way people have been treating you, change the way you act.

I learned a long time ago that I can change me a whole lot faster than I can ever change you. If I do not like the way you are treating me, I cannot do much about you, but I can change me right away. I cannot remain depressed when I think about His goodness and what He's done for me. The devil hates a smile, and he'll train you to frown if you let him. He will pull a cloud of doom over your every thought, relationship and situation if you do not resist him.

Change the channel of your life today, and resist the devil in everything you say and do. "Submit yourselves therefore to God. Resist the devil, and he will flee from you" (James 4:7). Know the wiles of the enemy. Rebuke his temptations at every turn.

_____

_____

_____

_____

_____

_____

_____

_____

"Ask the Lord to change you from glory to glory."

Boldly Make Decisions That Magnify Christ

According to my earnest expectation and my hope, that in nothing I shall be ashamed, but that with all boldness, as always, so now also Christ shall be magnified in my body, whether it be by life, or by death. (Philippians 1:20)

Don't be afraid of boldly making decisions, because the devil wins all standoffs. God teaches us through our mistakes. Your steps will be ordered of the Lord if you seek Him in every endeavor. Don't allow the devil to gain a toehold in your life through procrastination and indecision.

The children of Israel stood on one side of a valley week after week—until a young shepherd boy with a slingshot came along and made a decision to do something about the situation.

D. L. Moody said, "It is yet to be seen what God would do through one man's life surrendered totally to Him. I determine to be that man."

Moody was never ordained, but he shook three continents with the power of God, because he realized all things are possible to those that believe . . . (Luke 1:37). He make bold decisions for Christ. How will you step out decisively today in boldness to magnify the Lord?

_____

_____

_____

_____

_____

_____

_____

_____

_____

_____

"Bold confidence will mark believers in the new millennium."

The Anointed Touch

And it came to pass, when he [Jesus] was in a certain city, behold a man full of leprosy: who seeing Jesus fell on his face, and besought him, saying, Lord, if thou wilt, thou canst make me clean. And he put forth his hand, and touched him, saying, I will: be thou clean. And immediately the leprosy departed from him. (Luke 5:12,13)

This leper had every right to give up all claims to his healing. Why would the Anointed One consider touching him? Every part of his body was infected with this terrible disease. He was a detestable sight to those around him and devastated by his life of exile. By law he was destined to be separated from society.

I believe that something within this leper said, "Cast not away therefore your confidence, which hath great recompense of reward" (Hebrews 10:35). He believed he was marked for a miracle. So upon seeing Jesus he cried out to him, "Will you make me clean?"

Jesus did not send an intern to deal with this leper. He did not refer him to His disciples for treatment. His healing was not postponed because of the leper's place or position in society. Jesus is no respecter of persons, and he ministers to all alike. This leper surely sensed the Great Physician's true feelings in His touch and response of great compassion.

What relief and excitement this man must have felt, for no one had touched him in so long. Through the touch of Jesus' hand, virtue flowed and drove out every sign of that sickening disease. He was no longer prisoner to a life of pain. The effects of his healing reached beyond the boundaries of this leper's everyday life. Verse 15 of Luke chapter 5 says, "But so much the more went there a fame abroad of him: and great multitudes came together to hear, and to be healed by him of their infirmities."

_____

_____

_____

_____

_____

"Ask the Anointed One to touch you."

Yes, Lord!

Teaching us that, denying ungodliness and worldly lusts, we should live soberly, righteously, and godly, in this present world. (Titus 2:12)

Moses was a prideful and arrogant man, ready to take care of God's people (his way) when he lived in Pharaoh's palace. God took all of that away when He sent him into the wilderness. Moses went from presiding in the palace to watching sheep in the desert.

It took God 40 years to purge Moses of everything that blocked His ability to use him to deliver the children of Israel. Forty long years in the desert changed haughtiness to humility and hostility to harmony with God.

God's purpose in our lives is to bring us to a realization that everything of value that we have is from Him alone. God has a plan and purpose for you, and He will remove anything that will hinder your effectiveness in fulfilling His plan—your job, your friends, your surroundings, your money—anything. God will break all threads of independence until we bow our knee and say, "Yes, Lord."

"No matter what the Lord asks, say, 'Yes, Lord.'"

Deposit His Word into Your Heart

And Jesus answering saith unto them, Have faith in God. For verily I say unto you, That whosoever shall say unto this mountain, Be thou removed, and be thou cast into the sea; and shall not doubt in his heart, but shall believe that those things which he saith shall come to pass; he shall have whatsoever he saith. Therefore I say unto you, What things soever ye desire, when ye pray, believe that ye receive them, and ye shall have them. (Mark 11:22-24)

The greatest thing that will ever happen to your faith is when the Word of God takes that eighteen-inch drop from mental assent in your head to believing faith in your heart.

When God engraves His Word in your heart, there isn't enough doubt, discouragement or disaster to ever remove it. The devil doesn't have an eraser big enough to remove God's Word from your spirit once He has placed it there.

Today, hide His word in your heart. Treasure and cherish the Word with your whole being.

_____

_____

_____

_____

_____

_____

_____

_____

_____

_____

_____

"Daily hide His Word in your heart."

Faith is Never Casual

But without faith it is impossible to please him: for he that cometh to God must believe that he is, and that he is a rewarder of them that diligently seek him. (Hebrews 11:6)

You may say, "How is it possible to believe before you ever come to God?" Because God gave every man the measure of faith (Romans 12:3).

Don't ever say, "I don't have faith to be healed, or for my family's salvation or for my finances to improve." God gave you the faith to believe!

You know this is true by the very fact that you are saved. With your heart you believed when you didn't know anything about God, because He gave you the ability to believe.

Believe what? That God IS. Wherever you are, God was there first.

God is not a rewarder of casual acquaintance. His Word was given to us so we could know Him. But don't base your faith on the Word of God; base it, instead, on the God of the Word.

Radical Christianity has at its root a deep intimacy with God. Describe how you have grown intimate with God:

_____

_____

_____

_____

_____

_____

_____

_____

_____

_____

_____

_____

"Faith leads you to desire deeper intimacy with God."

Godly Character

And God said, Let us make man in our image, after our likeness: and let them have dominion over the fish of the sea, and over the fowl of the air, and over the cattle, and over all the earth, and over every creeping thing that creepeth upon the earth. (Genesis 1:26)

Your character is the sum total of every decision you have ever made; there is no such thing as an unimportant decision. God never intended for man to be a slave of circumstances. We were given dominion on the earth, and dominion only comes through exercising our will to make decisions.

Emotional decisions are broken over the knee of adversity. But if your decisions line up with the will of God for your life . . . though all hell breaks loose, you will weather the storm. You will set your chin like flint and say, "I am going to the other side! I don't care about the lightning or that my boat of life is being tossed to and fro. I know who rides in my vessel, and I will fear no harm. He will keep me safe."

Your decisions today should not be based upon your emotions but rather by decisions that are rooted in God's truth.

_____

_____

_____

_____

_____

_____

_____

_____

_____

_____

"Godly character is shaped by decisions based on truth, not feelings."

No More Crumbs!

Then king David sent, and fetched him out of the house of Machir, the son of Ammiel, from Lodebar . . . So Mephibosheth dwelt in Jerusalem: for he did eat continually at the king's table; and was lame on both his feet. (2 Samuel 9:5,13)

Lo-debar—nothing was there. Mephibosheth never intended for this to be a destination or a dwelling place. However, Lo-debar had become his prison of emptiness and isolation. It was his hell of existence—not life, but a living death. There was only one way out of Lo-debar. The only way out required that a prior promise be remembered and a cherished covenant be fulfilled.

When in Lo-debar it seems that existing on stale crumbs is the only option. Lo-debar's residents are tempted to believe the lie that there is nothing beyond its boundaries. For Mephibosheth, Lo-debar seemed like the end of the journey, the final chapter in a tragic existence. Lame and alone, the king's descendant appeared doomed to an existence devoid of hope or harvest. He may have been born royalty, but he would die an outcast. Or would he?

Against all hope, overcoming every circumstance and beyond Mephibosheth's wildest dreams, the impossible was happening. He was riding out of Lo-debar and from that moment on, there would be: *No More Crumbs!*

_____

_____

_____

_____

_____

_____

_____

_____

"You are royalty. Therefore dine at the King's table."

Divine Health

For ye were as sheep going astray; but are now returned unto the Shepherd and Bishop of your souls. (1 Peter 2:25)

God promises divine health to those who not only hear His commands but are faithful to obey them. Our heavenly Father's redeeming provision for us is as vast as the consequences of the fall. He provides forgiveness for sin, eternal life for death and healing for sickness. What an awesome God we serve!

Jesus revealed God's will in action as He went to the cities and villages around Galilee "healing every sickness and every disease" (Matthew 9:35), and His atoning death on the Cross sealed the matter. We have been redeemed, spirit, soul and body.

Once you have a revelation of Jehovah Rophe—the Lord who heals all our diseases—no infirmity, sickness nor disease will ever have power over you again.

_____

_____

_____

_____

_____

_____

_____

_____

_____

_____

_____

"God desires for you to enter into the new millennium in divine health."

Guard Your Heart

And it came to pass in an evening tide, that David arose from off his bed, and walked upon the roof of the king's house: and from the roof he saw a woman washing herself; and the woman was very beautiful to look upon. (2 Samuel 11:2)

We are never out of reach of the tentacles of temptation. You can be in a crowd of thousands or alone in your thoughts, and temptation will sit down beside you.

Was the seed of temptation already in David's heart, or was he only seeking a place of solitude when temptation overtook him? Instead of fleeing from the roof when he saw Bathsheba, he fed temptation by inquiring about her. The result of allowing temptation to stay in your heart will be as devastating to you as it was to him.

Guard your heart with all diligence (Proverb 4:23). Do not feed your spirit with the chaff of this world, but keep it strong through reading and meditating on the Word of God and communing with your heavenly Father.

"As you walk through this year, continually guard your heart all the time."

God Provides

And Abraham called the name of that place Jehovah Jireh: as it is said to this day, In the mount of the Lord it shall be seen. (Genesis 22:14)

God's plan is to establish your future and to do you no harm (Jeremiah 29:11). Just as He provided the ram to take Isaac's place in Genesis 22:8, God the Father provided God the Son to take your place.

Jehovah Jireh, "the One who provides," sent Jesus to be our mediator (Hebrews 8:6), our guarantee (Hebrews 7:22) and our messenger of the covenant (Malachi 3:1).

You are not bound to this world system. What your boss or the banking system has planned for you has nothing to do with your Father's plan.

Decide which kingdom you are living in. In God's kingdom there are no limits. He can bring the increase to break the yoke of poverty, and He can deliver you from every sickness and infirmity. Thank Him today for His plan for you and your family.

_____

_____

_____

_____

_____

_____

_____

_____

_____

_____

_____

_____

"God's vision and plan for you is accompanied by His provision."

To Live is Christ

According to my earnest expectation and my hope, that in nothing I shall be ashamed, but that with all boldness, as always, so now also Christ shall be magnified in my body, whether it be by life, or by death. For to me to live is Christ, and to die is gain. (Philippians 1:20,21)

Jesus was Lord in the apostle Paul's life, and his example to us today is unparalleled. His entire purpose in life was to boldly speak forth for Christ's sake and to become more like Him with each passing day. Paul disciplined himself, setting goals and priorities to glorify God.

Each one of us has the same amount of time before us today, but how we use that time is going to determine just how far we go in the things of God. We are each responsible for the depth of our own lives.

Set your sights today on living your life as Paul did, magnifying Christ in everything you set your hands to do, everywhere your feet go and with your every breath.

_____

_____

_____

_____

_____

_____

_____

_____

_____

_____

_____

"Live for Christ Jesus with every breath that you take."

Dependence Is Constant Contact

But we had the sentence of death in ourselves, that we should not trust in ourselves, but in God which raiseth the dead: who delivered us from so great a death, and doth deliver: in whom we trust that he will yet deliver us.
(2 Corinthians 1:9,10)

Remember the times God has set you free, the times He has moved on your behalf, the times He has come through when it seemed no answer would or even could come.

He is not going to begin failing you today. He will answer your prayer today, because He never changes. God will turn your tragedy into triumph and your trial into a testimony when you trust and depend upon Him.

Dependence on Him is not defeat; dependence is simply staying in constant contact. Trusting God means realizing He is the source of your deliverance and then staying within calling distance of Him.

List all the ways in which you keep in constant contact with the Lord.

_____

_____

_____

_____

_____

_____

_____

_____

_____

_____

_____

_____

_____

"Keep in constant contact with the Lord."

I Know the Lord

Behold, I and the children whom the Lord hath given me are for signs and for wonders in Israel from the Lord of hosts, which dwelleth in mount Zion. (Isaiah 8:18)

Pharaoh asked scornfully, "Who is the Lord?" (Exodus 5:2) At God's command, Aaron threw down his rod and it became a snake. Pharaoh's magicians laughed as their rods also turned into snakes, but the laughter died when Aaron's snake (rod) devoured theirs.

God proclaimed, "I will harden Pharaoh's heart, and multiply my signs and my wonders in the land of Egypt" (Exodus 7:3). As 10 plagues ravaged the land, Pharaoh, his magicians and all of Egypt came to know beyond a doubt who the Lord is.

God is multiplying His signs and wonders in our generation. Just as in the days of Moses, God is revealing himself to the scoffers, the doubters, the cynics and the sinners who scornfully ask, "Who is the Lord?"

On the other hand, radical, sold-out Christians marching into the new millennium confidently declare, "I know the Lord. I see the Lord high and lifted up." How will you lift up the Lord today?

_____

_____

_____

_____

_____

_____

_____

_____

_____

_____

"Know the Lord and lift Him up continually."

Shine, Jesus, Shine

And it came to pass, when Moses came down from mount Sinai with the two tables of testimony in Moses' hand, when he came down from the mount, that Moses wist not that the skin of his face shone while he talked with him. (Exodus 34:29)

Moses spent 40 days in the mountain with God. When he finally returned to camp with the Ten Commandments inscribed on stones, he had to cover his face because it shone with the glory of God (v.33). Moses shone with the tangible presence of God—everyone who looked at Him knew He had been with God.

If you will leave everything else behind . . . if you will be bold and persevere in your times of prayer, God will meet with you and talk to you just as He did with Moses. Scripture tells us that the veil covering our hearts is removed when we turn to the Lord and reflect His glory (2 Corinthians 3:14-18).

Stay in the mountain with God until you shine with His glory. Don't leave your house without His presence. Get in the mountain with God and receive His glory. How is Jesus shining through you?

_____

_____

_____

_____

_____

_____

_____

_____

_____

_____

"Shine through me, Lord Jesus."

Profess Victory

Seeing then that we have a great high priest, that is passed into the heavens, Jesus the Son of God, let us hold fast our profession. (Hebrews 4:14)

Whatever you talk about is your confession. If you are continually confessing how much trouble the devil is causing, how bad your finances are or how rotten your spouse is, rest assured that your words will ring true.

When the Bible directs us to "hold fast" to our profession, we are being told to hold onto what the Bible says about our situation with bulldog faith—the kind that does not let go.

You are going to have trouble in this life, but if you will hold fast to your confession of faith you can be assured of victory, because you have been blessed with every spiritual blessing (Ephesians 1:3). You have been redeemed, forgiven, and are a recipient of His lavish grace (Ephesians 1:7,8). And you have been delivered (rescued) from the domain of darkness (Satan's rule) and transferred to the kingdom of Christ (Colossians 1:13). Finally, you have been given a spirit of power, love and sound mind (2 Timothy 1:7).

How has Jesus delivered you from darkness into light?

_____

_____

_____

_____

_____

_____

_____

_____

_____

_____

_____

_____

"March through the night of tribulation into the light of His victory."

By Faith

So then faith cometh by hearing, and hearing by the word of God. (Romans 10:17)

You have faith in what you can see, touch and understand. You did not stand in front of your chair and debate whether or not it would hold you before you sat down. Why? You trusted the chair. You had prior experience with the chair and knew the chair had always held you safely. Your knowledge surpassed your fear that the chair would fail. You had faith.

Faith in God comes through the study of His Word, learning who He is, how He behaves and that He is a rewarder of those who diligently seek Him. As the Holy Spirit leads you into truth, you learn that God loves you and is ready to do anything for you. That knowledge produces understanding, understanding produces trust and trust produces the faith to believe for your miracle.

Seek Him in His Word. Learn about Him. Let the Holy Spirit show you the Father's heart. Faith is simply knowing God. Faith says, "I can trust Him to be who He says He is. I can trust Him to do what He says He will do."

_____

_____

_____

_____

_____

_____

_____

_____

_____

_____

_____

_____

"By faith, radically trust Him for everything in your life."

Your True Source

And thou say in thine heart, my power and the might of mine hand hath gotten me this wealth. (Deuteronomy 8:17)

When things are going well, it could be easy to take credit for your prosperity. You may think it is your job or your college education that has given you the ability to get wealth. Your intelligence and common sense are not the source of your supply, God is.

During times of great need, you can't depend on anything of this world, including your job or your education. People who hold several degrees and have worked for corporations for decades have been fired from their jobs, thrown into the job market, and are finding that their age and experience are not a help but a hindrance.

The woman sick with an issue of blood spent her living—everything she had—on physicians, relying on their intelligence and education, but she only grew worse (Matthew 9:20). If we forget God in our abundance, or we will eventually lose everything.

Realize exactly how dependent you really are on God, for He alone is your true source. Describe how God is your one and only source.

_____

_____

_____

_____

_____

_____

_____

_____

_____

_____

_____

"God is your source. There is no other!"

He Can Do Anything

But if thou canst do any thing, have compassion on us, and help us. (Mark 9:22)

In this Scripture Jesus explained to the desperate father, "It's not a question of what I can do." God flung the stars into the heavens, put the oceans in their boundaries, sprinkled sand around the shores, and then He sent the world spinning and commanded the oceans not to spill a drop. It was this blind man healer, this leper-cleansing man, this water-walking Jesus who said, "Light be" . . . light was and it has never ceased to be, because He never commanded it to stop. He is a supernatural, miracle-working God. He can do anything.

There is no mountain high enough to keep Him from getting to the other side. The devil can't come up with a problem in your life that God can't solve. It is never a question of what God can do, but only of what you believe He can do. Believe He can work miracles, He can make your feet like hind's feet, and that you too will leap and bound over every obstacle the enemy puts in your path!

The question you must answer as you enter a new millennium is this: What do you believe God can do in and through you? Only one answer passes the radical test: *Everything!*

_____

_____

_____

_____

_____

_____

_____

_____

"Get radical. Choose to believe that God will work miracles in your life."

Take Hold

Now we have received, not the spirit of the world, but the spirit which is of God; that we might know the things that are freely given to us of God.
(1 Corinthians 2:12)

Most Christians do not know much about the realm of the Spirit. It is as if they are separated from the Promised Land by the Jordan River. Once in a while, when no giants are around, they may rush across the water and take some fruit from the trees and then run back. This is a long way from dwelling in the land!

Perhaps they hear a rousing sermon by a strong evangelist. For a brief time their spirits are stirred up, and they reach out and take hold of their healing, their strength, their joy, their peace or their deliverance. But when the stirring fades, they go back to walking in the natural.

We were not meant to rush in and out of the spiritual realm; we are meant to live there. Why wonder where your spiritual blessings are. They are in the spiritual realm. Enter in and take hold of what is yours. Describe what God has given you and what you will take hold of:

_____

_____

_____

_____

_____

_____

_____

_____

_____

_____

_____

_____

"What keeps you today from taking hold of all that God has for you?"

No Man, Just Jesus

For an angel went down at a certain season into the pool, and troubled the water: whosoever then first after the troubling of the water stepped in was made whole of whatsoever disease he had. And a certain man was there, which had an infirmity thirty and eight years. (John 5:4,5)

Jesus asked the man if he wanted to be made whole, and he answered, "Sir, I have no man." He was so caught up with thinking he needed someone to help him, he could not see that his miracle was standing right in front of him!

When you have no man to help you—nowhere to turn but God—you are a prime target for a miracle! No man can do for you what Jesus can do for you.

When you quit depending on your job, the preacher, your family or the next healing line, you are positioned for your breakthrough. Family may let you down, the preacher may disappoint you and your friends may forsake you; but Jesus is the friend who sticks closer than a brother. Rely on Him and Him alone, and He will meet you at the very point of your deepest need. What are the deep needs He is meeting in your life today?

_____
_____
_____
_____
_____
_____
_____
_____
_____
_____

"No man—just Jesus—can meet your deepest needs."

Wilt Thou Be Made Whole?

When Jesus saw him lie, and knew that he had been now a long time in that case, he saith unto him, Wilt thou be made whole? (John 5:6)

Jesus asked the man beside the Pool of Bethesda if he wanted to be made whole. This may seem to be an odd question, but it really is not. Many appear to be seeking a miracle, but do not really want a miracle. They have grown comfortable with their condition, enjoying their self-pity and the attention they receive. Or they may be wishing for a miracle, but don't really expect one to come.

How long will you wait on the bank, while the rivers of living water course past you? Say good-bye to sympathy and complacency. Cast aside the maybe, the perhaps and the someday syndromes. Do not allow yourself to become an impotent Christian, lying by the water, too blind to see God, and with no power to overcome.

Take the initiative. Get to know Jesus. Get to know His Word. Stop waiting for a man to help you. Stretch out your hand, and allow Jesus to lift you up. How are you stretching out to Jesus today?

_____

_____

_____

_____

_____

_____

_____

_____

_____

_____

_____

"Only Jesus can make you whole."

Revival Is Coming

They that dwell under his shadow shall return; they shall revive as the corn, and grow as the vine: the scent thereof shall be as the wine of Lebanon. (Hosea 14:7)

Before Jesus returns, revival is coming. I see hospitals emptying. I see people running down the hallways and running out into the parking lot. I see church services that start on Sunday and go for three months on end, twenty-four hours a day.

I see that which was Pentecostal, apostolic authority being restored to the church of Jesus Christ. That which was shall be again. There will be tongues like fire sitting on you; jail cells bursting open; chains falling off; dead people's eyes popping open; and there will be liars and hypocrites falling dead in the middle of a praise and worship service. He's going to do it before we leave here. He said, I'm not sending Jesus until I restore everything to the church.

Say to yourself, "Revival begins with me." What needs revived in your life?

_____

_____

_____

_____

_____

_____

_____

_____

_____

_____

_____

_____

_____

_____

"Lord, let revival in this new millennium begin with me."

Get Ready for Your Healing

He brought them forth also with silver and gold: and there was not one feeble person among their tribes. (Psalm 105:37)

The Bible says God led the children of Israel out of Egypt, six million strong, and there was not a feeble one among them. Get ready to throw away those glasses; watch that silver hair grow raven black; watch your back straighten up; watch the pain of arthritis leave your body. Before Jesus splits that eastern sky He's going to heal every one of us.

List all the ways He is healing you today.

_____

_____

_____

_____

_____

_____

_____

_____

_____

_____

_____

_____

_____

_____

_____

"Praise God for your healing."

Preach and Heal

And as ye go, preach, saying, The kingdom of heaven is at hand. Heal the sick, cleanse the lepers, raise the dead, cast out devils: freely ye have received, freely give. (Matthew 10:7-8)

Heal the sick, cleanse the lepers—while you're at it, raise the dead, cast out devils. Freely you've received, freely give.

Jesus commanded us to preach, "The kingdom of heaven is at hand." Then He commands us to heal the sick. He didn't say, "Try to." He didn't say that only healing evangelists would heal people. He sent all his disciples out to heal the sick.

Notice He did not say, "Pray for the sick." He said, "Heal the sick." Start doing what God said to do. Watch the progression of Peter in the book of Acts 3. Peter, first of all at the Gate Beautiful said, "Silver and gold have I none but such as I have give I thee in the name of the Lord Jesus Christ of Nazareth. Rise up and walk."

The next time you find Peter doing the same exact thing except he said, "In the name of Jesus Christ, rise and walk." The next time he shortened it up a little bit and he just said, "Get up."

How will you preach and heal the sick today?

_____

_____

_____

_____

_____

_____

_____

_____

_____

_____

"Preach the Gospel and heal the sick."

Endure!

And ye shall be hated of all men for my name's sake: but he that endureth to the end shall be saved. (Matthew 10:22)

There is a struggle of light and darkness going on and it is only important that you know what side of the fence you're on; because no matter what you're going through, He's going to take you through whatever it is to where He said you'd go.

Jesus said in Matthew 10 that believers would be hated of men for His name's sake, but He who endures to the end the same shall be saved. Now, it actually translates this way, "The saved ones endure to the end."

Another translation, "Only the ones who are truly saved will endure to the end. Only the saved ones endure." Let me give you the reverse translation, "If you don't endure, you're not saved."

Get ready to endure to the end, no matter what the price.

_____

_____

_____

_____

_____

_____

_____

_____

_____

_____

_____

_____

_____

_____

_____

"Endure to the end."

Anointing Authority

Now when the sun was setting, all they that had any sick with divers diseases brought them unto him; and he laid his hands on every one of them, and healed them. And devils also came out of many, crying out, and saying, Thou art Christ the Son of God. And he rebuking them suffered them not to speak: for they knew that he was Christ. (Luke 4:40,41)

The authority of having an earth suit gives you the opportunity to manifest miracles, but the anointing gives you the <u>ability</u> to manifest miracles.

Immediately following the proclamation that He was the Messiah and the anointing was upon His life, Jesus entered into Peter's house and ministered to his mother-in-law. One thing you must realize about devils is that they are liars. Satan is the father of all lies (John 8:44). He never tells the truth unless telling the truth is to his advantage.

The demon hordes of hell were actually saying, "You can't torment us. You are the Son of God; you have no authority on the earth. We know you. You are God, and you don't have any authority in the earth realm." But Jesus' response was, "Shut up and come out of him!"

These demons were challenging Jesus' authority. They were saying, "You are the Son of God. You can't do this. In Matthew 8:29, these same demons said, "Don't torment us, thou Son of God. It is not the time. You can't torment us before the time."

He couldn't have tormented them if He was just the Son of God, but He wasn't just the Son of God. He wasn't just Spirit. He was born of a virgin; He came through the door (John 10:1). He also had authority as a man on the face of this earth!

The same anointing which empowered Jesus has been given to you. You have authority in every area of your life!

"You have anointing authority in your life!"

Shine With His Light Today

In him was life; and the life was the light of men. (John 1:4)

Our Commander Himself declares, "I am the light of the world" (John 9:5). We march under the banner of light. Christ as the true light invades the darkness, and darkness cannot overcome His light. The Word proclaims, "In him [Christ] was life; and the life was the light of men. And the light shineth in darkness; and the darkness comprehended it not" (John 1:4-5).

Go forward with the church who gets up with the morning light and walks in the former and latter rains of God. Remember, no matter how hot the night has been, the dawn is always accompanied by a cool, moist breeze. It will cool your fevered brow. A fresh breeze of God's Spirit is issuing forth today over the sapphire sill of heaven's gate for those who raise high the standard of Jesus Christ. Those under His banner are rejoicing every morning as they rise up saying, "This is the day which the Lord hath made; we will rejoice and be glad in it" (Psalm 118:24). The greatest day, the greatest dawn, the greatest morning that the church has ever seen lies straight ahead.

The church marches into the new millennium under Christ's banner of light dispelling darkness wherever she goes and establishing His revolutionary kingdom of light. Today, dispel the darkness with the light of Christ wherever you go.

_____

_____

_____

_____

_____

_____

_____

"Darkness flees when you march under Christ's banner of light."

Don't Deny Jesus

So when they had dined, Jesus saith to Simon Peter, Simon, son of Jonas, lovest thou me more than these? He saith unto him, Yea, Lord; thou knowest that I love thee. He saith unto him, Feed my lambs. (John 21:15)

Dr. Martin Luther King said, "The true measure of such a man or woman is not how he stands in times of comfort and convenience, but rather whether he is still standing in times of challenge and controversy" (*The Strength to Love,* New York: Harper & Row, 1963. p.20).

Watch Peter. See him warming himself by the fire of the world. Hear him deny his Lord three times, "I never knew the man." People around us will accuse us of being like Jesus. We might protest, "No, it must have been somebody else."

Watch Peter cower in fear and deny his Lord three times before the cock crows; but don't count him out, he's one of the saved ones. Watch him climb up on a soapbox on the Day of Pentecost. Watch him preach the first evangelistic crusade of the infant church and watch five thousand people respond to the altar call.

You may have denied the Lord in the past. Repent and receive His forgiveness. You were down, but you are not out. Live radically for Jesus this year and into the new millennium.

_____

_____

_____

_____

_____

_____

_____

_____

_____

_____

"Tell Jesus right now that you love Him and will serve Him to the end."

Write Down the Vision

I was in the Spirit on the Lord's day, and heard behind me a great voice, as of a trumpet Saying, I am Alpha and Omega, the first and the last: and, What thou seest, write in a book.
(Revelation 1:10,11)

Take John the beloved and boil him in blistering oil, and when he refused to die the first time, throw him in again. And when he won't die a second time throw him in again. And when he won't die a third time banish him fifty miles off the coast of Ephesus on the island called Patmos, with nothing but the wild beasts for company—but you had better not leave him pencil and paper.

The last living apostle sees visions . . . he sees Jesus. No amount of isolation or torture can prevent him from seeing Jesus. When you have a vision, write it down. "Write the vision, and make it plain upon tables, that he may run that readeth it" (Habakkuk 2:2).

When God gives you a vision, write it down. Seal it in your heart. March forward into the future with the power of Christ. Don't let anything keep you from living in the vision of God. Write down the vision God has given to you for the new millennium:

_____

_____

_____

_____

_____

_____

_____

_____

_____

"The vision of God will inspire, motivate and guide you into the new millennium."

Overshadowed by the Anointing

And by the hands of the apostles were many signs and wonders wrought among the people; (and they were all with one accord in Solomon's porch. And of the rest durst no man join himself to them: but the people magnified them. And believers were the more added to the Lord, multitudes both of men and women.) Insomuch that they brought forth the sick into the streets, and laid them on beds and couches, that at the least the shadow of Peter passing by might overshadow some of them. (Acts 5:12-15)

Not only did the tangible anointing fall during the days of the apostles, but also it is falling throughout the church today.

Several years ago there was a little girl in our congregation who was dying of an incurable disease. Her parents had spoken to my wife, Joni, and asked if I could pray over one of her bed sheets. They were then going to put it on her bed so she could sleep on it.

I took that bed sheet and wrapped it around my shoulders and preached an entire service, then I gave it back to the mother. Within a week that baby was up, running around and talking! The anointing is tangible!

Today is the acceptable time. Today is your time! What transpired in the book of Acts will look like a Sunday school picnic compared to what is going to happen when we begin to realize we are overshadowed by the anointing. We are marked for miracles!

_____

_____

_____

_____

_____

_____

_____

_____

"You are marked by the anointing for miracles."

Down but Not Out

Therefore, my beloved brethren, be ye stedfast, unmoveable, always abounding in the work of the Lord, forasmuch as ye know that your labour is not in vain in the Lord. (1 Corinthians 15:58)

Heroic giant-slayer David was hated by Saul and pursued as a criminal. He was down but not out. Elijah had to run for his life when Jezebel threatened to kill him. He was down but not out. Esther faced a death decree signed by the King. She was down but not out. Peter was beaten and thrown into prison by the angry Jewish leaders. He was down but not out. Paul was stoned outside the city gates and left for dead. He was down but not out.

All of these were down but not out, they were in the tomb of failure but still available to be revived and resurrected. You may be down but you are not out. This year may be the toughest you have ever faced, but rejoice. You will overcome every adversity, in the name of Jesus.

_____

_____

_____

_____

_____

_____

_____

_____

_____

_____

_____

_____

_____

"Our risen Savior gives us the victory over every circumstance."

God Seeks Us

Neither by the blood of goats and calves, but by his own blood he entered in once into the holy place, having obtained eternal redemption for us. (Hebrews 9:12)

In Rome's Sistine Chapel looms Michelangelo's classic work. Though it is titled "Creation," it aptly captures man's struggle. Suffering humanity, cut off from the Father's love and protection, sought to bridge that gulf and again experience the life-giving reality of God. Ever reaching toward God, the hands never touch; the distance is too great.

Over and over in the Old Testament, man tried to close the rift caused by sin with animal sacrifices and good works. Yet the blood of all the animals in the world could never erase man's guilt.

Before Adam ever sinned, God set His plan of redemption in motion. Before the need ever existed, God had a remedy. Jesus was the Lamb slain before the foundation of the world to return us to a place of fellowship with God and to repair the breach that man's sin created.

"God is reaching out to you."

Build a Bridge

The Spirit of the Lord is upon me, because he has anointed me to preach the gospel to the poor; he hath sent me to heal the brokenhearted, to preach deliverance to the captives, and recovering of sight to the blind, to set at liberty them that are bruised, to preach the acceptable year of the Lord. (Luke 4:18,19)

I believe the day has come for God's people to put on their whole spiritual armor and expose Satan's and his minions' evil plans. There is a remnant people in our generation who are being called by God to rebuild what Satan has destroyed. Like Christ they will say: *The Spirit of the Lord is upon me* . . . .

The Lord is looking for a people who will reach down to the fallen with one hand and reach up to the Father with the other—and unite the two! You are called to build the bridge and restore the breach between the lost and Jesus. Are you building bridges or barriers?

_____

_____

_____

_____

_____

_____

_____

_____

_____

_____

_____

_____

"The Spirit of the Lord is upon you.
Step forth to break bondages, in Jesus' Name."

Separate from the World

For as many as are led by the Spirit of God, they are the sons of God. (Romans 8:14)

The Lord wants to sanctify you *positionally* (to separate you from the world); *experientially* (allowing God's Spirit within you to separate your mind and body to the Word of God) and *ultimately* (at the Rapture of the church).

Many Christians attempt to see how close to sin they can come and still be saved. We cannot afford to love the world or the things in the world. Holiness begins by entering into the presence of a holy God.

Enter into His presence today. Spend the next millennium worshiping in the awesome presence of the Lord.

_____

_____

_____

_____

_____

_____

_____

_____

_____

_____

_____

_____

"Enter into His presence and stay there."

God's Kingdom is at Hand

Repent: for the kingdom of heaven is at hand.
(Matthew 4:17)

We must restore the message of the Gospel to the body of Christ. Satan has attempted to steal it, but we are putting it back.

The world must know that Christ is the only begotten Son of God. He came from heaven to earth to shed His sinless blood on the Cross to free us from our sin. He was buried, but rose on the third day—victorious over death, hell and the grave (1 Corinthians 15:4).

And something more. Because He lives, we can live also! By His Spirit and through His risen presence, Christ is *at hand*. He is at your right hand and left to guide and direct you. He is leading you by the hand. Take His hand and walk boldly into the new millennium.

_____

_____

_____

_____

_____

_____

_____

_____

_____

_____

_____

_____

"Christ is at hand. Ask Him to lead you."

Your Advocate

And to Jesus the mediator of the new covenant, and to the blood of sprinkling, that speaketh better things than that of Abel. (Hebrews 12:24)

Satan can condemn you all he chooses, but when you try pleading your case before God, Christ comes to your rescue and becomes your advocate, speaking on your behalf to the Father.

We have all sinned and come short of the glory of God (Romans 3:23). But Christ paid the price for our iniquity. We are guilty, yet we are free. We are condemned to death, yet we live. "And he is the propitiation for our sins: and not for ours only, but also for the sins of the whole world" (1 John 2:2).

How can we find redemption when we are at fault? By accepting the price that was paid at Calvary. It is futile to attempt to cover the problem of sin with religion, good works or self-sufficiency. Only by crying out for mercy can the story of our lives be rewritten.

Jesus is your Advocate with the Father. Ask Him to take your needs to the throne of God.

"Your Advocate awaits your prayer so that He may plead your case."

Jesus, the Door

I am the door of the sheep. All that ever came before me are thieves and robbers: but the sheep did not hear them. I am the door: by me if any man enter in, he shall be saved, and shall go in and out, and find pasture. (John 10:7-9)

Demonic activity is rampant in our world. Millions are being held hostage by Satan's evil deception and perversion. He has stolen the plank of freedom from our lives and is now holding us in bondage.

Who is going to come forward and declare, "In the name of Jesus, it is time for deliverance"? Who is going to demand that Satan return what is rightfully ours?

In the beginning, God gave dominion of the earth to Adam and his descendants. Through deceit, Satan stole from mankind what rightfully belonged to us. Jesus restored our position of authority; and as His army, we must now see to it that the devil stays in his place. We must say once and for all, "Enough is enough!" Resist the enemy, and declare that where you are, is holy ground. Describe your rebuke of Satan.

_____

_____

_____

_____

_____

_____

_____

_____

_____

_____

_____

"Cry out with authority and power in Jesus' name,
'Devil, enough is enough!'"

God is Omnipotent

He rebuked the fever; and it left her: and immediately she arose and ministered unto them. (Luke 4:39)

We serve an omnipotent God. *Omni* means "all" and *potent* means "powerful." There is potential in God that we have not yet seen on earth. I believe we are on the brink of a great revival. The Lord intends for us to take back what is ours and exercise authority over the forces of darkness.

It is time for God's people to tell the devil, "Stop it! That's enough! You have stolen enough power from the church and have weakened the basic tenets of faith until people are stumbling as they attempt to cross the bridge of grace!"

Since God is all-powerful, you can do all things through Christ who strengthens you. Where do you need a manifestation of God's power in your life? Declare His power and Satan's defeat!

_____

_____

_____

_____

_____

_____

_____

_____

_____

_____

_____

_____

_____

"Serving an omnipotent God means that all power belongs to Him and no one else."

Grace!

For by grace are ye saved through faith; and that not of yourselves: it is the gift of God: not of works, lest any man should boast. (Ephesians 2:8,9)

How do we have faith to believe God for spiritual power, authority and deliverance? The secret lies in one word: Grace.

Faith is by grace. It is not something you must work to acquire. "Therefore it is of faith, that it might be by grace"(Romans 4:16).

For too long Christians have accepted a gospel of humanism that says favor with God is a result of our personal effort. Scripture tells us faith comes through grace—the unmerited favor of God—which produces the availability of God's power to not only deliver you, but also the power to move mountains.

Grace is the gift you receive before your faith. Without it you would never have found salvation. Without it you can never know God's deliverance.

Ask the Lord for grace to do all things by His power.

_____

_____

_____

_____

_____

_____

_____

_____

_____

_____

_____

_____

_____

"Grace is a gift you cannot earn and you do not deserve."

Faith Mercy and Grace!

Let us therefore come boldly unto the throne of grace, that we may obtain mercy, and find grace to help in time of need. (Hebrews 4:16)

God has given you a spirit of unlimited belief. When you hear an anointed message or read God's Word, something deep within you says, "Yes, I believe!"

Then a battle begins. Your mind, your will and your emotions say, "No, that just isn't possible." "For we walk by faith, not by sight" (2 Corinthians 5:7).

Remember this: When you feel as if you do not have enough faith to believe, God is still flooding your spirit with grace and mercy. Even in your weakness His grace is sufficient.

Trusting God opens your heart to receive His grace and mercy. Write down some of the ways you have experienced His mercy.

_____

_____

_____

_____

_____

_____

_____

_____

_____

_____

_____

_____

_____

"Everything we have is the result of the mercy of God."

Capturing Thoughts

Casting down imaginations, and every high thing that exalteth itself against the knowledge of God, and bringing into captivity every thought to the obedience of Christ. (2 Corinthians 10:5)

You may drive down the road and see a picture of a seductive woman on a billboard with cheap wine in her hand. In the flesh, the thought can come into your mind, "Boy, that looks good." It's just a thought at that point. What do you do with the thought? Scripture commands us to *take every thought captive!*

Your thoughts can only attack you if you allow it. You have the will to think whatever you wish. So the Bible says, "If there be any virtue . . . think on these things" (Philippians 4:8). What things? Whatsoever things are pure, and whatsoever things are lovely.

When you are tempted to think impure and unlovely things, don't! Refuse to dwell on negative, wicked thoughts. Fix your mind and your heart on the things of the Spirit and you will reap a harvest in the Spirit that will produce the mind of Christ in you.

_____

_____

_____

_____

_____

_____

_____

_____

_____

_____

_____

"Today, take every thought captive."

Stop Limiting God

Simon, Simon, behold, Satan hath desired to have you, that he may sift you as wheat: but I have prayed for thee, that thy faith fail not: and when thou art converted, strengthen thy brethren.
(Luke 22:31,32)

Why does God have more faith in us than we have in ourselves? Because He knows the Christ who lives on the inside of us and God knows He will never back down to the devil.

The Lord has given you the power to command the forces of darkness to leave you alone, and He is waiting for you to exercise that power. When the task seems beyond our ability, we can rely on the God of the Word that declares, "Now unto him that is able to do exceeding abundantly above all that we ask or think . . ."(Ephesians 3:20).

Stop limiting God by the level of your faith or belief. He is still the God of the impossible. He still performs miracles and is ready to bring you abundance, health, victory, vitality, joy, peace and security.

"Jesus was only limited by unbelief.
Is there something in you which limits Him?"

Satan Must Return It

We know that whosoever is born of God sinneth not; but he that is begotten of God keepeth himself, and that wicked one toucheth him not. (1 John 5:18)

Don't just ask for Satan to leave you alone; demand that he return what he has taken from you. By the power of the Holy Spirit, you have the awesome authority to tell the devil what to do. Put Satan in his place. Jesus never "counseled" out demons. He boldly confronted them and cast them out!

A battle line has been drawn between God and Satan. You should demand that everything the devil has taken or disrupted be put back on God's side of the line. Even more, tell him to stay in his place and leave you alone.

_____

_____

_____

_____

_____

_____

_____

_____

_____

_____

_____

_____

_____

_____

_____

"It's time for Satan to return all he has stolen from you. Demand the return!"

Endued With Power

For these are not drunken, as ye suppose, seeing it is but the third hour of the day. But this is that which was spoken by the prophet Joel; And it shall come to pass in the last days, saith God, I will pour out of my Spirit upon all flesh: and your sons and your daughters shall prophesy, and your young men shall see visions, and your old men shall dream dreams: and on my servants and on my handmaidens I will pour out in those days of my Spirit; and they shall prophesy: And I will shew wonders in the heaven above, and signs in the earth beneath; blood, and fire, and vapour of smoke. (Acts 2:15-19)

It is time to lose our inhibitions and once again begin to experience the compassion of Jesus, to cry for the lost souls of the world and weep for those trapped in sin. Our churches need to be filled with manifestations of the gifts of: tongues and interpretation of tongues, prophecy, the word of wisdom, the word of knowledge, discerning of spirits, wonder-working faith, the gift of the working of miracles and the gifts of healing (1 Corinthians 12:8-10).

Satan has robbed us long enough. We desperately need the Holy Spirit and His gifts back in our theology and in our lives. "For as many as are led by the Spirit of God, they are the sons of God" (Romans 8:14).

We have two choices. We can either continue to sit quietly in our little churches while the world rushes headlong into hell, or we can declare, "I am going to get everything God promised me. I am going to become endued with power from on high."

_____

_____

_____

_____

_____

_____

"It's time to be endued with power from on high."

Total Immersion

And they were all filled with the Holy Ghost, and began to speak with other tongues, as the Spirit gave them utterance. (Acts 2:4)

The baptism in the Holy Ghost is not the work of man; it comes straight from heaven. When His power touches your life He will set you on fire with the things of God. He will give you a love for the Word of God that is insatiable. He will give you a spiritual hunger that cannot be quenched.

To *baptize* means "to immerse fully, to bury."

The Lord is ready to immerse you, to overshadow your life with His power and move you into the realm of the supernatural. He wants to baptize you into Himself and give you power over devils, sickness and sin.

It is time to let the rivers of living water flow into your life and to experience a baptism of fire and power. Yield every member of your body to the Holy Spirit—your heart, your mind, and yes, even your tongue.

"Let living waters flow out of you."

Healing Will Be Manifested

And Jesus went about all the cities and villages, teaching in their synagogues, and preaching the gospel of the kingdom, and healing every sickness and every disease among the people.
(Matthew 9:35)

We may not want to admit it, but we are in the midst of an onslaught from hell called sickness and disease. Satan has tried to steal divine healing from the church.

While the church expounds experimental theology and looks for new answers to old questions, there are suffering, bleeding, dying people in the world around us. Where are the miracles we read about in Scripture?

Once the church understood the truth of Calvary. Christ died for our sin, and there is healing in the atonement (Isaiah 53:3-5). Today, however, millions of people who inhabit our churches accept salvation but no longer accept divine healing. They ignore the Word that says, "Who his own self bare our sins in his own body on the tree, that we, being dead to sins, should live unto righteousness: by whose stripes ye were healed" (1 Peter 2:24).

People read about God's provision for healing of the human body, but as they see the overwhelming amount of sickness and disease and observe an apparent absence of healing manifestations, their logic reasons that since they do not see divine healing, it must not be for today.

_____

_____

_____

_____

_____

_____

_____

_____

"Healing will be manifested in the revolutionary church."

According To Your Faith

But he was wounded for our transgressions, he was bruised for our iniquities: the chastisement of our peace was upon him; and with his stripes we are healed. (Isaiah 53:5)

There is also the question of faith. Again and again, when Christ healed those who were sick, He said, "Be it done according to your faith." Remember this: Faith begins where the will of God is known! It *is* God's will to heal you.

Your heavenly Father has one objective concerning your healing, and that is His will to heal you. Healing is not a promise. It is a fact.

The same blood that washed away your sins took the pain out of your body. Jesus bore every disease—from the common cold to cancer. Today, let your faith arise. Tell Satan you are restoring the bridge to your healing and, by faith, accept the total work of Calvary.

Exercise your faith for healing. Walk in your healing as you count down toward the new millennium.

_____

_____

_____

_____

_____

_____

_____

_____

_____

_____

_____

"Your healing is not a wish; it is a reality through the cross of Christ."

Heaven's Floodgates

Bring ye all the tithes into the storehouse, that there may be meat in mine house, and prove me now herewith, saith the LORD of Hosts, if I will not open you the windows of heaven, and pour you out a blessing, that there shall not be room enough to receive it. (Malachi 3:10)

Whether the world likes it or not, I serve a God who promises He will supply all my needs and who continues to release His abundance.

The floodgates of heaven stand wide open to me as I tithe and give offerings unto the Lord who is my source and meets my every need. When I do all that I can do, He does the rest. His provision far exceeds my wildest imaginations.

In this new millennium, sowing and harvest will happen in the same season. You will sow from one hand and reap in another. Your blessings will overflow, and you will be blessed in order to bless others.

Make it your aim to give, for you can never outgive God. You can never outgive God. What are you prepared to sow into the kingdom of God today?

_____

_____

_____

_____

_____

_____

_____

_____

_____

_____

_____

_____

"The floodgates of heaven open wide this year to pour out heaven's blessing upon you."

The Lord Remembers

And she vowed a vow, and said, O LORD of hosts, if thou wilt indeed look on the affliction of thine handmaid, and remember me, and not forget thine handmaid, but wilt give unto thy handmaid a man child, then I will give him unto the LORD all the days of his life, and there shall no razor come upon his head. (1 Samuel 1:11)

Hannah was barren and prayed for years that somehow she could have a child. It was to no avail. She finally reached the point where she did not care what others thought. She was going to boldly approach God.

A few verses later we read these marvelous words: ". . . and the Lord remembered her" (v. 19).

After years of praying, God not only answered, but also opened the floodgates of heaven and gave her a blessing she could scarcely contain. She bore a son—and five more children besides!

Hannah also understood the law of sowing and reaping. You must plant what you lack. If you want apples, plant apple seeds. If you lack oranges, plant orange seeds. Hannah lacked children, so she agreed to sow her first child back to God. God remembers your faithfulness in sowing and will bring your harvest in due season. Boldly approach His throne with your needs.

_____

_____

_____

_____

_____

_____

_____

_____

_____

"God remembers your sowing and will usher in your harvest."

Praying and Giving

There was a certain man in Caesarea called Cornelius, a centurion of the band called the Italian band, a devout man, and one that feared God with all his house, which gave much alms to the people, and prayed to God alway. (Acts 10:1,2)

In the Book of Acts you can read about a man named Cornelius, who learned what happens when mixing praying and giving.

One day, as he was praying, an angel appeared to Cornelius and said, "Thy prayers and thine alms are come up for a memorial before God. And now send men to Joppa, and call for one Simon, whose surname is Peter" (Acts 10:4,5).

The Lord not only answered the prayer of Cornelius, but prepared Peter in a vision to come to the man's home and to introduce the message of salvation, healing and deliverance to the entire Gentile world! Prayer and giving are a powerful, explosive combination. Today, what will you pray? What will you give?

_____

_____

_____

_____

_____

_____

_____

_____

_____

_____

*"Two mighty weapons which destroy
the enemy's strongholds are prayer and giving."*

Financial Freedom in Christ

Give and it shall be given unto you; good measure, pressed down, and shaken together, and running over. (Luke 6:38a)

We need to stop being timid with our requests to the Lord. The giver of all gifts says, "Ask and it shall be given you"(Matthew 7:7).

The world has come to the conclusion that the only way to become financially prosperous is to lie, cheat and steal. The Lord has another plan.

It is time for God's people to say, "Satan, you didn't give it to me, and you are not going to take it away. It is none of your business how I am blessed. I am the apple of God's eye. I am the righteousness of God in Christ. Jesus shed His blood for me, and my God created more than enough for all of us."

In this new millennium, declare your financial freedom! List the blessings God has already provided for your freedom:

_____

_____

_____

_____

_____

_____

_____

_____

_____

_____

_____

_____

"This is the day to declare financial freedom in Christ Jesus!"

The Pillar of Faith

If ye have faith as a grain of mustard seed, ye shall say to this mountain, Remove hence to yonder place; and it shall remove; and nothing shall be impossible unto you. (Matthew 17:20)

How strong is your faith? Has it been weakened and worn away by the constant attacks of unbelievers? Has Satan planted seeds of doubt that have grown into weeds of uncertainty and distrust?

Many people believe it takes a mountain of faith to move the smallest problem, when just the opposite is true.

There is no alternative for a simple, deep-rooted faith that is anchored in Almighty God. Stop looking. You have found the answer: faith in God!

Many people make the fatal mistake of building their lives on decisions. The problem, however, is that we can make the *wrong* decisions. Instead, build your life on a solid foundation of Jesus Christ.

"Stop trusting your decisions. Trust Christ."

Faith's Beginning

How then shall they call on him in whom they have not believed? And how shall they believe in him of whom they have not heard? (Romans 10:14)

I have met people who have attempted to call upon God before they even knew Him. Faith begins when you hear the message of Christ. Next comes believing. When you receive God's message as your own, you are in a position to call upon Him. By taking these steps, you will hear God say, "Call unto me, and I will answer thee, and shew thee great and mighty things, which thou knowest not" (Jeremiah 33:3).

Oh, the power of miracle-working faith—it can cool the fevered brow of your infant child. It can put bread on your table when you don't have a dollar to your name. Faith can turn your midnight into dawn.

Today is the day for calling upon the Lord not just when you need something but when you need Him. Call upon Him at home, at work, at school and at play. Don't hang up . . . make your call continuous and ongoing.

_____

_____

_____

_____

_____

_____

_____

_____

_____

_____

_____

_____

_____

"Call upon the Lord every moment of today."

Hope in the Lord

Why art thou cast down, O my soul? And why art thou disquieted within me? Hope thou in God: for I shall yet praise him for the help of his countenance. (Psalm 42:5)

Hope is not the result of self-produced wishing or dreaming. It is anchored in God Himself. As the psalmist wrote, "My soul, wait thou only upon God; for my expectation is from him"(Psalm 62:5).

Hope is not projecting my expectations on God. It is not a wish list and God is not a Santa Claus. Rather, hope is expecting God. Hope expects God to act and fulfill His promises in His sovereign way.

Hope in the Lord. Fill up today with hope and expectation to meet God at every turn.

_____

_____

_____

_____

_____

_____

_____

_____

_____

_____

_____

_____

_____

_____

_____

_____

"Hope expects God to act in His way."

Risen!

He is not here: for he has risen, as he said. Come see the place where the Lord lay. And go quickly, and tell his disciples that he is risen from the dead. (Matthew 28:6,7a)

Can you imagine how the disciples felt when they saw Christ being nailed to the cross? Their hopes were shattered. Their dreams were crushed. It seemed everything they had envisioned had suddenly disappeared. Their agony did not last long, however.

On the third day, Mary Magdalene and the other Mary came to the sepulcher. "And behold, there was a great earthquake: for the angel of the Lord descended from heaven, and came and rolled back the stone from the door, and sat upon it"(Matthew 28:2).

And the angel said to them, "He is not here: for he has risen, as he said. Come see the place where the Lord lay. And go quickly, and tell his disciples that he is risen from the dead" (Matthew 28:6,7).

Christ stands as the apex of our hope; the crown jewel of our faith. He lives! He lives in this year and into the new millennium. Meet Him today and spend time in His presence.

_____

_____

_____

_____

_____

_____

_____

_____

_____

_____

_____

"He lives. Meet Him everywhere you turn."

No Shame!

And hope maketh not ashamed; because the love of God is shed abroad in our hearts by the Holy Ghost which is given unto us. (Romans 5:5)

Hope is the adrenal gland of the spirit. Just the simple act of thinking about something God has in store for the saints sets off a dynamic chain reaction within us that is difficult to describe. We are suddenly "quickened."

The anchor of hope is in the power of the resurrection. Because He lives, we too shall live. As believers we know that death is not the end, but a miraculous beginning.

Without expectation and belief we become slaves to apathy, indifference and perpetual gloom. Expectation changes pessimism to confidence in an instant. Live boldly and confidently today. This is your season to hope in the Lord.

"You can live positively and confidently in hope."

Love Your Enemies

But I say unto you which hear, Love your enemies, do good to them which hate you, bless them that curse you, and pray for them which despitefully use you. And unto him that smiteth thee on the one cheek offer also the other. (Luke 6:27-29a)

The world seems to talk endlessly about love, but we see very little demonstrated. Instead, as a nation we have worshiped at the shrine of hatred and violence. Even Christians, it seems, derive enjoyment from watching dramatic stories filled with conflict and hate.

Why are our children violent? It is a direct result of their training. I am told that by the time a child in America is 16, they have watched on television 200,000 acts of violence, including over 100,000 cold-blooded murders.

The theme of God's Word is the direct opposite. Moses taught that we must love our neighbor. Jesus added something more. He said that we are not only to love our neighbor, but we must love our enemy, too.

Think of an enemy that you need to forgive and to love today. Refuse to go into the next millennium with offense or unforgiveness in your heart. Write down whom you need to forgive and love:

_____

_____

_____

_____

_____

_____

_____

_____

_____

_____

"Decide to forgive and love your enemies today."

Revival Begins in Us

Though I speak with the tongues of men and of angels, and have not charity, I am become as sounding brass, or a tinkling cymbal.
(1 Corinthians 13:1)

Here is one of the most startling revelations in Scripture. We know that the great revival at the end of time will ride on the wings of the gifts of the Holy Spirit. How does your life measure up to God's Word?

What happens in the pulpit does not impress God. I am sure there are times the Lord must place His hands over His ears and declare, "The way you live is talking so loudly I cannot hear what you are saying."

The Bible says, "If a man say, I love God, and hateth his brother, he is a liar: for he that loveth not his brother whom he hath seen, how can he love God whom he hath not seen?" (1 John 4:20)

If your heart is yearning for revival, let it begin with you. Find people who are lonely and tell them, "Jesus loved you so much that He refused to live without you. He died on the Cross to make you His own." Who will you tell about Jesus today?

_____

_____

_____

_____

_____

_____

_____

_____

_____

_____

*"On the other side of your obedience
is a soul waiting to hear the Gospel."*

Let's Party With God

Then saith he to his servants, The wedding is ready, but they which were bidden were not worthy. Go ye therefore into the highways, and as many as ye shall find, bid to the marriage.
(Matthew 22:8,9)

Jesus knew how to party in style. He performed his first miracle at a wedding feast in Canaan of Galilee where He turned water into wine. And when He pronounced a perpetual party as He stood in the synagogue and proclaimed, "It's Jubilee," He became the life of the party.

There's another party in preparation—the marriage feast of the Lamb. The curtain is rising on the last act of human drama. The party of the ages is about to commence. The proclamation has been published! The invitations have all been sent and they read, "Let all who will come." The stage is set. The participants are in place. The time is now, and I want to announce the place is here! Let us declare: "Let the party last all night. Jehovah God stands guard over our celebration" (Psalm 5:11 TMB).

_____

_____

_____

_____

_____

_____

_____

_____

_____

_____

_____

"The Bridegroom has prepared a feast for you.
Have you accepted the invitation to come?"

God's Abundance

For I know the thoughts that I think toward you, saith the Lord, thoughts of peace, and not of evil, to give you an expected end. (Jeremiah 29:11)

Just as water flows along a steady course, God, your Father, has a well-designed plan for you. You need to know that He has been working on your situation before you were born.

God wants you to live in abundance more that you want to be there! In the prophetic words written on these pages you will discover provision, protection, supply and security. The Bible declares: "Beloved, I wish above all things that thou mayest prosper and be in health, even as thy soul prospereth (3 John 2). Today, prosper and be in health.

_____

_____

_____

_____

_____

_____

_____

_____

_____

_____

_____

_____

_____

_____

_____

_____

"The abundance of God will overflow your life today."

Covenant Blessing

For ye know how that afterward, when he would have inherited the blessing, he was rejected: for he found no place of repentance, though he sought it carefully with tears. (Hebrews 12:17)

The last bastion of satanic resistance is your money, and though you will tolerate lack, Jesus will not. Today we do not offer animal sacrifices, but instead we wrap our money in leather purses and wallets. Don't leave your finances back in Egypt, because once you surrender this to God, He has everything.

There is a great price to pay when we make the wrong exchange. Esau, the firstborn son of Isaac and Rebekah, came home after a long, unsuccessful hunting expedition, weary to the point of exhaustion. Jacob, knowing how hungry his brother was, offered to feed him, on one condition. He said, "Sell me this day thy birthright" (Genesis 25:31). Esau pulled the piece of paper out and agreed to the exchange.

The covenant blessing is our birthright as children of God, to be treasured like a precious diamond. Never let it go, for it holds the promise of God's continual supply. What will you do this year to hold onto your covenant blessing?

_____

_____

_____

_____

_____

_____

_____

_____

_____

_____

"Perpetual provision flows through God's covenant blessing for you."

Exchange and Repentance

I beseech you therefore, brethren, by the mercies of God that ye present your bodies a living sacrifice, holy, acceptable unto God, which is your reasonable service. And be not conformed to this world: but be ye transformed by the renewing of your mind, that ye may prove what is that good, and acceptable, and perfect, will of God. (Romans 12:1,2)

The process of exchange begins with repentance. Repentance means to change your mind about God and toward God.

This transformation includes a mind that is renewed and a heart that is cleansed by the blood of Christ. To victoriously exchange your old sin habits for God's kingdom, your mind needs to be totally free of confusion or double-mindedness. Renew your mind in Christ daily.

_____

_____

_____

_____

_____

_____

_____

_____

_____

_____

_____

_____

_____

_____

_____

_____

"A renewed mind and new heart are necessary for radical faith."

The Process of Possession

And it shall be, when thou art come in unto the land which the LORD thy God giveth thee for an inheritance, and possessest it, and dwellest therein.
(Deuteronomy 26:1)

God's abundance is available to all, but Deuteronomy 26:1 reveals that you have to possess your spiritual territory. If you ask any army strategist, you will discover that possession means to drive out and spoil the previous tenants. Colossians 2:15 declares, "And having spoiled principalities and powers, he [Jesus] made a shew of them openly, triumphing over them in it."

Everything around us is moving speedily toward the consummation of all things when Jesus Christ will return and we will reign with Him for 1000 years. Satan will be bound, the lion will lay down with the lamb and peace will be ours. But, if you look around, you will notice we are still in a battle against the enemy of our souls.

Fight the good fight of faith into the new millennium. Don't quit. Determine to endure until Jesus returns.

_____

_____

_____

_____

_____

_____

_____

_____

_____

_____

_____

"This year, drive Satan out of his stronghold and possess your land."

Submit Your Finances to Christ

But let him ask in faith, nothing wavering. For he that wavereth is like a wave of the sea driven with the wind and tossed. For let not that man think that he shall receive any thing of the Lord. A double minded man is unstable in all his ways. (James 1:6-8)

The double-minded man is in a struggle between his soul and his spirit, between his mind and his heart. In order to rid your life of this problem forever, you must submit to God's line of authority to totally govern your life.

If you will submit your financial future to the headship of Christ, you will experience the freedom and security His authority brings, and say good-bye to both confusion and double-mindedness. Describe the ways you will submit to the headship of Christ in your finances:

_____

_____

_____

_____

_____

_____

_____

_____

_____

_____

_____

_____

_____

_____

"It's time to submit all your finances to the headship of Christ."

Counteract Fear with Faith

Fear thou not, for I am with thee: be not dismayed; for I am thy God: I will strengthen thee; yea, I will help thee; yea I will uphold thee with the right hand of my righteousness. (Isaiah 41:10)

You must counteract fear with faith. Faith and fear cannot coexist in the same heart. Abraham was strong in faith, because he did not waver or vacillate. In other words, he did not slide back and forth between two opinions. This is a common problem among Christians. When they receive their paychecks on Friday their faith is at an all-time high, but by the time they balance their checkbooks, fear has replaced their expectation.

Where there is doubt concerning God's will to prosper you, perfect faith cannot exist. Why is this true? When the will of God is known, faith comes alive, and fear dies. Psalm 35:27b says, "Let the LORD be magnified, which hath pleasure in the prosperity of his servant." If He had not wanted you to prosper, He would not have created prosperity. Abundance is not a promise; it is a fact.

Describe how expectation and faith have replaced fear in your life:

_____

_____

_____

_____

_____

_____

_____

_____

_____

_____

_____

"In the revolutionary church, doubt is crushed by faith."

It's Yours!

The land was not able to bear them, that they might dwell together: for their substance was great. (Genesis 13:6)

In Leviticus 27:16 the ancient Hebrews measured their land by the amount of seed it would take to sow it. Lot and Abraham separated, because the land was not sufficient to support both of them.

God is not concerned about how much land you own, but rather, how productive you are. Results are more important than acreage. The Lord not only provides provision, but He also provides protection.

What fruit is your life producing? Christ will protect you this year so that your life might bear the good fruit of giving, witnessing and serving. Describe how you will give, witness and serve Him today:

_____

_____

_____

_____

_____

_____

_____

_____

_____

_____

_____

_____

_____

_____

_____

_____

"How productive are you for Jesus Christ?"

You Are Protected

Verily, verily, I say unto you, If a man keep my saying, he shall never see death. (John 8:51)

The meaning of these words in the Greek is that we are placed in a position of absolute protection, chaperoned, as a father would protect his virgin daughters.

God will drive off those who would steal the seeds from the land you possess and protect your field from intruders. He is concerned about your finances, your family and your marriage—every aspect of your life.

God is protecting you, your family and every part of your life today. Describe the many ways you have experienced God's protection:

_____

_____

_____

_____

_____

_____

_____

_____

_____

_____

_____

_____

_____

_____

_____

_____

"God jealously protects you from the enemy."

Redeemed By Your Kinsman

And the women said unto Naomi, Blessed be the LORD, which hath not left thee this day without a kinsman, that his name may be famous in Israel. And he shall be unto thee a restorer of thy life, and a nourisher of thine old age: for thy daughter in law, which loveth thee, which is better to thee than seven sons, hath born him. (Ruth 4:14,15)

Boaz fell in love with Ruth, but there was another near kinsman who had the right, but not the will, to redeem her. This kinsman took off his sandals, symbolizing his unwillingness to walk on the stony ground. This was a sign to Boaz that he could sow the seed necessary to redeem the land of Ruth's dead husband. In order to take possession and provide protection, you not only need the legal right, but also the will to redeem.

Jesus had both the right and the will to redeem lost humanity. God was willing to sow the necessary seed, through His only Son, Jesus, in the borrowed tomb of Joseph of Arimathea. That seed sprang to life and remains alive today. Romans 8:29 says that Jesus became the firstborn among many brethren. His seed greatly multiplied, and we are the harvest on that seed sown.

_____

_____

_____

_____

_____

_____

_____

_____

_____

"Jesus is your Kinsman Redeemer."

Planting Peas

And after him was Shammah the son of Agee the Hararite. And the Philistines were gathered together into a troop, where was a piece of ground full of lentiles: and the people fled from the Philistines. But he stood in the midst of the ground, and defended it, and slew the Philistines: and the LORD wrought a great victory.
(2 Samuel 23:11-12)

There was a pea farmer who lived in the time of David by the name of Shammah. Year after year he planted his crops, nurtured and watered them, and waited expectantly for his harvest. But each year when it was time to reap the toil of his hard labor, he would look up in the noonday sun and see empty wagons coming over the hills. They were the wagons of his adversaries, the Philistines, who came to rape and ravage his harvest.

One day Shammah was toiling in his field. He was practically exhausted when he looked up and saw the Philistines, again looking to plunder his crops. Scripture records that Shammah "stood in the midst of the ground and defended it" (2 Samuel 23:12).

Shammah planted his feet and determined that he would not be plundered by these Philistine thieves and God was with him! Jehovah Shammah, the Lord who is always present with you, showed up, fought on his behalf and defeated Shammah's adversaries.

You cannot allow anything to threaten your seed. Jehovah Shammah will stand with you as you tell Satan, "Stop. Don't come one step closer."

_____

_____

_____

_____

_____

_____

_____

_____

"Defend the seed that you have planted."

Recount What God Has Done

And he hath brought us into this place, and hath given us this land, even a land that floweth with milk and honey. And now, behold, I have brought the first fruits of the land, which thou, O LORD, hast given me. And thou shalt set it before the LORD thy God, and worship before the LORD thy God: And thou shalt rejoice in every good thing which the LORD thy God hath given unto thee, and unto thine house, thou, and the Levite, and the stranger that is among you. (Deuteronomy 26: 9-11)

Start the process of watering your seed. After claiming your inheritance, after possessing the land and after presenting your gifts to God, it is time to make a declaration and speak to your seed. The children of Israel reminded God of four things.

1) They recounted their origin. Do you remember where the Lord brought you from? The Bible speaks of a time when you "were without Christ" (Ephesians. 2:12).

2) They recounted the persecution. Talking about your past is an opportunity to speak with humility about your experiences. Hebrews 10:32 says, "Call to remembrance the former days."

3) They remembered their deliverance. Egypt was behind them, and the promised land was before them. They had been redeemed. When you recount your deliverance, you are watering your seed.

4. The Israelites recounted their possession of the land. Write down how God is helping you recount God's promises:

_____

_____

_____

_____

_____

_____

"Recount and remember all that God has done in your life."

Hunger and Thirst

Blessed are they which do hunger and thirst after righteousness: for they shall be filled. (Matthew 5:6)

What is your hunger in life? Hungering for physical things only satisfies for a moment, but hungering for spiritual things satisfies eternally.

Your hunger determines how you grow. When you hunger for food and eat constantly, you grow physically. When you hunger for righteousness, then you will grow in acting, speaking and thinking righteously.

How are you growing spiritually? It depends on your hunger. Feed today on God's Word.

_____

_____

_____

_____

_____

_____

_____

_____

_____

_____

_____

_____

_____

_____

_____

_____

"Fill your day with a hunger for His righteousness."

God's Word Is Not Bound

Wherein I suffer trouble, as an evil doer, even unto bonds; but the word of God is not bound.
(2 Timothy 2:9)

When Paul was imprisoned in Rome, he wrote to Timothy. Paul knew deep inside that when he spoke the Word, there were no chains that could keep his body down. We will reap tomorrow the seeds of the words we sow today.

In Jeremiah, chapter 1, the Lord asked Jeremiah, "What do you see?" The prophet responded, "I see a rod of an almond tree" (Jeremiah 1:11). He saw it blossoming and bearing fruit in the middle of winter.

Why do we offer sacrifices of praise to God? When the fruit of our lips gives thanks to His name, He gives perpetual abundance throughout the entire year, regardless of what season it is. The process of watering your seed includes faith, belief and confession. Praise God for the fact that your soil is being watered and your harvest is on the way. Write your praise:

_____

_____

_____

_____

_____

_____

_____

_____

_____

_____

_____

_____

"Offer God the sacrifices of praise."

Sow and Possess

Isaac sowed in that land, and received in the same year an hundredfold: and the LORD blessed him.
(Genesis 26:12)

This principle has been practiced by farmers since the first field was cleared and the first crop was planted. In ancient Israel, there was once a famine so great that Isaac was ready to flee to Egypt. There was no rain. The fields were bare. There was nothing but parched, dry ground.

But the Lord had another plan. He appeared to Isaac and said, "Dwell in the land which I shall tell thee of" (Genesis 26:2).

Following the Lord's command, Isaac tilled the soil and planted seed. He reaped an abundant harvest and he possessed the land. Are you sowing and possessing?

_____

_____

_____

_____

_____

_____

_____

_____

_____

_____

_____

_____

_____

*"Sowing good seed and possessing the land
is your purpose in the new millennium."*

Offices of Authority

And he gave some, apostles; and some, prophets; and some, evangelists; and some, pastors and teachers. (Ephesians 4:11)

Christ is our High Priest, but He has designated and ordained His representatives here on earth, and set some in office according to the fivefold ministry found in Ephesians.

To God, the office is much more important than the officeholder. What is an office? It is the place where the work of the Lord is done.

Ask yourself this question. Is Ronald Reagan or George Bush the President of the United States? No. These men are no longer in office. The person who occupies the White House only *functions in* the office of the President. He has been given the constitutional authority to function in that role. The office is far more powerful than the men who hold that office.

In order to operate in the proper spiritual authority and have the blessing of God operating in our midst, it is imperative that any person who holds an office in our churches must be called and chosen by the Lord.

People don't understand that when you have been chosen by the Lord to hold an office in His kingdom, an astounding thing happens. He gives you not only the authority and the responsibility, but He also supplies the knowledge, wisdom, understanding and skills necessary to perform the tasks. Has God chosen you to occupy an office?

_____

_____

_____

_____

_____

_____

_____

_____

_____

"The revolutionary church has God's chosen people in the offices of authority."

Giving Millions

Now consider how great this man was, unto whom even the patriarch Abraham gave the tenth of the spoils. (Hebrews 7:4)

Abraham, returning from the defeat of five kings, met Melchisedec, the king of Salem, and priest of the most high God. When they met, Abraham presented not a small bounty but possessions worth millions. He was giving his tithe to a man he had never seen before. He had no idea how the priest was going to use the funds, nor did he question him as to what he intended to do with it. That was not Abraham's responsibility. He was only told to obey.

When we obey in the natural, something transpires in the realm of the supernatural. The priest to whom you hand God's tithe and your offering is temporary, but in the Lord's sight, the spirit of that office is eternal.

"Make certain the priest to whom you give your tithe is serving the Most High God."

Walk in Unity

You are cursed with a curse: for ye have robbed me, even this whole nation. (Malachi 3:9)

Thousands of people can suffer at the expense of someone taking what belongs to God. The Lord spoke through the prophet Malachi that the people had robbed Him in tithes and offerings.

Even though some gave, God considered it a national sin. I strongly believe that one of the main reasons we are not seeing a mighty revival across America and around the world today is because so many Christians are disobedient in their giving. The moment the body of Christ gets this revelation and begins to walk in unity, we will have the blessing promised to us in Psalm 133:1-3:

"Behold, how good and how pleasant it is for brethren to dwell together in unity! It is like the precious ointment upon the head, that ran down upon the beard, even Aaron's beard: that went down to the skirts of his garments; As the dew of Hermon, and as the dew that descended upon the mountains of Zion: for there the LORD commanded the blessing, even life for evermore."

"Walk in the blessing Christ has promised you."

You Are Anointed!

You shall also decide and decree a thing, and it shall be established for you; and the light [of God's favor] shall shine upon your ways . . . You shall also decide and decree a thing, and it shall be established for you; and the light [of God's favor] shall shine upon your ways. (Job 22:28,30 AMP)

What can Satan do to you? How can he affect your life or your family? When the alien armies of the Antichrist assail themselves against you in full battle array, and they see the blood painted upon your life and your loved ones, they will have to pass over!

You may say, "I need a job;" or "I need a healing in my body;" or "I need to be free from addiction;" or "I need renewal in my spirit." God is in the healing and delivering business. By His anointing He wants to deliver you from sin, sickness, disease, depression and every devastating blow of the enemy! Job 22 declares that God's favor will shine upon your ways.

Through His Anointing, it is the deep desire of the Lord to touch every area of your life with the oil of His Spirit. He wants to restore families and marriages everywhere. God wants to paint those in pain with His healing anointing. God wants to paint those with broken hearts with a healing balm.

The Holy Ghost's radar is locked in on you right now. You may not know how you will survive the insurmountable mountain facing your life, but God has already planned your escape and anointed you to receive your breakthrough! You are anointed!

_____

_____

_____

_____

_____

_____

_____

"You are anointed to fulfill God's plan."

Abundant Rain

There is a sound of abundance of rain.
(1 Kings 18:41b)

Your situation may look hopeless, and the winds may seem to be blowing you farther away from the shore of your miracle, but keep walking in the Word!

Elijah's servant had heard the same words 6 times before, "Go again"(1 Kings 17 and 18). The command from the prophet was clear, concise and confronting. The words came 3 years after this same man cried out to God and ordered the rain to cease.

Famine swept the land, and nothing remained of the once fertile ground. Fields of grain had turned to dust, and the leaves had withered on their trees. Signs of life were drowned out by the overcoming forces of death. But on that day Elijah had experienced great victory. Fire had fallen; the prophets of Baal had been slain. God had once again displayed his mighty arm against His enemies.

In the midst of famine, standing at the top of Mount Carmel, Elijah cried out, "There is a sound of abundance of rain" (1 Kings 18:41b).

_____

_____

_____

_____

_____

_____

_____

_____

_____

_____

_____

"Be refreshed in the abundance of rain falling on you from heaven."

Unclean Seed

Whosoever committeth sin transgresseth also the law: for sin is the transgression of the law.
(1 John 3:4)

What does the word unclean mean? It means to use your seed for anything other than its intended purpose.

How can you expect to have a field of golden grain when you plant rows and rows of diseased, contaminated seed? The root of the problem is much too deep for that.

Across the world there is a great deal of confusion regarding sin, but the Bible gives us this definition:

"Whosoever committeth sin transgresseth also the law: for sin is the transgression of the law" (1 John 3:4).

Sin is lawlessness. In other words, it is not a regulation or an ordinance. Instead, it is a deed. It is not the absence of law, but rather, the breaking of the law that produces iniquity. God sets a standard for our moral and physical behavior. It is a "mark" that our actions are measured against.

_____

_____

_____

_____

_____

_____

_____

_____

_____

_____

_____

_____

"This year stop sowing unclean seed."

Two Reasons For Lack

But every man is tempted, when he is drawn away of his own lust, and enticed. Then when lust hath conceived, it bringeth forth sin: and sin, when it is finished, bringeth forth death. (James 1:14,15)

There are two reasons for lack in your life:

1) The first reason is because **you don't ask God for what you want.** The Bible says: "Ye lust, and have not: ye kill, and desire to have, and cannot obtain: ye fight and war, yet ye have not, because ye ask not" (James 4:2).

2) The second reason for lack is that **you ask amiss.** James 4:3 declares, "Ye ask, and receive not, because ye ask amiss, that ye may consume it upon your own lusts. "

I have stated it before—faith begins where the will of God is known. To ask amiss means to ask with wrong, evil or selfish motives.

Missing the mark is the result of breaking God's law. When that happens, it is sin. James 1:14,15 offers the process which leads down the road to sin.

_____

_____

_____

_____

_____

_____

_____

_____

_____

_____

_____

"God gives you the provision which will eliminate lack in your life."

God Cannot Bless What is Cursed

I have not eaten thereof in my mourning, neither have I taken away ought thereof for any unclean use, nor given ought thereof for the dead: but I have hearkened to the voice of the LORD my God, and have done according to all that thou hast commanded me. (Deuteronomy 26:14)

After Moses taught that God wants our seed to be sown in time of famine and not to be used for anything unclean, he admonishes us in Deuteronomy 26:14 that we should not give *ought thereof for the dead*.

In the sight of God, gifts offered to dead idols, or dead works, is cursed. God gave a warning in Ezekiel 14:8 to those who would set up a stumbling block, such as an idol.

God cannot bless what He has cursed and neither can you. Following the lesson God taught regarding our giving, the Lord gave Moses 12 specific warnings, or curses, upon those who disobey His Word (Deuteronomy 27:15-26). When we attempt to live contrary to that Word and touch what God has cursed, there is nowhere for us to turn.

"Do not expect God to bless what you do, only what He does through you."

Your Breakthrough is Today!

For though we walk in the flesh, we do not war after the flesh: (For the weapons of our warfare are not carnal, but mighty through God to the pulling down of strong holds;) Casting down imaginations, and every high thing that exalteth itself against the knowledge of God, and bringing into captivity every thought to the obedience of Christ. (2 Corinthians 10:3-5)

Your breakthrough will occur when you receive the advanced knowledge of God which will propel you through every line of Satan's defenses.

Your breakthrough does not depend upon your ability, only your availability to be used of God for His purposes. Your breakthrough doesn't depend on weapons of flesh but on spiritual weapons—the sword of the Spirit and the penetrating power of prayer.

Determine that today will be the time and place for a breakthrough in your relationships, finances and faith. Don't wait another moment for your breakthrough. Only 90 days are left until the new millenium. Receive your breakthrough today!

_____

_____

_____

_____

_____

_____

_____

_____

_____

_____

"Seek God for your breakthrough today."

You Are Normal

And he said unto them, Ye are from beneath; I am from above: ye are of this world; I am not of this world. (John 8:23)

Jesus was not of this world. Neither are we. Our kingdom is one of light, not darkness; of the Spirit, not of the flesh; of surrender, not control and of love, not hate.

The kingdom of the world wars against the children of light. As a child of light, you have been born of Spirit and water into God's kingdom, which knows no end. To the world, you now look abnormal. Rest assured it is the world who is abnormal. Radical Christians following Jesus are normal.

Declare today, "I'm not an abnormal person living in a normal world . . . I'm a normal person living in an abnormal world." You are in the world as salt and light . . . you are not of the world. Stop conforming to the world around you and be transformed by Jesus Christ. List all the ways you will no longer conform to the world and then list the way you are conforming to Christ Jesus.

_____

_____

_____

_____

_____

_____

_____

_____

_____

_____

_____

_____

_____

"As a radical follower of Christ, you are truly normal."

Move the Mountain

For verily I say unto you, That whosoever shall say unto this mountain, Be thou removed, and be thou cast into the sea; and shall not doubt in his heart, but shall believe that those things which he saith shall come to pass; he shall have whatsoever he saith. (Mark 11:23)

Right now you can make a decision.

You can allow your mountain to move your faith…
OR
You can allow your faith to move your mountain.

So, what will you decide? Are you tired of sitting at the foot of a mountain and going nowhere? Stop waiting to exercise your faith. Faith acts.

What mountains do your faith need to move today? List them and then act in faith, trusting Christ to destroy every mountain and restore you.

_____

_____

_____

_____

_____

_____

_____

_____

_____

_____

_____

_____

"Choose to have faith in Christ that will move your mountains."

Not Of The World

They are not of the world, even as I am not of the world. (John 17:16)

You are in the world but you are not of the world. So why are you trying to live so close to the world? Too many Christians are trying to walk a fine line between holiness and worldliness; between purity and immorality; and between surrender and selfishness.

No Christian can stand with one foot in the world and the other in the Kingdom. You are either sold out to Christ or you have sold out to the world. Quit trying to see how close you can live to the world and still be saved. It is time to get sin out of your life and to walk the highway of holiness.

Decide today that you will walk in the Kingdom of light, avoiding darkness at every turn. Write a prayer of repentance confessing to the Lord all those areas of compromise with the world in your life. Ask Him for forgiveness and then ask the Holy Spirit to empower you to avoid those "worldly" areas in the future.

_____

_____

_____

_____

_____

_____

_____

_____

_____

_____

_____

*"Stop living on the edge. Move away from
the world and toward holiness."*

We Need The Holy Spirit

And my speech and my preaching was not with enticing words of man's wisdom, but in demonstration of the Spirit and of power: That your faith should not stand in the wisdom of men, but in the power of God. (1 Corinthians 2:4,5)

In a time when a powerless Pentecost has been the norm and not the exception, with more perversion than power, more playboys than prophets and more compromise than conviction . . . we need the Holy Ghost who condescends to indwell mortals and fill us full of Himself.

We need the Holy Ghost because He manifests Himself in holiness and purity. In Him is substance, not style. We need the presence of God's Spirit to empower us to live what we preach and walk what we talk.

Ask the Holy Spirit to fill and empower you today.

"Holy Spirit, fill me with your power."

To See Jesus

The same came therefore to Philip, which was of Bethsaida of Galilee, and desired him, saying, Sir, we would see Jesus. (John 12:21)

Honestly, it would not really matter to me if the gates of heaven were made of wood and if they swung on leather hinges.

It would not matter to me if there was mud in the streets knee-deep and the mansions were nothing more than cardboard shanties.

Because, when I look down to the end of that muddy street, to the end of that heavenly boulevard, I will see the One who took my place. Radical faith hungers to see the Savior and to passionately love the One who died for us. Is your faith radical?

"Desire this: to see Jesus."

Understand Revelation

Fear none of those things which thou shalt suffer: behold, the devil shall cast some of you into prison, that ye may be tried; and ye shall have tribulation ten days: be thou faithful unto death, and I will give thee a crown of life. (Revelation 2:10)

So many people are confused about the last book of the Bible, but there is no reason to be confused about it.

In fact, if there is any generation in the history of the world that should understand the book of Revelation—it is this one. We are the end time generation. We stand in this countdown to the millennium on the precipice of eternity.

The end approaches and Revelation calls for a radical church willing to endure suffering and martyrdom in order to serve the King of kings. Are you willing to serve Him? Are you passionately hot for Jesus? Are you an overcomer?

_____

_____

_____

_____

_____

_____

_____

_____

_____

_____

_____

_____

_____

"Revelation calls us to become radical and revolutionary for Christ."

The Lamp of His Word

Thy word is a lamp unto my feet, and a light unto my path. (Psalm 119:105)

We are watching prophecy be fulfilled every day. We don't need the evening news to interpret the signs of the times. Just read the Bible, and you will know the news before it happens.

There will be earthquakes and famines. There will be disease and war. There will be signs in the heavens and false Christs running around everywhere. The Bible painted an accurate picture of the approaching millennium. Use it as your spiritual roadmap into the new millennium.

"Let the Word be your guide in the new millennium."

God Heals

Surely he hath borne our griefs, and carried our sorrows: yet we did esteem him stricken, smitten of God, and afflicted. But he was wounded for our transgressions, he was bruised for our iniquities: the chastisement of our peace was upon him; and with his stripes we are healed. (Isaiah 53:4,5)

There are still those who ask,

"Is God able to heal?"

Able?!

God set the world spinning on its axis and commanded the oceans not to spill a drop. When your body isn't functioning correctly, who better is there to turn to that the One who created you?

You are fearfully and wonderfully made (Psalm 139:14). Ask the Great Physician to heal your today. When you receive your healing write down your praise for all He has done.

_____

_____

_____

_____

_____

_____

_____

_____

_____

_____

_____

_____

_____

"God heals. It's not a hope . . . it's a fact."

Spirit-Frilled

And when Simon saw that through laying on of the apostles' hands the Holy Ghost was given, he offered them money, saying, Give me also this power, that on whomsoever I lay hands, he may receive the Holy Ghost. But Peter said unto him, thy money perish with thee, because thou hast thought that the gift of God may be purchased with money. Thou hast neither part nor lot in this matter: for thy heart is not right in the sight of God. Repent therefore of this thy wickedness, and pray God, if perhaps the thought of thine heart may be forgiven thee. (Acts 8:18-22)

Many who claim they have experienced the baptism of the Holy Ghost are more dead than alive, more off than on, more wrong than right.

Some are more spirit "frilled" than spirit filled. They have been used to the "outer fringe of His works" and have forgotten the "inner essence of His power."

We must avoid Simon the Magician's example of seeking the gifts more than the giver and the power more than the presence of God's Spirit. What will you do to seek His presence today?

_____

_____

_____

_____

_____

_____

_____

_____

_____

_____

_____

_____

"Seek the Spirit's presence, not His presents."

Deal Quickly and Thoroughly with Sin

If we confess our sins, he is faithful and just to forgive us our sins, and to cleanse us from all unrighteousness. If we say that we have not sinned, we make him a liar, and his word is not in us.
(1 John 1:9,10)

Sin is sly. It works much like a cat playing with a ball of yarn. It's fun for a little while, but before you know it, its cords of death will have wrapped around you, and you will find yourself entangled by your despair.

When you sin, the best action to take is confession. Remember, the only sin God cannot forgive is unconfessed sin.

Take an honest look at yourself today. Is there unconfessed sin in your life? If so, confess it and deal with sin quickly and thoroughly.

_____

_____

_____

_____

_____

_____

_____

_____

_____

_____

_____

_____

_____

_____

"Now is the time to confess sin. Do not let it get a foothold in your life."

Obey and Avoid Satan's Snare

Surely he shall deliver thee from the snare of the fowler, and from the noisome pestilence. He shall cover thee with his feathers, and under his wings shalt thou trust: his truth shall be thy shield and buckler. (Psalm 91:3,4)

When a mother loudly says, "No!" or slaps her baby's hand as it reaches for a hot oven, she is protecting her child.

When God gave His commandments to His children, He was doing the same thing. The commandments of God were given for our protection.

Obeying God is the only sure way to avoid the devil's trap. Trying to sidestep obedience will lead you directly into Satan's snare.

Obey God and live. Disobey, and face the consequences of sin, which all end in death. Choose to obey God today.

"Obedience becomes a protective shield from sin."

A Heart for God

But now thy kingdom shall not continue: the LORD hath sought him a man after his own heart, and the LORD hath commanded him to be captain over his people, because thou hast not kept that which the LORD commanded thee. (1 Samuel 13:14)

In the midst of the trials of life, it is one thing to know God. It is another thing to have God say, "I know this man. I know his heart. I know he will faithfully serve me."

Let your desire be to have a broken and contrite heart.

Ask God's Spirit to break your heart of stone and give you a heart of flesh. Seek a new heart from the Lord so you will be called, "a man after the heart of God."

"Lord, give me a heart after Yours."

Fasting

Moreover when ye fast, be not, as the hypocrites, of a sad countenance: for they disfigure their faces, that they may appear unto men to fast. Verily I say unto you, they have their reward. But thou, when thou fastest, anoint thine head, and wash thy face; that thou appear not unto men to fast, but unto thy Father which is in secret: and thy Father, which seeth in secret, shall reward thee openly. (Matthew 6:16-18)

Fasting is not a hunger strike against God—trying to persuade Him to do something, or wanting Him to feel sorry for you because you haven't eaten.

Instead, fasting is a denial of self that brings you to a point where you can align your spirit with what God already intends to do.

Are you willing to fast today or this week so that you can spend time with the Lord and listen to His voice? If so, write down when and why you will fast.

_____

_____

_____

_____

_____

_____

_____

_____

_____

_____

_____

_____

"Fast so that you may hear more clearly the voice of God."

Mighty in Battle

Lift up your heads, O ye gates; and be ye lift up, ye everlasting doors; and the King of glory shall come in. Who is this King of glory? The LORD strong and mighty, the LORD mighty in battle. Lift up your heads, O ye gates; even lift them up, ye everlasting doors; and the King of glory shall come in. Who is this King of glory? The LORD of hosts, he is the King of glory. (Psalm 24:7-10)

If you want to experience God's abundance, find a church where their sword is not just being polished but is dripping with the blood of the enemy—where it has pierced the heart and soul of the demonic forces of hell.

Get involved with those who are in the heat of the battle. The revolutionary church of the new millennium is marching into battle under Christ's banner. Retreat is not an option. To be in the church means to be in the battle.

In what ways are you battling alongside those in your church?

_____

_____

_____

_____

_____

_____

_____

_____

_____

_____

_____

_____

_____

"March behind the King of glory into the battle."

Seeing the Unseen

While we look not at the things which are seen, but at the things which are not seen: for the things which are seen are temporal; but the things which are not seen are eternal. (2 Corinthians 4:18)

Faith sees what cannot be seen and hears what cannot be heard. Faith changes you into a human being who can believe what cannot be believed, who can see what cannot be seen, and who can hear what cannot be heard.

Decide to walk by faith and not by sight (2 Corinthians 5:7). Today you will be required to exercise your faith when your action doesn't feel right or look reasonable. But faith can surmount human experience and transport us into the realm of the supernatural and miraculous. Walk by faith and see the miraculous power of God.

_____

_____

_____

_____

_____

_____

_____

_____

_____

_____

_____

_____

_____

_____

"Only those who walk by faith can see the invisible."

Signs and Wonders

And these signs shall follow them that believe; In my name shall they cast our devils; they shall speak with new tongues; they shall take up serpents; and if they drink any deadly thing, it shall hurt them; they shall lay hands on the sick, and they shall recover. And they went forth, and preached every where, the LORD working with them, and confirming the word with signs following. Amen. (Mark 16:17,18,20)

Once you grasp God's vision for your life you will no longer be satisfied with church as usual.

You won't be satisfied with a six-foot icicle standing behind the pulpit spouting his three points and a poem. When God shows up, His power manifests. The sick are healed. The oppressed and possessed are delivered. The lost are saved. And the presence of the Holy Ghost fills, anoints, baptizes, cleanses and empowers His people.

You will cry, "Where are the signs and wonders? Where are the miracles? Where is the revelation and the demonstration?"

You will never be the same once you grasp God's vision for your life. Write down God's vision for you:

_____

_____

_____

_____

_____

_____

_____

_____

_____

_____

_____

"A vision of God will give you a deeper hunger for His presence."

The Veil Was Rent

And, behold, the veil of the temple was rent in twain from the top to the bottom; and the earth did quake, and the rocks rent. (Matthew 27:51)

The Holy God, the Creator of the universe, gives us free access into His presence!

The veil that hung in the temple, four inches thick, woven without seam, twenty feet wide, and forty feet high, was torn from top to bottom by God, and He said,

"I am coming out,
and you are coming in."

Today your High Priest, Jesus, is ushering you into the Holy of Holies through His blood. You are cleansed, forgiven, healed and whole. Offer to Him the sacrifice of praise for being your High Priest.

Write a prayer of thanksgiving for the access the blood of Jesus gives you into the Holy of Holies.

_____

_____

_____

_____

_____

_____

_____

_____

_____

_____

_____

_____

_____

"You have access to the Holy of Holies by the blood of Jesus."

The Cornerstone

Unto you therefore which believe he is precious: but unto them which be disobedient, the stone which the builders disallowed, the same is made the head of the corner, And a stone of stumbling, and a rock of offence, even to them which stumble at the word, being disobedient: whereunto also they were appointed. (1 Peter 2:7,8)

We have not been building on the foundations of faith, hope and love with Christ as the cornerstone.

Instead, we have been building on fear and panic, putting our hope in political masterminds who have manipulated the unthinking, undiscerning masses to the perpetuation of their own perversion.

Rebuke fear, control, intimidation and legalism in your life now. Return to your one sure foundation—Jesus Christ. When the storms of the new millennium rage, He alone will be there to see you through.

_____

_____

_____

_____

_____

_____

_____

_____

_____

_____

_____

_____

_____

_____

"Build your life on the foundation of Jesus Christ."

Confess the Word

If ye abide in me, and my words abide in you, ye shall ask what ye will, and it shall be done unto you. (John 15:7)

The Bible is God's Word to us. It is an operator's manual, given to mortal men by an eternal God. God and His Word are alive and inseparable. His Word does not change, nor can it fail, nor will it return unto Him without accomplishing what it was sent to do. (Isaiah 55:11).

When you confess what God's Word says about you, you are agreeing that what He has said concerning you is true. There is infinite power in that agreement.

Decree that you have what God says you have. Proclaim that you are what God says you are. God said He would hasten after His Word to perform it, to bring it to pass in your life.

When you speak the Word, angels hearken to that command (Psalm 103:20), and all of heaven will back you up. You have God's written guarantee.

_____

_____

_____

_____

_____

_____

_____

_____

_____

_____

_____

_____

"Confess His Word today."

Jesus is Coming

And great earthquakes shall be in divers places, and famines, and pestilences; and fearful sights and great signs shall there be from heaven.
(Luke 21:11)

Worldwide famine in these days when there should be none tells us that Jesus is coming. The major wheat producers grow enough food to feed every starving person in the world, yet famine abounds.

There have been more earthquakes worldwide in the last 15 years than in the other 8 decades of this century. New and powerful strains of bacteria emerge to mock the efforts of doctors to fight them.

Jesus warned us that in these times men's hearts would fail them for fear (Luke 21:26), but He was not talking about you. The people who fear the turbulent events of these times are those who do not understand what is happening—but you do! Every newscast that tells us of these events is a reminder to us of our blessed hope—Jesus will come soon to take His church to heaven. Are you ready to meet Jesus?

_____

_____

_____

_____

_____

_____

_____

_____

_____

_____

_____

_____

*"As we approach the new millennium,
we live in the end times. Jesus is coming soon."*

Marriage on the Rock

For thou art my rock and my fortress; therefore for thy name's sake lead me, and guide me.
(Psalm 31:3)

My wife and I made a covenant with God when we married that the word d-i-v-o-r-c-e would never be mentioned in our home. For us, it is simply not an option. When you marry you not only forsake all others, but you forsake your right to be right. Divorce is a product of a home ruled by selfish wants and desires and is a satanic tactic to overthrow the throne of God.

Turn off television programs depicting adultery and marital strife. If you don't, these spirits will invade your mind and, subsequently, your home. "For as he thinketh in his heart, so is he" (Proverb 23:7).

Fill your home with the presence of God. Speak words of unity and love to one another. Paul said that we should in honor prefer one another above ourselves. (Romans 12:10). Prefer your mate's needs and desires above your own. Center your relationship around Christ. Build it on a sure foundation. Marriages built on the Rock never go "on the rocks."

_____

_____

_____

_____

_____

_____

_____

_____

_____

_____

_____

"Build your marriage on the Rock."

Evangelize the World

For God sent not his Son into the world to condemn the world; but that the world through him might be saved. (John 3:17)

Go back to the purity of the first hour you knew Jesus . . . when you felt as if everyone in the world should have a chance to feel what you felt and know what you knew. Everyone in the world should have the opportunity to feel washed clean by the blood of Jesus and know they are on their way to heaven.

Keep that hunger and that purity that reaches out a hand and says, "I'll pray for you. I'll believe God for your miracle." We are the only hope to evangelize this world. We are the generation destined to reach out in this last hour to the depraved and the destitute with the life-changing Gospel of Jesus Christ. From the uttermost to the guttermost, take a stand and declare, "This is the Bible, and it is the answer for everything!"

Jesus commissioned us saying, "Go ye into all the world, and preach the gospel to every creature" (Mark 16:15). We are all called to be witnesses, and God has given us an anointing and a calling to reach the lost. People are hungry to know God, and you have the answer.

_____

_____

_____

_____

_____

_____

_____

_____

_____

_____

_____

"We're God's only hope to evangelize the world."

Go Up!

And David enquired of God, saying, Shall I go up against the Philistines? And wilt thou deliver them into mine hand? And the LORD said unto him, Go up; for I will deliver them into thine hand.
(1 Chronicles 14:10)

David had ascended the throne of Israel when the Philistines again attacked. Before sending his troops against them, he asked the Lord for His will in the situation. David wanted to know if he was commissioned from heaven to engage them in battle—"the steps of a good man are ordered of the Lord" (Psalm 37:23).

He knew it was his destiny to purge the Philistines; but David wanted to be sure that God would go before him to give him the victory. David understood God's perfect timing.

Once you have God's Word on the matter, you can go into battle expecting to be victorious. Determine to acknowledge Him in all your ways. Be sure His hand is on whatever you set your hand to do, and you will have total victory throughout the year.

_____

_____

_____

_____

_____

_____

_____

_____

_____

_____

_____

"With God's Word you can enter into any battle and win."

The Mind of Christ

I beseech you therefore, brethren, by the mercies of God, that ye present your bodies a living sacrifice, holy, acceptable unto God, which is your reasonable service. And be not conformed to this world: but be ye transformed by the renewing of your mind, that ye may prove what is that good, and acceptable, and perfect, will of God. (Romans 12:1,2)

As you mature in Christ, there are some things you need to accept, even though you may not understand them.

When everything in you cries, "No, Lord, no," and you say, "How could God want me to go through this?" . . . that is the time for you to bow your knee and declare, "Yes, Lord, yes." God will allow you to walk through the fire to prove that the power to deliver you is of Him and not of yourself.

He is the God who brought you in; and He is the God who will bring you out. Let no thought of defeat enter your mind, but rather, "Let this mind be in you, which was also in Christ Jesus" (Philippians 2:5).

_____

_____

_____

_____

_____

_____

_____

_____

_____

_____

_____

"Walk through this year with the mind of Christ—servanthood."

Kingdom Priorities

And if ye go to war in your land against the enemy that oppresseth you, then ye shall blow an alarm with the trumpets; and ye shall be remembered before the LORD your God, and ye shall be saved from your enemies. (Numbers 10:9)

In His last discourse on earth, Jesus instructed His disciples to go and preach the Gospel to all nations (Matthew 28:19). His first priority for His followers was to bring the good news of salvation to as many people as possible.

He followed this instruction with the assurance, "And these signs shall follow them that believe; in my name shall they cast out devils" (Mark 16:17).

Jesus not only intended for the Gospel to be made available to all mankind, but for His manifested presence to continue to destroy the works of the enemy.

The presence of Jesus Christ is alive and active in every born-again believer . . . and we have a divine mandate to set the captives free and to tear the devil's kingdom down! Keep the kingdom priorities ever before you. List your kingdom priorities:

_____

_____

_____

_____

_____

_____

_____

_____

_____

_____

"Keep your kingdom priorities before you all year."

Keep Satan Underfoot

Behold, I give unto you power to tread on serpents and scorpions, and over all the power of the enemy: and nothing shall by any means hurt you.
(Luke 10:19)

On his way to Rome the apostle Paul was shipwrecked on the island of Malta. As he was gathering wood to make a fire, a deadly viper suddenly sank its fangs into his hand.

The natives watched in horror, knowing Paul would surely die from the poisonous venom, but the apostle merely shook the snake off into the fire.

You need not walk in fear of the devil. In that moment on Calvary, Jesus stripped the devil of his stolen power and restored it to mankind.

Genesis 3:15 says, God said unto the serpent, "Her seed; it shall bruise thy head, and thou shalt bruise his heel." As a born-again believer you have power to trample him under your feet. Don't give Satan a foothold to sin in your life today.

_____

_____

_____

_____

_____

_____

_____

_____

_____

_____

_____

_____

_____

"Christ defeated Satan on the cross.
Any power the devil has is what you give him."

Destroy Doubt

And immediately Jesus stretched forth his hand, and caught him, and said unto him, O thou of little faith, wherefore didst thou doubt? (Matthew 14:31)

Doubt says, "I wonder if it could be." Unbelief says, "I know that it is not." Doubt is not nearly the obstacle that unbelief is. On the day of Pentecost, many in the crowd doubted the testimony of Peter and the disciples, but 3,000 were added to the Church that very day. Doubt does not stop the mighty wind from heaven.

Doubt offers God the opportunity to prove Himself. He sent Elijah into an idolatrous land to challenge the priests of Baal to a contest. God was more than willing to prove himself to the doubters, and when the fire fell from heaven, no doubt remained (1 Kings 18).

Peter doubted when He took his eyes off Jesus. He saw the waves of misfortune and felt the wind of disaster beating against him. As he began to sink, he cried out to Jesus . . . and immediately Jesus reached out His hand and caught him (Matthew 14:24-33). Jesus was there to lift him up—and He'll be there for you, too. List all the ways that you will trust Jesus today.

_____

_____

_____

_____

_____

_____

_____

_____

_____

_____

_____

_____

_____

"Cast all doubt aside and radically trust Jesus today."

Surrender Unconditionally

But when he saw Jesus afar off, he ran and worshipped him. (Mark 5:6)

Jesus said, "All power is given unto me in heaven and in earth" (Matthew 28:18).

When Jesus arrived in the country of the Gadarenes, immediately he was confronted by a man who was possessed by so many demons that the man called himself Legion.

These demons were not only many, but also they were powerful. "No man could bind him, no, not with chains. Because that he had been often bound with fetters and chains, and the chains had been plucked asunder by him, and the fetters broken in pieces: neither could any man tame him" (Mark 5:3,4).

Yet when the demoniac saw Jesus coming from a distance, he flung himself at Jesus' feet. Absolute, unconditional surrender!

Any time you think about the devil, immediately add the word defeated. Is the devil attacking you? No, the defeated devil is attacking you. Call on the One who holds all power in heaven and in earth, and drive the defeated devil out of your life. Surrender unconditionally and absolutely so you may live this year victoriously.

_____

_____

_____

_____

_____

_____

_____

_____

_____

_____

_____

"Unconditional surrender brings complete victory."

Pray Boldly

Let us therefore come boldly unto the throne of grace, that we may obtain mercy, and find grace to help in time of need. (Hebrews 4:16)

The prayer of intercession is urgent prayer on behalf of a pressing need. We live in a world filled with pressing needs!

God said, "I sought for a man among them, that should make up the hedge, and stand in the gap before me for the land, that I should not destroy it: but I found none" (Ezekiel 22:30). What a tragedy that for a lack of even one person who would pray, destruction fell on many!

The Day of the Lord is drawing near. Judgment such as the world has never known is coming upon this earth.

God is looking for spiritual warriors who will stand in the gap for the hurting, the helpless and the hopeless. Will you join the ranks? Ask the Lord to lead you into intercession today.

_____

_____

_____

_____

_____

_____

_____

_____

_____

_____

_____

_____

_____

"Stand in the gap through intercession."

Give Into the Storehouse

Behold the fowls of the air: for they sow not, neither do they reap, nor gather into barns, yet your heavenly Father feedeth them. Are ye not much better than they? (Matthew 6:26)

You rarely see a hungry bird, or a bird with no feathers, or a bird with no tree to sleep in. Birds never sow, reap or gather into barns. All they have is what they need at the moment. Our heavenly Father takes care of them on a daily basis.

He has an even greater plan than that for us. He doesn't just take care of us on a day-to-day basis. He is Jehovah Jireh, the God of more than enough. He gives us the ability to plant, to harvest and to gather the abundance into the storehouse (Malachi 3:10).

Your abundance belongs in the storehouse that God has provided—the ministry where you are being fed and ministered to. Bring your abundance into the place where God has put His name. Start sowing, reaping and gathering into the storehouse—so the Gospel of Jesus Christ may be preached in all the earth.

Only 60 days remain until the new millennium. In the new millennium, the radical church will be filled with radical givers. Determine in the next 60 days to grow in your radical giving to the Lord.

_____
_____
_____
_____
_____
_____
_____
_____
_____

"Are you giving so that the storehouse may prosper?"

You Are a Miracle

For in Him we live, and move, and have our being; as certain also of your own poets have said, For we are also his offspring. (Acts 17:28)

You are a walking, living, breathing miracle, because God lives inside of you. If you do not allow the life of God to live through you, death will creep into every area of your life—your family, your finances, your home, your marriage and your future.

The crowd stood at the base of the cross watching Jesus die. While they looked for the sensational, they missed the supernatural. You do not have to wait on God to do something supernatural; you are living supernaturally every day.

Get in touch with the supernatural life residing within you. God has given you all power over devils sent to discomfort, dissuade and disconnect you. Tap into His life today and walk in victory. Give thanks for His victory in your life right now.

_____

_____

_____

_____

_____

_____

_____

_____

_____

_____

_____

_____

_____

"God has given you all power.
Walk in His authority, defeating every foe."

God's Mercy

Therefore seeing we have this ministry, as we have received mercy, we faint not. (2 Corinthians 4:1)

You have probably heard all your life that grace is the unmerited favor of God. But Jesus sprinkled His blood on the mercy seat, not the grace seat. It is mercy—not grace—that is the result of His unmerited favor.

Jesus' blood paid the price for our sin, because we are guilty. We were without God, without hope and deserving of an unending hell. If your very life substance could not pay the price for your deliverance, what makes you think your prayers, your penance or your good works can ever help you?

In this life you are going to walk through some things where no one can encourage you, no one can bless you and no one can help you. When you do, you will cry out for His mercy to forgive you when you don't deserve to be forgiven; to love you when you are unlovable; and to accept you when you are unacceptable. Because of His unmerited favor . . . He will. Proceed into the new millennium through His mercy.

_____
_____
_____
_____
_____
_____
_____
_____
_____
_____
_____
_____

"His mercy is all we need to walk into the new millennium."

Speak Faith

And they overcame him by the blood of the Lamb, and by the word of their testimony . . . .
(Revelation 12:11a)

God has dealt every man the measure of faith, including you. (Romans 12:3).

The devil cannot penetrate the Word of God spoken in faith. When we confess what the Word says, we unlock the door of our faith.

Whatever you are believing for your family, stand in faith on what the Word of God says about them. Your neighbors may say your kids are lost, but the Bible says they shall be saved (Acts 16:31).

The devil can't read your mind. Words of life, victory and deliverance are going to have to come from YOUR mouth.

Silent faith is dead faith. For faith to operate, you must confess your faith out loud. Speaking the Word gives life to our faith. Speaking the Word binds the devil from our families and our homes. Write down the Word you will speak today.

_____

_____

_____

_____

_____

_____

_____

_____

_____

_____

_____

_____

_____

"Speak the Word of faith. Let His Word abide on your tongue."

Keep Your Heart

Keep thy heart with all diligence; for out of it are the issues of life. (Proverb 4:23)

The word "keep" in this passage means "to set armed guards around." Imagine for a moment a priceless diamond on display in a museum. On either side of the display case stands an armed guard, carefully watching every person who approaches. No thief can open the case and remove the diamond as long as the guards are protecting it. The Bible cautions us to guard our hearts with the same vigilance.

Be watchful against evil ideas and the people who express them to you. Be careful what influences you allow to come into your home. The devil will use any opportunity he can find to gain a foothold in your heart (Deuteronomy 11:16).

Your heart shall live forever (Psalm 22:26b). Your heart is a precious treasure; keep it safe from demonic plundering! Guard your heart as you march into the new millennium.

_____

_____

_____

_____

_____

_____

_____

_____

_____

_____

_____

_____

_____

_____

"Keep your heart from all input except that which comes by His Spirit."

Our Sure Refuge

God is our refuge and strength, a very present help in trouble. Therefore will not we fear, though the earth be removed, and though the mountains be carried into the midst of the sea; though the waters thereof roar and be troubled, though the mountains shake with the swelling thereof. Selah.
(Psalm 46:1-3)

A security camera recorded the reactions of customers in a grocery store during an earthquake. Bottles and boxes fell to the ground as people ran for cover. In the middle of the chaos, one woman remained in the aisle, trying to prevent cans of peas from falling off a shelf.

As the close of the age draws near, God is shaking the world. Some Christians do not understand and become confused when the events of their lives become chaotic. Many try to hold onto the very things God is trying to shake out of their lives. They do not realize they are clinging to the things God is telling them to let go.

Let Him shake loose anything and everything that is keeping you from a deeper walk with Him. Hold tight; when the shaking is over, you will be on solid ground.

"Stop holding on to that which Christ commands you to loose."

Receive His Grace

And with great power gave the apostles witness of the resurrection of the Lord Jesus: and great grace was upon them all. (Acts 4:33)

God graces people who are determined to make it through. His grace becomes an asbestos suit for those walking through the fiery furnace of the trials of human existence.

You can find out what grace is when you find out who receives grace. Everybody receives mercy, but everybody doesn't receive grace. Only a very select group of people ever receive God's spirit of grace—those who have humbled themselves before Him and walk uprightly. (Zechariah 12:10; Psalm 84:11; Proverb 3:34; James 4:6; 1 Peter 5:5).

Humility is not living in poverty or wearing last century's clothes. Humility is knowing who you are, who God is and giving Him the glory for the difference. Great grace to endure is given to those who acknowledge Him as Lord of all. Ask the Holy Spirit to show you any areas where you need humility.

_____

_____

_____

_____

_____

_____

_____

_____

_____

_____

_____

"Ask the Holy Ghost for the grace to endure."

Rise Up Against Darkness

He hath not beheld iniquity in Jacob, neither hath he seen perverseness in Israel: the Lord his God is with him, and the shout of a king is among them. (Numbers 23:21)

When the children of Israel entered into the Promised Land, they camped in the plains of Moab near Jericho. The inhabitants of the land were terrified by this vast assembly of people and wanted to drive them out.

The Moabite king, Balak, summoned the prophet Balaam and ordered him to call down curses on the Israelites. But Balaam could not utter one word against them. He told Balak he could not curse what God had blessed, for "the shout of a king is among them." The triumphal war cry of their King silenced every curse before it could be uttered.

In these last days the church is rising against the powers of darkness. The devil will try to bring curses against us, but he will fail—for the shout of the King of kings is among us! He will turn pale with fear and flee before the righteous, who advance upon his strongholds, filled with the Holy Ghost and power.

March with the radical, revolutionary church in these last days. Be filled with the power of the Holy Ghost.

"Join with the saints and rise up above the kingdom of darkness."

Exalt Jesus Always

Sing praises to God, sing praises: sing praises unto our King, sing praises. For God is the King of all the earth: sing ye praises with understanding. God reigneth over the heathen: God sitteth upon the throne of his holiness. (Psalm 47:6-8)

This Scripture is only one of many throughout the Bible where God tells us that He is the supreme ruler of the universe.

In this age of the false gospel of humanism, man has attempted to minimize the difference between himself and God by trying to exalt himself and bring God down to his level. In today's society we value things based on their availability; we only hold precious that which is in short supply. Gold is more valuable than silver, because there is less gold available to us.

There is only one God, and He is matchless in value! He is greater than all men, all ideas and all religions. There are many of these, but only one of Him.

Psalm 89:6 asks, "For who in the heaven can be compared unto the Lord?" The answer is no one! We are to always be decreasing that He might increase and be exalted in all things. Write down what needs to decrease in your life today that He might be exalted.

_____

_____

_____

_____

_____

_____

_____

_____

_____

_____

_____

"Lord, I must decrease so that You might increase in my life."

Whole-hearted Devotion

Surely none of the men that came up out of Egypt, from twenty years old and upward, shall see the land which I sware unto Abraham, unto Isaac, and unto Jacob; because they have not wholly followed me: Save Caleb the son of Jephunneh the Kenezite, and Joshua the son of Nun: for they have wholly followed the Lord. (Numbers 32:11,12)

Too many Christians today are like the Israelites, wandering in the wilderness, because they are not fully committed to the God they say they serve.

God is looking for a people who will serve Him with wholehearted devotion and a willing mind (2 Chronicles 16:9). We are to serve God wholeheartedly—not like the religious, uncommitted scribes and Pharisees. Jesus said, These people honor me with their lips, but their hearts are far from me (Matthew 15:8).

You may spend a few minutes reading your Bible, but are you sincerely seeking Him, asking Him to guide your every step? Bow your knee and make Him Lord of all today.

_____

_____

_____

_____

_____

_____

_____

_____

_____

_____

"Worship Him today with wholehearted devotion."

Jesus Is Lord

Jesus said unto him, Thou shalt love the Lord thy God with all thy heart, and with all thy soul, and with all thy mind. (Matthew 22:37)

Lordship means total commitment to a sovereign Lord. That means much more than praying to receive Christ in your heart, or reading your Bible or showing up for church on Sunday morning.

Your life belongs to God, and He is your Master. See His will for your life, and bring glory to Him in all that you do.

Lordship is a relationship expressed in loving obedience to God. Actions speak louder than words. It is easy to sing about how much we love Jesus and testify to our friends and family of our unwavering love without really loving Him.

John 14:21 says, "He that hath my commandments, and keepeth them, he it is that loveth me." If we truly love God, we will obey His Words and apply them in our lives. Father, help us today to let your words be a lamp unto our feet, to guide us in obedience to your commands.

_____

_____

_____

_____

_____

_____

_____

_____

_____

_____

_____

_____

"True love obeys the Lord in all things."

We Must Pray

He that believeth on me, the works that I do shall he do also; and greater works than these shall he do; because I go unto my Father. (John 14:12)

We have authority over the devil because we have the indwelling presence of the Holy Ghost. We should be doing the same works as Jesus did, and even greater. Yet, too often it seems as if the devil is winning the war. We cannot do what Jesus did, because we do not do what Jesus did—pray.

When Jesus taught and healed among the multitudes, He prayed (Luke 5:16). When He stood among mourners at the tomb of Lazarus, He prayed (John 11:41,42). When He awaited His betrayal and faced the ordeal of the cross, He prayed (Luke 22:41).

Jesus frequently withdrew for private times of communion with His Father, each time returning refreshed and refilled with the power of the Holy Ghost.

There is power to destroy cancer, eradicate AIDS and save our families in prevailing prayer. But we must do as Jesus did—we must pray!

_____

_____

_____

_____

_____

_____

_____

_____

_____

_____

_____

_____

"In radical Christianity, prayer is never an option—it's always a must!"

Acknowledge Jesus

That the communication of thy faith may become effectual by the acknowledging of every good thing which is in you in Christ Jesus. (Philemon 6)

The key to spiritual warfare is found in 1 John 3:8, "For this purpose the Son of God was manifested, that he might destroy the works of the devil." How then are the works of the devil destroyed? By Spirit-filled Christians acknowledging Jesus! When we bring Him into the battle, the devil is doomed.

When the attack is heavy and anxiety runs high, turn to Jesus. Divert your attention from all distractions and fix your mind on Him. Speak His name aloud. Thank Him for His blessings and His promises. Shout your praises to Him for His matchless love and unfailing strength.

Acknowledge that He is more powerful than depression and mightier than temptation. Acknowledge that you were once on your way to hell, but now you are on your way to heaven. Acknowledge that Jesus is Lord of all and that the devil is under your feet. In all your ways, acknowledge Him. Write down all the ways you will acknowledge Jesus as Lord today:

_____

_____

_____

_____

_____

_____

_____

_____

_____

_____

_____

"Acknowledge that Christ in you is greater than any attack against you."

Prayer Is Not Dead

Call unto me and I will answer thee, and shew thee great and mighty things, which thou knowest not. (Jeremiah 33:3)

A prominent theologian stated, "Prayer is doomed," and "I don't see that the church of the 20th century will have any more need of prayer than it does any other form of magic."

Well, I disagree. The Bible says God hears our prayers and He will answer—but there are some keys to prayer. First of all, you must know the will of God. Go to the Scriptures to find out what the will of God is for your situation. Decide specifically what you want God to do for you.

I used to just pray for a wife, until I saw some of the candidates that were showing up. When I learned to pray specifically, God brought Joni into my life.

Decide what you want; know the will of God; verbalize your request and bind doubt and unbelief. After you have prayed, here is the major key: give thanks. Rejoice that God has heard and answered your prayer. Because we know He hears us, we have confidence that He has granted our requests. Now write down your prayer.

_____

_____

_____

_____

_____

_____

_____

_____

_____

_____

_____

"Prayer verbalizes your petitions to God."

Prepare to Praise

Speaking to yourselves in psalms and hymns and spiritual songs, singing and making melody in your heart to the Lord; Giving thanks always for all things unto God and the Father in the name of our Lord Jesus Christ. (Ephesians 5:19,20)

Prepare your heart to praise the Lord. Prepare to give thanks for all the blessings He has bestowed upon you—your home, your family, your job and your very life! For everything, give thanks.

Praise Him when you rise in the morning. Praise Him as you go to work and as you return home. Praise Him in the evening for another day finished. Praise Him before you go to sleep for a restful night and a new sunrise when you awaken.

The more you praise Him and give thanks, the more the devil flees from your presence. Praise and prayers of thanks to the Lord are your greatest defenses against the wiles of the devil.

"What shall I render unto the Lord, for all his benefits toward me?" (Psalm 116:12). Give God thanks today for His boundless grace and mercy in your life. Praise Him today with your whole being. Praise Him! Write down your praise for today.

_____

_____

_____

_____

_____

_____

_____

_____

_____

_____

"Radical Christians fill their days with praise."

The Trumpet Sounds

For the Lord himself shall descend from heaven with a shout, with the voice of the archangel, and with the trump of God: and the dead in Christ shall rise first. (1 Thessalonians 4:16)

The Jewish fall holy days begin with the shofar (a trumpet made from a ram's horn) blasting its call to regather to a pure faith in God. The same shofar gathered the troops of biblical times for battle and to hail their king's arrival.

The word translated "sound" in this verse and "shout" in 1 Thessalonians 4:16 is more accurately translated the "alarm blast of the shofar."

The Feast of Trumpets points to the time when we will gather to meet Him in the clouds. The signal of the gathering will be the sound of the shofar, the blowing of the trumpet. When the trumpet sounds, we who have received Jesus Christ as Savior will respond to that glorious sound and hail our long-awaited King.

The trumpet is sounding in the heavens announcing our wake-up call to repentance. As this millennium draws to a close . . . we draw closer to our Kings' return. Jesus is coming. Listen for the shofar!

"As the new millennium approaches, constantly watch for Jesus' return."

Guilty but Blameless

For by grace are ye saved through faith; and that not of yourselves: it is the gift of God. (Ephesians 2:8)

When you cried out, "God I'm a sinner," God replied, "That's all right, I'm a Savior." He sent His Son to save from the uttermost to the guttermost. To God, you can be living on the streets, without a dollar for food or a place to put your head, and He will love you just as much as if you were an international celebrity of worldwide acclaim!

He made a way for us to be reconciled from sin and saved from eternity in hell through Jesus Christ His Son who shed His sinless blood on Calvary, was resurrected on the third day and now sits at the right hand of the Father continuously pleading that precious blood on our behalf!

"Blameless" is an old English word that is rarely used in our court systems anymore. The jury finds a man "guilty," but the judge can declare him "blameless." That means he committed the crime, but is not going to be sentenced for it.

As a sinner, you are as guilty as a fox in a chicken coop, but God looks at the blood of Jesus Christ and holds you blameless. By the blood of Christ and your faith in the finished work of Calvary, you are held blameless.

_____

_____

_____

_____

_____

_____

_____

_____

_____

_____

_____

"His blood pleads mercy for you!"

Let the Spirit Lead

If we live in the Spirit, let us also walk in the Spirit. (Galatians 5:25)

The greatest asset today's family has is the leading of the Holy Spirit. We must all learn to discern the prophetic voice of God and learn to obey Him. A gentle nudging of the Holy Spirit to pray may make the difference between life and death in your family. You may only hear a gentle "Do not go to the store right now; stay and worship me." While you are worshiping Him, the devil's plan to meet you head-on with a swerving truck is thwarted because you heard and obeyed His voice.

Satan hates a godly family because he knows its spiritual strength. The devil would like nothing better than to sow strife and discord into your family life, opening the door for him to attack.

Determine to join hands with your family members every morning and to pray a hedge of protection around each other before anyone leaves the house! Write a prayer of protection for your family now.

_____

_____

_____

_____

_____

_____

_____

_____

_____

_____

_____

"Pray a hedge of protection daily for your family."

Abide In Christ

If a man abide not in me, he is cast forth as a branch, and is withered; and men gather them, and cast them into the fire, and they are burned.
(John 15:6)

In Ohio we have a lot of clay reserves. In some areas the topsoil is very thin, while underneath there is a hard layer of clay called a "hardpan." We can have an all-out downpour, and within hours the topsoil will be as dry as powder.

Some Christians shout victory on Sunday, but by Monday they have no joy, no victory and no peace. They are as hardhearted as our Ohio clay, and their fruit withers on the vine. They are without patience, mercy, gentleness, meekness, temperance or compassion. They are just going through the motions.

Others wither as soon as the hot winds of temptation, trouble and tribulation blow their way.

Keep your faith fresh and alive by constantly tilling the soil of your heart. Pray for the Holy Ghost to send the rain. Stay in union with the source of all life, and your faith will blossom and bear fruit in season.

_____

_____

_____

_____

_____

_____

_____

_____

_____

_____

"Keep your faith fresh and alive."

Be Filled with the Holy Ghost

And they were all filled with the Holy Ghost, and began to speak with other tongues, as the spirit gave them utterance. (Acts 2:4)

The rushing wind that blew into the room that day was the unexpected fulfillment of an expected promise and prophecy. Isaiah and Joel had both foretold the coming of this day (Isaiah 28:11, Joel 2:28,29). Jesus had told them to wait on it and to watch for it.

Though he had denied Christ only days before, a downcast Peter waited with the others. When the wind came, Peter changed. He became steadfast and bold in Christ. He spoke in languages he didn't even know! He became a man whose shadow would heal the sick. In spite of his shortcomings, Peter had been filled with the Holy Ghost!

It is the commandment of God—and the privilege of God's people—to be filled with His Spirit, in spite of our shortcomings. When we are immersed in Him, we are given supernatural power, grace and ability. The church needs Pentecostal power for these last days. Invite Him to fill you and transform you today. Write down your invitation to the Holy Ghost.

_____

_____

_____

_____

_____

_____

_____

_____

_____

_____

"Be filled with the Holy Ghost."

The Anointing

Thou preparest a table before me in the presence of mine enemies: thou anointest my head with oil; my cup runneth over. (Psalm 23:5)

Psalm 23 is often called "The Shepherd's Psalm," because it describes the loving care the Lord provides for His flock. David said in the first verse, "The Lord is my Shepherd, I shall not want," because you will never experience a need our heavenly Father will not supply.

David went on to say, "Thou anointest my head with oil" (v.5). He was alluding to the way shepherds poured oil on the heads of their sheep before they were sent out to graze. The oil soaked into their wool; and if they happened to cut their heads on stones while grazing, the healing oil was already there to soothe and cleanse the wound.

God is not only the loving Jehovah Rohi, (the Lord our Shepherd), but He is also Jehovah Jireh, the God of more than enough who provides for your every need before your need arises. Experience today the provision of His anointing.

_____

_____

_____

_____

_____

_____

_____

_____

_____

_____

_____

_____

_____

_____

"Let the provision of His anointing flow over you today."

Complete Honesty

Behold, thou desirest truth in the inward parts: and in the hidden part thou shalt make me to know wisdom. (Psalm 51:6)

God wants nothing less than complete honesty from us. He who comes to God with the acknowledgment of his sin comes in truth—a sinner saved by grace. His grace requires nothing more than truth from the truly repentant.

A sincere heart is not a perfect heart, a holy heart or even one dedicated to service—it is a heart willing to reveal itself just as it is and nothing more.

You need not be afraid of shocking God. There is nothing about you He does not already know. Even the hairs of your head are numbered.

Be honest with God. He who searches the hearts of men will never withhold His grace and mercy from you. Complete honesty with God reveals your heart to you!

_____

_____

_____

_____

_____

_____

_____

_____

_____

_____

_____

_____

_____

_____

"Be completely honest today with God."

Obey the Spirit

Thy kingdom come. Thy will be done in earth, as it is in heaven. (Matthew 6:10)

Jesus came to bring the kingdom of heaven to earth; to establish godly, heavenly authority in the hearts and lives of all humanity.

God said, "I will put my laws into their mind, and write them in their hearts: and I will be to them a God, and they shall be to me a people: And they shall not teach every man his neighbour, and every man his brother, saying, Know the Lord: for all shall know me, from the least to the greatest" (Hebrews 8:10,11).

We do not live in a kingdom cut off from the king, nor do we live bound by impersonal laws that control every aspect of our lives. In the kingdom of heaven, Jesus Christ dwells inside every spirit-filled believer, teaching us and guiding us every step of the way. As our indwelling constant companion and counselor, the Holy Spirit reveals to us the heart of the Savior.

Jesus came to bring heaven to earth, to bestow the gift of sonship and to bring you into relationship with your heavenly Father. Thank the Father for the Son and the gift of sonship.

_____

_____

_____

_____

_____

_____

_____

_____

_____

"Celebrate your sonship in Christ."

Take His Yoke

Take my yoke upon you, and learn of me; for I am meek and lowly in heart: and ye shall find rest unto your souls. (Matthew 11:29)

Jesus' earthly ministry included preaching, healing, miracles and teaching. You may have bowed your knee to call Him Savior, but do you know Him as "Teacher?"

The disciples sat under His instruction for three years before their spirits were truly teachable and ready to receive the baptism of the Holy Spirit.

A teachable spirit seeks the Spirit of the Lamb of God, meek and lowly in heart. Jesus' entire work in us is a divine teaching. The Holy Spirit who dwells in us, the very Spirit of Christ, shall teach us all things (John 16:13) if we submit our spirits to become meek and teachable.

Take up His yoke today and learn His meekness and lowliness of heart, because with that learning comes the teachable, pliable spirit that does nothing of its own will, but says, "Not my will, but thine be done."

Describe His will for you today:

_____

_____

_____

_____

_____

_____

_____

_____

_____

_____

_____

_____

_____

"His yoke and His will for you today is all that matters."

Pray Always   *Pray without ceasing.* (1 Thessalonians 5:17)

Prayer is our communication link with God. We need to stay in constant touch with our Father. Without continual communication—praying without ceasing—we cannot know His voice or follow His way.

When that line of communication is down, our spirit man cannot receive direction from God. We become vulnerable to the enemy and are subsequently motivated by our flesh instead of our spirit. Our ears become deafened to the still, small voice of the Holy Spirit, and the whispered lies which the enemy bombards us with begin to sound believable.

When you pray, you have access into the spirit realm, where God is, and He will reveal to you the root cause of any battle you are facing.

Prayer in private equals power in public. Battles are won in your prayer closet on your face before God interceding, seeking His wisdom and receiving His direction. Write down your private prayer for today.

_____

_____

_____

_____

_____

_____

_____

_____

_____

_____

_____

_____

_____

"Public power only arises from private prayer."

Declare the Gospel

And it shall come to pass afterward, that I will pour out my spirit upon all flesh; and your sons and your daughters shall prophesy, your old men shall dream dreams, your young men shall see visions. (Joel 2:28)

The church of Jesus Christ has withstood the deadening blows of the God-haters throughout the ages. In every generation scoffers have denied the existence of God or invented their own religions to accommodate their sin. In our own generation we are seeing the fulfillment of 2 Timothy 3.

But God promised He would preserve a remnant church of the faithful, and in the last days this remnant church would rise up in Holy Ghost power. That time is now!

The church is beginning to come out from the world and be separate. A Bible-believing remnant is leaving behind the compromising, sin-infested church of man to take up the standard of Jesus Christ. Together we will call out to God and march forward to bring His glorious Gospel to the ends of the earth.

The revolutionary, remnant church marching into the new millennium will conquer every foe and storm the gates of hell. Are you ready?

_____

_____

_____

_____

_____

_____

_____

_____

_____

_____

"Take His glorious Gospel to the ends of the earth."

Be Set Free From The Past

Brethren, I count not myself to have apprehended: but this one thing I do, forgetting those things which are behind, and reaching forth unto those things which are before, I press toward the mark for the prize of the high calling of God in Christ Jesus. (Philippians 3:13-14)

Many people need to be delivered from the skeletons of their past. "Those things which are behind" may include failed marriages, broken promises, failures, disappointments, setbacks and betrayals.

You can be standing waist high in ocean water and watch as water begins to ebb quietly away from you . . . then the force of the wave begins to increase, propelling you forward.

Just as the tide pulls the water back, forming a wave of power, God draws you to Himself.

Don't fight against God's pulling and tugging at your spirit. Allow yourself to be drawn to Him and enveloped in His presence. Trust Him with your very life, and He will propel you forward into your destiny. Describe the destiny that Christ has for you:

_____

_____

_____

_____

_____

_____

_____

_____

_____

_____

_____

"Don't fight God, but rather yield to Him as He draws you unto Himself."

Pursue the Holy Ghost

And thou say in thine heart, My power and the might of mine hand hath gotten me this wealth. (Deuteronomy 8:17)

The proof of your desire for the Holy Ghost in your life is in your pursuit. If you want to activate His power in your life and operate in the power of the gifts of the Spirit, then pursue your desire!

One way to pursue the Holy Ghost is to pray in the Spirit constantly. When you begin to pray in the Holy Ghost, you release your God-given power to operate in His will for your life.

Desire the Spirit today. Pray in the Spirit. Activate His power in your life.

"Desire the Holy Ghost today."

The Thief

But if he [the thief] be found, he shall restore sevenfold; he shall give all the substance of his house. (Romans 10:17)

Satan will try to steal from you anything he can. If anything has been stolen from your life, Satan is the culprit.

The word "thief" in the King James version of the Bible is the Greek word "kleptes." We get the word "kleptomaniac" for this Greek word. It means, "a thief by nature" or "a compulsive thief."

The devil is a calculating, deceptive plunderer who moves freely in and out of unsuspecting lives. Every individual in some way has been defrauded or robbed by this indiscriminate thief.

One good thing about identifying Satan as the thief is that God's Word tells us that if the thief is caught, he must restore what he has taken sevenfold!

List below all that the enemy must restore sevenfold to you today.

my covenant husband; husband of my youth
my marriage; I want a new & fresh start
my family (I want it made whole!)
my husband's love; make it new & strong
my farm land
my retirement & financial security
my way of life
my time I can spend with my children & grandchild...
my health (my painful knees!)

"In Jesus' name, make the enemy restore sevenfold what has been stolen."

Listen to the Spirit

The same heard Paul speak: who stedfastly beholding him, and perceiving that he had faith to be healed, Said with a loud voice, Stand upright on thy feet. And he leaped and walked. (Acts 14:9,10)

A man, lame from birth, sat in the crowd the day Paul preached the Gospel in Lystra. The Bible doesn't tell us what Paul said, but whatever he said produced faith in this man.

"Heard" as it is used in this verse, implies the abiding results of a past action—the preaching of the Word. Paul's preaching gave birth to faith, and it began to grow in the man the more he heard Paul expound. "Faith cometh by hearing, and hearing by the word of God" (Romans 10:17).

The seed of the Word of God was planted in this man's spirit. Paul continued to exhort the crowd when suddenly that seed of faith blossomed.

The man began acting as if he were already healed. Paul was able to see beyond his outward expression and see the condition of his heart. Paul, speaking words of faith, commanded him to stand; and he did, to the glory of God. Listen to God's Word which is building your faith.

_____

_____

_____

_____

_____

_____

_____

_____

_____

_____

_____

"Are you hearing what God is speaking to you to build your faith."

The Wine of Joy

And the floors shall be full of wheat, and the fats shall overflow with wine. (Joel 2:24)

God intends for our hearts to overflow with His joy. He fills you with joy as a result of your spirit man being in tune with Him.

Nehemiah 8:10 says, "The joy of the Lord is your strength." His joy sustains you when the doctor says you have to die and cannot live, when your kids are on crack, or when you don't have a dollar to change. True joy is unaffected by your circumstances.

When you become filled with the Holy Spirit, you receive His joy. In Acts Chapter 2, those present in the Upper Room became "intoxicated" with the Holy Ghost, causing the crowd to believe they were drunk with wine. But Romans 14:17 says, "The kingdom of God is not meat and drink; but righteousness, peace and joy in the Holy Ghost." They became drunk with joy! Thank Him for His incomparable joy permeating your spirit.

Rejoice that the new millennium will bring your many opportunities to become drunk in the Spirit. In our countdown to the new millennium, only 30 days remain for you to be completely filled to overflowing with His Spirit.

_____

_____

_____

_____

_____

_____

_____

_____

_____

_____

_____

"Rejoice in the Lord always, and again I say rejoice!"

Spiritual Strength

Then said David to the Philistine, Thou comest to me with a sword, and with a spear, and with a shield: but I come to thee in the name of the LORD of hosts, the God of the armies of Israel, whom thou hast defied. (1 Samuel 17:45)

David knew he had the right weapon, and he was ready to use it. David also knew he had the right hand of God—the very Lord of Hosts, and he was ready to serve Him!

Like David, we need to know what our right spiritual weapons are, and we must develop our spiritual strength in order to properly use those weapons. Strength is always developed through disciplined exercise.

No matter how skillful a soldier is with his weapon, an exhausted ninety-eight pound weakling cannot defeat his foe over the long course of battle.

You need constant and continual spiritual exercise to build and maintain your strength. Exercise today by reading the Word, praying, and lifting up your praise to God.

_____

_____

_____

_____

_____

_____

_____

_____

_____

_____

_____

"Are you exercising spiritual discipline in order to build spiritual strength?"

Labor in the Lord

Therefore, my beloved brethren, be ye steadfast, unmoveable, always abounding in the work of the Lord, forasmuch as ye know that your labour is not in vain in the Lord. (1 Corinthians 15:58)

I receive letters every day from pastors and church workers concerning the rough road they face in the ministry. Many times people look at this church and our television ministry and wish they had what I have been privileged to be a part of for so many years.

Let me encourage you with these words, "It has not always been this good." I remember starting with just seventeen people. I sometimes preached until my throat was so dry I coughed up blood. At one time doctors told me I had to stop preaching; but I knew I was born to have "a microphone in one hand and a Bible in the other."

To labor in the Lord is to serve Him whenever He calls and doing whatever He commands. Even when strength ebbs and emotions are drained, God will give you the strength to continue in your fruitful labor for Him.

Wherever you are, draw a line in the spiritual sand and say, "Devil, I'm pressing on, no matter what you say; nothing can stop me and my God." Be steadfast and unmovable, and you will abound in the Lord's work. What is your labor for today?

_____

_____

_____

_____

_____

_____

_____

_____

_____

"Your labor in the Lord is not in vain."

Follow Jesus to the Father

For my thoughts are not your thoughts, neither are your ways my ways, saith the Lord. (Isaiah 55:8)

God's ways differ from our ways. We cannot reason our way through to a conclusion or muscle our way through to a victory. His way always leads us to His Son—the Way.

God has not only revealed Himself to us through His Word, but through the life and ministry of Jesus, who was the Word of God incarnate (John 1:1). As we read His Words and observe His life—the mind, the heart and the ways of God are revealed to us.

Follow Jesus and let Him lead you to the Father. As you study and meditate on the life and ministry of Jesus in the Gospels, you will have a more intimate relationship with Him. Where is Jesus leading you this year? Where will He lead you in the new millennium? To the Father!

_____

_____

_____

_____

_____

_____

_____

_____

_____

_____

_____

_____

_____

"Jesus is leading you back to the Father who loved and formed you in the womb."

Ask for Prayer

Is any sick among you? let him call for the elders of the church; and let them pray over him, anointing him with oil in the name of the Lord: and the prayer of faith shall save the sick, and the Lord shall raise him up; and if he have committed sins, they shall be forgiven him. (James 5:14,15)

Throughout the Bible, God continually met people at their level of faith. He will always meet you where you are, but He doesn't want you to stay where you are.

"Calling for the elders" is healing at the lowest level of faith. The literal translation of this verse reads, "The prayer of faith will save the weak one, and if he has committed any sin, God will forgive him."

We are to call for the elders only when we are too weak and defeated to pray for ourselves. What if everyone in the church was at that level, unable to express their faith? Don't become complacent with your faith. Look where He has brought you from, and let him lift you to where He wants you to be.

_____

_____

_____

_____

_____

_____

_____

_____

_____

_____

_____

_____

_____

"Exercise your faith today."

His Wings are Beneath Us

As an eagle stirreth up her nest, fluttereth over her young, spreadeth abroad her wings, taketh them, beareth them on her wings. (Deuteronomy 32:11,12)

The Bible compares God's relationship with Israel, and the care with which He came to their relief, to the eagle who observes the feathers of its young to determine when they are ready to fly—and then deliberately disturbs them out of the nest.

God may be disturbing your nest today. He may be nudging you out of comfortable habits and ways and into ways that stretch and challenge you.

A bird leaving the nest for an initial flight must depend on the wings of its mother for support. Likewise, the Lord never disturbs the nest without providing strength and support to go beyond your comfort level. In what ways is He stirring you today to go beyond your comfort zone?

_____

_____

_____

_____

_____

_____

_____

_____

_____

_____

_____

_____

_____

_____

"He stretches and challenges you."

Pray In His Will

Having the same spirit of faith . . . I believed, and therefore have I spoken; we also believe, and therefore speak. (2 Corinthians 4:13)

I have met people who believe the Bible teaches that whatever we ask we can have . . . with no strings attached. They obviously have not read 1 John 5:14: "And this is the confidence that we have in him, that, if we ask any thing <u>according to his will</u>, he heareth us."

We can't ask outside the will of God and expect an answer. But when our request lines up with His will, we have the guarantee that He will not only hear us, but also that our answer is on the way.

Your hope and expectation will never rise above your level of confession. You will reap tomorrow the harvest of the words you sow today. Release your confession from a heart full of faith and belief in the God of the Word, and rest in confidence that He will hear and respond.

Write your prayers for today:

_____

_____

_____

_____

_____

_____

_____

_____

_____

_____

_____

_____

_____

"Are you willing to pray His will and not your own today?"

Total Freedom

And he was sad at that saying, and went away grieved: for he had great possessions. And Jesus looked round about, and saith unto his disciples, How hardly shall they that have riches enter into the kingdom of God! (Mark 10:22,23)

When the children of Israel set out for the Promised Land, the last thing to leave the kingdom of darkness and the land of bondage was their cattle. Their herds represented their finances. Our finances are the last bastion of satanic resistance to TOTAL freedom.

Before you can receive what is in God's hand, you must first unclench your fist and offer the Lord what is in your hand.

God tells us, in Malachi 3:10, to bring our finances to Him and PROVE that He will open the windows of heaven, and pour out a blessing so great we will not even be able to contain it. You will never enter God's kingdom by keeping one foot in the world. Don't be bound by what you own. Resolve to cooperate fully with God's plan for your life. Remember, when you let go of what you have, God will release what He has.

What do you need to release into the Father's hands today?

_____

_____

_____

_____

_____

_____

_____

_____

_____

_____

_____

"When you release what you grasp, your hands then open to receive."

His Kingdom Not Ours

Jesus went about all Galilee, teaching in their synagogues, and preaching the gospel of the kingdom. (Matthew 4:23)

God's kingdom is not a democracy. Christ is our king, and we are His loyal subjects. When we accept His Lordship, we accept His provision and His protection. When we refuse His reigning presence, we are assured of destruction. You are only the trustee of what you possess. Everything you have belongs to your king.

Again and again Jesus taught us that if we will be good stewards of what God gives us, when He returns, we will be greatly rewarded.

The power to create wealth is one of God's gifts under the covenant. Jesus only intensified the terms of the covenant. If we will live faithfully under the New Covenant, we will be even more effective than those who operated under the Old Covenant. If you will submit your finances to the headship of Christ, you will experience the prosperity, blessing, freedom and security His authority brings.

"In God's Kingdom, we are not owners, only stewards of what is His."

Establish Yourself in God

And he shall be like a tree planted by the rivers of water, that bringeth forth his fruit in his season; his leaf also shall not wither; and whatsoever he doeth shall prosper. (Psalm 1:3)

God established His covenant in the earth, but if you are not established in His covenant, it will never do you any good. Our hearts must be established in His Word, which is His bond.

The psalmist gives us a perfect description of those whose hearts are established: men who fear the Lord and delight in His commandments are blessed with abundance that cannot be taken away. You will reap the fruit of whatever your heart is established in—fear or faith; sickness or health; poverty or prosperity; sin or righteousness. As Joshua prepared for battle, God said if he would meditate in His Word, he would prosper and be successful (Joshua 1:8).

Spend time in the Word; establish it in your heart. Through it He will chart the course for His abundance to be released into your life.

_____

_____

_____

_____

_____

_____

_____

_____

_____

_____

_____

_____

"Lord, I desire to be established and rooted in you."

Examine Yourself

Examine yourselves, whether ye be in the faith; prove your own selves. Know ye not your own selves, how that Jesus Christ is in you, except ye be reprobates? (2 Corinthians 13:5)

Is Christ truly the Lord of your life? Are you ready to accept and act upon His Word? Are you willing to invest the time and effort necessary to receive what God has for you? Will you acknowledge the source of your supply? Can you be trusted with what He places in your hands?

God's truth about abundance only comes alive in your life when you are ready to receive it. If you said "no" to any of these questions, you need to get serious with God. Seek Him in prayer for His life-changing power to come into your heart.

But if you have said "yes" to God and "no" to the world; if your heart is ready to receive and act on His Word; if you are ready to invest your time and energy to receive all He has for you; if you acknowledge Him as your true source and will be a worthy steward of all He gives—prepare to embark on a course of abundant life and blessing!

"Say Yes to God and No to the world."

Get Rid of Yesterday

. . . Take up the ashes which the fire hath consumed with the burnt offering on the altar, and he shall put them beside the altar. (Leviticus 6:10)

God is saying, "Take yesterday's ashes off the altar and get them out of my presence." He is saying, "Lay yesterday's spiritual experience aside." For too many, their first experience with the baptism in the Holy Ghost is their last. If we have not had a fresh experience with God today, we are late. If we did not receive a renewed infilling today, we are lagging behind.

Not only are God's mercies renewed daily, but also He wants to refresh our spirits so that we remain overflowing with Holy Ghost power and anointing. God has new frontiers for us to conquer. Yesterday's flame is growing dimmer. Get re-ignited in the Spirit!

To dwell in the presence of God requires fresh fire every day! Humble yourself before Him and say, "I am not ready to go forth until I have first been prepared by You. Touch me today."

Let the fire of the Holy Ghost daily purify and prepare you, and give you fresh passion for Him. What ashes from yesterday do you need to release?

_____

_____

_____

_____

_____

_____

_____

_____

_____

_____

*"The ashes of yesterday can poison today's water.
Drink only from fresh wells."*

Watch Out, a Thief Prowls

But know this, that if the goodman of the house had known in what watch the thief would come, he would have watched, and would not have suffered his house to be broken up. (Matthew 24:43)

The devil wants to grieve you by taking your loved ones and your most treasured possessions. He wants to torment you by taking your peace and security. He wants to rob you of your health, your finances and your cherished dreams. Most of all, he wants to shake your faith in the Word of God, so you will be powerless to stand against him. He will strike at your life, taunting, "Why didn't God prevent this?" He will laugh at your sorrow and sneer, "Curse God and die!"

A thief does not have to be strong to steal. All he has to do is wait until there is no one home! This is what the devil does. He preys on people who are not "at home" spiritually. He stalks those who do not believe he is real, because he knows they will not be on guard against him. He lurks behind Christians who believe he is real—but leave themselves open to his oppression.

Be watchful, stay alert and stand guard! What do you need to guard against the enemy's attack? Pray about that now.

_____

_____

_____

_____

_____

_____

_____

_____

_____

"Guard by prayer all that is valuable."

The Trial of Faith

That the trial of your faith, being much more precious than of gold that perisheth, though it be tried with fire, might be found unto praise and honour and glory at the appearing of Jesus Christ.
(1 Peter 1:7)

Nowhere in God's Word are we guaranteed we will not have to face trials after we are born again. While God promises us refuge from temptation and sin (Psalm 91), His purpose is to be God to you and for you to be His child. Whatever God allows in your life reveals His infinite love for you and your infinite need for Him.

When you are tempted, it is the desires of your heart that are on trial. Tried in this verse means "to prove or examine." While God will never tempt us with evil, He will allow what the devil means for evil to establish our hearts in righteousness.

At some time we will all be tested, just as Jesus was tested in the wilderness, as to whether our hearts can be divided to follow the lusts of the flesh and the world. God has promised to deliver us from every trial and to be a refuge to all who run to Him. What is the Lord testing in your life today?

_____

_____

_____

_____

_____

_____

_____

_____

_____

_____

"As the millennium approaches, the tests of your faith will increase to prepare you."

His Rod and Staff

Yea, though I walk through the valley of the shadow of death, I will fear no evil: for thou art with me; thy rod and thy staff they comfort me. (Psalm 23:4)

God is with us in danger, in difficulty and even death . . . and because He is with us, we need fear no evil thing. A "rod" was a weapon of defense or discipline and symbolizes God's power and authority. The staff was used to draw sheep close to the shepherd, to keep them from straying down dangerous paths and to rescue them from trouble.

God wants to be a constant companion to you. He will dwell within your heart and soul, and guide you every step of the way, but there's a catch—you have to be willing to let Him be your guide. You have to be willing to submit, to listen and to go where He tells you to go.

When you rebel against your Shepherd's leading, you rebel against the very best for your future. Remember this the next time you are tempted, then submit to God's gentle and loving correction. What areas of your life is God correcting today?

_____

_____

_____

_____

_____

_____

_____

_____

_____

_____

_____

_____

"Lord, I welcome your loving discipline and correction today."

Problems Drive us to Jesus

The Lord is good, a strong hold in the day of trouble; and he knoweth them that trust in him. (Nahum 1:7)

Problems should not devastate us, but should instead serve to drive us closer to the Cross. If you are not rooted and grounded in the Word, you are easy prey for the adversary. Sink your roots deep into God's fertile soil and let His faithfulness strengthen you for every battle.

Keep His praises ever on your lips and in your heart, and you will never hear Him say, "I never knew you: depart from me, ye worker of iniquity" (Matthew 7:23).

If you stay in close contact with Him, you will not yield to your emotions and be moved by what you see or hear. You will not regress, retreat or accuse God of abandoning you when hardship comes. You will be able to stand steadfast and declare as Abraham did, being fully persuaded that what He had promised, He was able to perform (Romans 4:21).

Is God your stronghold day by day? You can be sure He is by talking to Him every day. Right now write a prayer communicating with the Father.

_____

_____

_____

_____

_____

_____

_____

_____

_____

_____

_____

"How will you communicate with the Father today?"

God Preserves You

The Lord shall preserve thee from all evil: he shall preserve thy soul. The Lord shall preserve thy going out and thy coming in from this time forth, and even for evermore. (Psalm 121:7,8)

When you trust in the Lord and turn your life over to Him, He promises to preserve you from all evil. He does not say you won't be confronted with temptation or troubles; but He promises to protect you when trouble comes. He will walk with you through the valleys and soar with you over the mountaintops.

In the midst of turmoil, He will give you an inner peace that passes all understanding. (Philippians 4:7). You will be able to sleep while the storm rages around you. You will have such sweet peace, you will be amazed at your ability to face what comes your way. When you trust in Him, restlessness, worry and strife are things of the past.

When you give Him your burdens, He gives you His peace. His comfort and protection are yours forever, when you give yourself totally to Him.

"Never fear, God will preserve you."

Love Others

Seeing ye have purified your souls in obeying the truth through the Spirit unto unfeigned love of the brethren, see that ye love one another with a pure heart fervently. (1 Peter 1:22)

Racism has been one of mankind's sins for as long as the earth has existed. Although in theory the barriers have been taken down, far too many people still judge others by the color of their skin.

Do you abide in the light of Jesus? Do you pray and help others? Do you love others . . . with no regard for the shade of their skin? If you can't answer yes to all three questions, you have a stumbling block before you.

"He that loveth his brother abideth in the light, and there is none occasion of stumbling in him" (1 John 2:10).

Until you can meet Jesus in prayer and repent of your prejudice, you are not walking in His light. We are all children of the one and only God, brothers and sisters of heart and soul. Jesus not only takes away sins of the flesh, but sins of the heart and spirit. All prejudice dissolves before the love of Christ. A revolutionary church cannot tolerate prejudice. Whom do you need to pray for today?

_____

_____

_____

_____

_____

_____

_____

_____

_____

_____

_____

"Lord Jesus, eradicate all prejudice from my life."

God is at Work for Good

And we know that all things work together for good to them that love God, to them who are the called according to his purpose. (Romans 8:28)

No matter what obstacle has upset your plans, we have a promise from our Father in heaven: EVERYTHING works together for good to them that love God.

While God has given us a free will, He still is sovereign. He knows everything that happens in our lives. Just as an earthly father may allow his child to make decisions while living under his roof, so our Father allows us to make free choices. You may think you are putting something over on God, but He will take your sinful acts and use them to accomplish His purpose on the earth.

He will even use the deeds of sinners to bring His plan for mankind to pass. He turned the evil of Joseph's brothers into the salvation of the entire Hebrew nation!

Are you striving to work according to His purpose or yours? Don't let yourself become upset over any interruptions to your plans, but rather, rejoice that God is in control of the situation. Describe how God is working for good in your life today.

_____

_____

_____

_____

_____

_____

_____

_____

_____

_____

"In everything, God works for good to those who love Him."

The Lord Is My Helper

So that we may boldly say, The Lord is my helper, and I will not fear what man shall do unto me. (Hebrews 13:6)

As Paul wrote to the Hebrews, "let brotherly love continue. Be not forgetful to entertain strangers: for thereby some have entertained angels unawares" (vv. 1,2).

We should always be ready to do the Lord's work without fear of what man will say or do. The prophets of old suffered more persecution and torture than we can ever imagine today; yet the spirit of fear still holds many back from speaking out for the Lord.

The anointing of God is sent to meet needs. If you never step out, you will never experience the help of His anointing. But for His grace, we could be the ones in need. Since God has blessed us with His help, we should be bold in service for Him. We should help those we can help and pray for those we can't.

Step out boldly for Christ, so that in the day of judgment He may step out boldly for you. How is He helping you today?

_____

_____

_____

_____

_____

_____

_____

_____

_____

_____

_____

"Reach out to God. He is waiting to help you."

Sing Joyfully

O come, let us sing unto the Lord: let us make a joyful noise to the rock of our salvation. Let us come before his presence with thanksgiving, and make a joyful noise unto him with psalms.
(Psalm 95:1,2)

Abraham made a pilgrimage from his home in Ur of the Chaldees, following God and riding on His promise; seeking a city whose builder and maker was God (Hebrews 11:10). Abraham's promise was put to the test on a rock located on Mt. Moriah, and there God proved Himself faithful. (Genesis 22:2).

American tradition tells us the Pilgrims first landed at Plymouth Rock, where they sojourned from their native England, seeking religious freedom. God led them here, where they laid the foundation for a government built on Christian principles.

Jesus is the Rock of our salvation, the Rock of Ages. Remember the Pilgrim who left heaven, came to earth and shed His blood to ransom and redeem us from an eternity in hell. He alone deserves to be celebrated. Be thankful unto Him, and bless His Holy Name!

_____

_____

_____

_____

_____

_____

_____

_____

_____

_____

_____

"Joyfully sing a new song of praise unto the Lord today."

Before a Miracle...

And the angel came in unto her, and said, Hail, thou that art highly favoured, the Lord is with thee: blessed art thou among women. And, behold, thou shalt conceive in thy womb, and bring forth a son, and shalt call his name JESUS. (Luke 1:28,31)

The story of Mary and the conception of Jesus reveals powerful keys to receiving God's miracle-working power.

Before you can receive a miracle, **you must receive a Word from God.** Whether it comes from the Bible, through anointed preaching, or from the Lord speaking in your spirit, you must receive the Word that speaks to your situation.

When God told the prophet Elijah to seek out the widow of Zarephath, He had a plan for her. He intended to provide for her needs and prosper her in a time of drought and famine. When Elijah came to her, she had not yet received that Word from God. The prophet had to put a demand on her faith to bring her into God's provision. She received God's Word through the prophet, and in so doing received her miracle (1 Kings 17).

Receive God's Word for your situation, and allow Him to conceive a miracle in your spiritual womb. What word have you received from the Lord?

_____

_____

_____

_____

_____

_____

_____

_____

_____

"Lord, speak your Word to me today.
I long to see your miracles in my life."

The Incarnate Word

In the beginning was the Word, and the Word was with God, and the Word was God . . . and the Word was made flesh, and dwelt among us.
(John 1:1,14a)

In the Old Testament, God had many visible signs of His presence. During the Exodus, it was a cloud by day and a pillar of fire by night (Exodus 13:21). After the tabernacle was built in the wilderness, the ark of the covenant became the visual symbol of His presence.

Today we have the precious gift of His presence through the Holy Spirit. But if Jesus had never been born, we would still be taking our sacrifices to a priest. We would stand outside the gate praying that it would be received and breathing a sigh of relief when he again appeared.

God allows us to do what even the most holy priests could never do—commune with Him personally. Christmas is much more than just a holiday to remind us of the Father. Christmas is a holy festival—a celebration of the incarnation of the Son of God.

Prepare for the new millennium. Ask Christ to be incarnated in your life.

_____

_____

_____

_____

_____

_____

_____

_____

_____

_____

_____

"When we commune with Christ, He imparts Himself to us."

A Savior Is Born!

For unto you is born this day in the city of David a Saviour, which is Christ the Lord. And this shall be a sign unto you; ye shall find the babe wrapped in swaddling clothes, lying in a manger.
(Luke 2:11,12)

When Jesus Christ was born in that manger, He brought with Him the good news that through Him we are saved from eternity in hell. Because of God's grace, we are instead given eternal life.

Do not allow yourself to become caught up in the religious tradition of a baby in a manger. Be thankful Jesus did not remain a babe in swaddling clothes.

He went from a child to a young man, teaching and ministering the love of the Father, to the humiliation of the Cross of Calvary.

At Christmas, it is especially important to realize just who was born in that stable. Never forget, when you celebrate Christ and His birth, you celebrate the God of all heaven and earth.

_____

_____

_____

_____

_____

_____

_____

_____

_____

_____

_____

_____

_____

"Celebrate the birth of the King."

Jesus, the Servant

But made himself of no reputation, and took upon him the form of a servant, and was made in the likeness of men: and being found in fashion as a man, he humbled himself, and became obedient unto death, even the death of the cross. (Philippians 2:7-8)

We always like to think of a cute, rosy-cheeked baby lying in a manger, born in peace and comfort. But His was not the case. Jesus was born into a world of adversity. His first breath placed Him under Roman rule. He lay in a feeding trough, wrapped in rough, inexpensive swaddling clothes, sharing a bed with animals used for common tasks.

Jesus came not to impress, but to identify personally with us. His presence in the world was not one of judgment, but of love and salvation. He came to save and offer new life to all who would believe in Him.

Jesus came from glory and wrapped Himself in flesh and blood for one purpose—to provide a way back to the Father for you. Thank Jesus for becoming a servant for your sake.

_____

_____

_____

_____

_____

_____

_____

_____

_____

_____

_____

"He came serve and not be served."

Purifying Fire

He is like a refiner's fire . . . and he shall purify . . . and purge them as gold and silver.
(Malachi 3:2b-3)

The Bible says three things about God.

- First, God is love—passion, heat.
- Second, God is light—principle, energy.
- Third, God is a consuming fire—the result of the combination of heat and light.

John the Baptist said, "I am baptizing you with water, but someone is coming whose shoes I am not even worthy to unloose. He will baptize you with the Holy Ghost and with fire. He'll put everything in its place before God, and everything false will be burned up like chaff." (Matthew 3:11,12).

Fire does one of two things to whatever it comes in contact with. It either destroys or purifies, baptizes or consumes. The difference between heaven and hell is only the condition of the heart subjected to the fire. Let your cry be, "Purify me until your will is mine, and I am molded in your image."

_____

_____

_____

_____

_____

_____

_____

_____

_____

_____

"Purify me, Lord."

Perfect Rest

My people shall dwell . . . in quiet resting places. (Isaiah 32:18)

Peace does not belong to the unredeemed. Jehovah Shalom, the God of Peace, gives perfect peace to all whose hearts are turned toward Him.

When the flood of God's wrath swept across the earth, Noah's family rested securely in the ark. The Israelites passed the night peacefully, covered by the blood of a spotless lamb, as the death angel passed over their homes.

Noah's family and the Hebrew children in Egypt had peace and rest—in the midst of death and destruction.

In this final hour of the age, as the world around us rages and all creation awaits its redemption, we too can rest in the promises of our God and the covenant of His grace. Jesus Christ is the quiet resting place for His people.

When we draw near to Him, He will draw near to us. When we abide in Him, He will abide in us. When we are filled with Him, we are filled with His perfect peace and enter into a place of rest.

_____

_____

_____

_____

_____

_____

_____

_____

_____

_____

_____

_____

"Draw near to Christ and enter into perfect rest."

Jesus is Lord Over All

Who, being in the form of God, thought it not robbery to be equal with God: but made himself of no reputation, and took upon him the form of a servant, and was made in the likeness of men. (Philippians 2:6,7)

God ordained a divine structure when He bestowed the lordship over the earth upon Jesus Christ. He is the ruling, reigning, sovereign Lord over all (Ephesians 1:20-22), and all things have been placed in submission to Him.

Jesus is Lord, whether you acknowledge Him or not; and He wants to be Lord of your life. Whether or not you submit to His lordship does not change anything. When we become caught up in the things of the world, pursuing our agendas and denying His, we miss our blessings as heirs of His kingdom.

The terrified disciples forgot who was with them in the storm-tossed boat. But when they called out to Him, He calmed not only the storm around them but the storm in their hearts.

Call out to Him to still the storm raging in your heart and your mind. Call out to Him and receive the peace He came to earth to give.

"Jesus demands Lordship over all your life as you enter into the new millennium."

The God of Hope

Now the God of hope fill you with all joy and peace in believing, that ye may abound in hope, through the power of the Holy Ghost. (Romans 15:13)

Paul preached again and again that there was no immortality apart from the resurrection.

For those outside of Christ, there is no hope. They are hopeless and helpless in a world without God.

But because of the redemptive work of Jesus on the cross, Satan will not have the last word in the lives of believers, and good—not evil—will triumph.

Hope beyond the scope of human limitation is the mark of the believer. It is what sets us apart from a doomed and dying world and gives us the courage to go on when dying would be easy.

Look forward to the New Year with renewed hope in your heart—for the future and for your children to come to the saving grace of Christ.

Abound in the hope that looks the devil in the eye, looks beyond your circumstances and compels you to declare "Devil, in the name of Jesus, I claim the victory!" The new millennium will be filled with hope in Christ.

"You have every reason in Christ to be filled with hope."

God's New Thing

Behold, I will do a new thing; now it shall spring forth; shall ye not know it? I will even make a way in the wilderness, and rivers in the desert. (Isaiah 43:19)

It is the eve of a new millennium. You cannot go into the New Year and the new millennium without a renewed commitment to Jesus Christ. What does that involve?

- **Get radical for Jesus Christ.**
- **March with the revolutionary church led by Jesus.**
- **Be empowered by the Holy Spirit.**
- **Be followed by signs and wonders.**
- **Pray boldly and without ceasing.**
- **Witness daily to the lost.**
- **Serve others with love—in Jesus' name.**
- **Forgive time and time again.**
- **Proclaim the acceptable year of the Lord.**
- **Turn the world upside down for Christ.**
  Write down all the ways you will be radical for Christ in the new millennium:

_____

_____

_____

_____

_____

_____

_____

_____

_____

_____

"God is doing a new thing in your life.
Get radical. Live boldly for Christ."

ABOUT THE AUTHOR

Rod Parsley began his ministry as an energetic 19-year-old in the backyard of his parent's Ohio home. The fresh, old-time Gospel approach of Parsley's delivery immediately attracted a hungry, God-seeking audience. From 17 people who attended Parsley's first 1977 backyard meeting, the crowds rapidly grew.

Today, as the pastor of Columbus, Ohio's 5,200–seat World Harvest Church, Parsley oversees World Harvest Christian Academy, World Harvest Bible College, Bridge of Hope missions, outreach and *Breakthrough*, World Harvest Church's daily and weekly television broadcast.

Pastor Parsley's preaching of the Gospel of Jesus Christ with old-fashioned, Holy Ghost power reaps a harvest of souls not only across North America, but also across the globe to nearly 136 nations via television and shortwave radio.

Rod Parsley currently resides in Pickerington, Ohio with his wife, Joni, and their two children, Ashton and Austin.

OTHER BOOKS BY ROD PARSLEY

Breakthrough Quotes
Bridge Builders' Bible, Ten Golden Keys Special Edition
God's Answer to Insufficient Funds
The Jubileee Anointing
New Direction
New Direction, Spanish Edition
No Dry Season (Best Seller)
No More Crumbs (Best Seller)
Repairers of the Breach
Ten Golden Keys to Your Abundance

For more information about *Breakthrough* or World Harvest Church or to receive a product list of the many books and audio and video tapes by Rod Parsley, write or call:

Breakthrough
P.O. Box 32932
Columbus, Ohio 43232-0932
614-837-1990
www.breakthrough.net

For information about World Harvest Bible College,
Write or call:

World Harvest Bible College
P.O. Box 32901
Columbus, Ohio 43232-0901
614-837-4088

If you need prayer, the *Breakthrough* prayer line
is open twenty-four hours a day, seven days a week.
614-837-3232

NOTES

NOTES

NOTES

NOTES

NOTES

NOTES

NOTES

NOTES

NOTES

NOTES

NOTES